STUDY GUIDE for

Lerner, Meacham, and Burns
Western Civilizations

TWELFTH EDITION

Volume 1

By Philip L. Ralph

W·W·NORTON & COMPANY

New York · London

W . W. Norton & Company, Inc., 500 Fifth Avenue, New York, N. Y. 10110
W. W. Norton & Company Ltd., 10 Coptic Street, London WC1A 1PU

ISBN   0-393-96209-1

1 2 3 4 5 6 7 8 9 0

Contents

To the Teacher and the Student

This *Study Guide* has been prepared specifically for the Twelfth Edition of *Western Civilizations*. New study questions and problems have been added and the selection of readings has been adjusted and expanded to reflect new emphases in the text.

As with the previous edition, the primary purpose of the revised *Study Guide* is to help the student in **mastering the material in *Western Civilizations* and to supply him with a means whereby he can test his mastery. It also affords a convenient guide for review as well as a basis for class discussion and tests. Before using it, both teachers and students should be aware of the following features of the guide:**

1. *The chapters vary in length, as do those in the textbook on which it is based.* The common plan of devoting the same number of pages to each chapter of a text, irrespective of its length, has been rejected in favor of placing greater emphasis on the important than on the trivial.

2. *The same general pattern is followed in each chapter, but not slavishly.* This typically includes chronology, identifications, study questions, problems, and geographical identifications. Where there is no particular accent on chronology in the textbook, however, there is no exercise on it in this *Study Guide*. The space devoted to chronology in the chapter on the Romans is necessarily greater than that given it with the Egyptians. The extent to which other devices appear (identifications and study questions, for example) varies as seems fitting according to the length and character of the corresponding chapter in *Western Civilizations*.

3. *A chapter usually begins with a review of chronology that aims to give the same emphasis to "dates" that the original chapter in the textbook does.* Like the identifications, these chronologies are intended primarily as study aids. Some, those on Chapters 2 and 3, for example, might be used as objective tests, but most are meant to be aids for learning rather than methods for testing in class.

4. *In most of the chapters the chronology is fol-* lowed by identifications. These may concern people or things or ideas or all three. They do not cover every name or term in the chapters of the textbook, for the result would be chaos. Occasionally, multiple-choice or completion questions are used for identifications.

5. *Every chapter has study questions.* Usually the questions are of the essay variety. The majority are based simply and clearly on the text. Others require a little more than merely accurate recollection of facts. In every case these questions can be answered from the textbook alone. They can be used by the student to test his comprehension of the material in the textbook or by the instructor for class discussion or tests. If the student has faithfully done the work provided by the guide up to this point, that is, has written the answers to objective questions and has gone over the study questions in his own mind, he will have mastered the textbook thoroughly.

6. *Every chapter has a section of problems.* Some of these offer controversial or speculative questions for the student to deal with. Others suggest topics of inquiry. In each instance some further reading is needed. For the most part the kind of outside reading required can be found in common reference books. Often an encyclopedia article will suffice. Many of the problems can serve as bases for class discussions, for outside papers, or for extra reading assignments. They are intended to be optional, for the teacher to use or not as he chooses.

7. *Most of the chapters include a list of geographical identifications.* These, by requiring the student to become familiar with the location of important cities, regions, and historical sites, enhance the usefulness of the maps in the text and help prepare the student for map exercises which the teacher may wish to assign.

8. *Each chapter contains a section of readings, selected to illustrate and supplement the text material.* The length and number of selections vary from chapter to chapter, but in no case are they too

extensive to be covered by the student along with his text assignment. Because the readings have been chosen largely from contemporary sources and with the organization and emphases of the text constantly in mind, they will help the student to visualize and better understand the material he is studying. To this end, questions to assist in analyzing the readings are provided.

9. *For each of the seven major parts of the textbook this guide includes a review, the first section of which is a map problem.* (Parts Six and Seven are covered by a single review following Chapter 31.) These map problems can be used earlier if the teacher so desires. The four maps in the review of Parts Six and Seven might very well be marked by the student as he reads the chapters upon which they are based. The second section of the review is a chronological check-up which coordinates material from several chapters. Emphasis is placed on the simultaneity of events and eras rather than on the recollection of a long list of exact (and usually meaningless) dates.

In short, this *Guide* is designed to be a concise aid which will neither consume all of the student's study time nor dictate to the teacher how he must teach the course.

The Earliest Beginnings

12,000   Page 13

IDENTIFICATIONS

You should be able to identify the following:

paleoanthropology "bipedality"
Louis Leakey *Homo erectus*
"Nutcracker Man" Neanderthal man
Homo habilis sympathetic magic

STUDY QUESTIONS

1. Why is a definition of history as "past politics" inadequate?
2. How have the discovery of fossil remains in East Africa during the past two decades altered our conception of human origins?
3. Explain the evolutionary anatomical changes that led to the emergence of *Homo habilis*.
4. Approximately how much time elapsed between the emergence of *Homo habilis* and the emergence of *Homo erectus*?
5. Cite the evidence for the superiority of *Homo erectus* over his predecessors.
6. Why may the ability to use tools for food gathering be regarded as the first step toward civilization?
7. Though his ways may seem primitive, *Homo erectus* was a very successful species. What is the proof?
8. During what period approximately was Neanderthal man dominant in much of Europe and neighboring continents?
9. Summarize the technical and cultural advances made by Neanderthal man.
10. What is the probable explanation for the Neanderthal custom of burying the dead?
11. Between 30,000 and 40,000 years ago a significant transition occurred in the earth's human population. What was it?
12. How do you account for the magnificent cave paintings found in parts of southern France and northern Spain?
13. Why is it unlikely that the transition in human society from food-gathering to food production was the result of conscious choice?
14. Identify the "momentous revolution" that occurred 4,000–3,000 years ago and explain why it was revolutionary.
15. Trace the stages in transition from a nomadic to an agricultural society.
16. What new handicrafts arose during the age of villages?
17. What are the basic differences between a village and a city? Explain the assertion that "cities existed to exploit villages."
18. What was the significance or the effect of the emergence of a priestly class in society?
19. What is the basis for claiming that a true civilization had begun in Mesopotamia by 3,000 B.C.?

PROBLEMS

1. If much of the past is irrecoverable, how can an attempt to reconstruct the past help us to better understand the present?
2. On the basis of reading in such books as Christopher Dawson, *The Age of the Gods*, B. Malinowski, *Magic, Science, and Religion*, and Edward Norbeck, *Religion in Primitive Society*, describe what you consider to be the essential character of primitive religion.
3. Explore further the origin of the state. Make use of such books as R. H. Lowie, *Primitive Society*, M. J. Herskovits, *Man and His Works*, and C. C. Lamberg-Karlovsky and J. Sabloff, *Ancient Civilizations*.
4. Explain the importance of each of the following to the rise of civilizations:
   a. The development of agriculture
   b. The development of organized religion
   c. The origin of the city
5. Read Ruth Benedict, *Patterns of Culture*, and see how many ancient peoples you can fit into her system of classification.

THE SUBJECTIVE ELEMENT IN HISTORY
Bernard Lewis

There are many ways of defining and subdividing history; traditionally, by who, and when, and where; then, in a more sophisticated age, by topic — by what, and how, and, for the intellectually ambitious, why; methodologically, by types of sources and the manner of their use; ideologically, by function and purpose — of the historian more than of the history, and many others. The classification used here, as will have emerged from the above remarks, is into three types, as follows:

(1) Remembered history. This consists of statements about the past, rather than history in the strict sense, and ranges from the personal recollections claimed by the elders to the living traditions of a civilization, as embodied in its scriptures, its classics, and its inherited historiography. It may be described as the collective memory of a community or nation or other entity — what it, or its rulers and leaders, poets, and sages, choose to remember as significant, both as reality and symbol.

(2) Recovered history. This is the history of events and movements, of persons and ideas, that have been forgotten, that is to say, at some stage and for some reason rejected by the communal memory, and then, after a longer or shorter interval, recovered by academic scholarship — by the study of records, the excavation of buried cities, the decipherment of forgotten scripts and languages, and the consequent reconstruction of a forgotten past. But reconstruction begs the basic question, and disguises what would be better described as construction. The word itself indicates the dangers of the process, and leads us to the third type of history.

(3) Invented history. This is history for a purpose, a new purpose differing from previous purposes. It may be invented in either the Latin or the English sense of the word, devised and interpreted from remembered and recovered history where feasible, and fabricated where not.

Remembered history of one kind or another is common to all human groups from the primitive tribe to the universal empire, from the tribal cult to the universal church. It embodies poetic and symbolic truth as understood by the people, even where it is inaccurate in detail, but it becomes false or is rejected as false when the desired self-image changes and the remembered past no longer corresponds to it or supports it. It is preserved in commemorative ceremonies and monuments, religious and later secular, and in the words and rituals associated with them — in pageantry and drama, song and recitation, chronicle and biography, epic and ballad and their modern equivalents, also in official celebrations, popular entertainment, and elementary education.

Recovered history is the result of the discovery and reassessment of the past by critical scholarship — basically a modern and European task. The ancients, with few exceptions, were not interested in ancient history; indeed most history, until the new curiosity of the Renaissance, was either remembered or contemporary and much of it still purposive.

The invention of history is no new invention. It is an ancient practice dating back to remote antiquity and directed to a variety of purposes. Again, it is common to all groups, ranging in type from the primitive heroic myths of nomadic tribes to Soviet official historiography or American revisionism.

Critical history begins with a dissatisfaction with memory and a desire to remedy its deficiencies. But there is more than one kind of dissatisfaction. The critical scholar may be dissatisfied with what remembered history offers him because he feels that it is inaccurate or deficient or misleading. But there are others whose dissatisfaction springs from a different cause. They would rather rewrite history not as it was, or as they have been taught that it was, but as they would prefer it to have been. For historians of this school the purpose of changing the past is not to seek some abstract truth, but to achieve a new vision of the past better suited to their needs in the present and their aspirations for the future. Their aim is to amend, to restate, to replace, or even to recreate the past in a more satisfactory form. Here we may recall two of the main purposes of remembering the past, for communities as for individuals. One is to explain and perhaps to justify the present — a present, some present — on which there may be dispute. Where there are conflicting loyalties or clashing interests, each will have its own version of the past, its own presentation of the salient events. As Dr. Plumb has remarked, "Warring authorities means warring pasts." It is such situations which lead and have led, from immemorial antiquity, to the invention of the past, that is, to the improvement of memory.

A second use of the past, from very early times, has been to predict and even to control the future. This is manifested in the oracle-bones of ancient China, the omen tablets of Babylon, the messianic tracts of the Jews, Christians, and Muslims, Nostradamus, Old Moore's Almanac, and the Marxist-Leninist classics of modern Communism. They are all equally reliable.

Invention is of several types, and has several functions. Broadly, its aim is to embellish — to correct or remove what is distasteful in the past, and replace it with something more acceptable, more encouraging, and more conducive to the purpose in hand. It may be spontaneous, as in the heroic sagas, romantic, as in a good deal of 19th- and 20th-century writing, or officially sponsored and even imposed.

Much of it is literary, and continues or imitates the tradition of the old heroic poems. The famous Portuguese epic, the Lusiads of Camoens, though derivative and neo-classical in form, deals with contemporary events and presents an idealized version of the great Portuguese discoveries and conquests, in which the poet himself was a proud participant. The events in Palestine in 1929 and in Kashmir in 1947 have been described in Arabic and Pathan war-songs, in the true heroic style; in a different key, the American opening of the West and conquest of the Indian have been similarly celebrated in legend and balladry, in the whole neo-epical and pseudo-epical cycles of cowboy and Indian stories, in song and verse, fiction and film. Through these, as well as through schoolbooks and children's literature, they occupy a place in American corporate self-awareness comparable with the heroic memories of Greece and the imperial consciousness of Rome. Of late there has been some revulsion from the traditional self-congratulatory view of the conquest of the American West, but it still falls far short of the change which took place in the Mexican view of the past, when, as part of their revolution, they began to distinguish between their Hispanic and Indian heritages and to identify themselves more and more with the latter. The European visitor to the United States and to Mexico cannot but be struck by the contrast between the attitudes of the two to the Indians. While Americans speak, with guilt or otherwise, of "what we did to the Indians," Mexicans, even of pure European descent, speak of "what the Spaniards did to us." The contrast is driven home in the vast historical murals painted by Diego Rivera for the Palacio Nacional in Mexico City.

It is not for nothing that a Soviet historian once remarked that the most difficult of a historian's tasks is to predict the past.

THE MIND OF PRELITERATE MAN
Franz Boas

The difference in the mode of thought of primitive man and that of civilized man seems to consist largely in the difference of character of the traditional material with which the new perception associates itself. The instruction given to the child of primitive man is not based on centuries of experimentation, but consists of the crude experience of generations. When a new experience enters the mind of primitive man, the same process which we observe among civilized man brings about an entirely different series of associations, and therefore results in a different type of explanation. A sudden explosion will associate itself in his mind, perhaps, with tales which he has heard in regard to the mythical history of the world, and consequently will be accompanied by superstitious fear. The new, unknown epidemic may be explained by the belief in demons that persecute mankind; and the existing world may be explained as the result of transformations, or by objectivation of the thoughts of a creator.

When we recognize that neither among civilized nor among primitive men the average individual carries to completion the attempt at causal explanation of phenomena, but only so far as to amalgamate it with other previous knowledge, we recognize that the result of the whole process depends entirely upon the character of the traditional material. Herein lies the immense importance of folk-lore in determining the mode of thought. Herein lies particularly the enormous influence of current philosophic opinion upon the masses of the people, and the influence of the dominant scientific theory upon the character of scientific work.

It would be vain to try to understand the development of modern science without an intelligent understanding of modern philosophy; it would be vain to try to understand the history of medieval science without a knowledge of medieval theology; and so it is vain to try to understand primitive science without an intelligent knowledge of primitive mythology. "Mythology," "theology" and "philosophy" are different terms for the same influences which shape the current of human thought, and which determine the character of the attempts of man to explain the phenomena of nature. To primitive man — who has been taught to consider the heavenly orbs as animate beings; who sees in every animal a being more powerful than man; to whom the mountains, trees and stones are endowed with life or with special virtues — explanations of phenomena will suggest themselves entirely different from those to which we are accustomed, since we still base our conclusions upon the existence of matter and force as bringing about the observed results.

A THEORY OF THE ORIGIN OF CIVILIZATIONS
Arnold J. Toynbee

We have now reached a point at which we can bring our present argument to a head. We have ascertained that civilizations come to birth in environments that are unusually difficult and not unusually easy, and this has led us on to inquire whether or not this is an instance of some social law which may be expressed in the formula: 'the greater the challenge, the greater the stimulus.' We have made a survey of the responses evoked by five types of stimulus — hard countries, new ground, blows, pressures and penalizations — and in all five fields the result of our survey suggests the validity of the law. We have still, however, to determine whether its validity is absolute. If we increase the severity of the challenge *ad infinitum*, do we thereby ensure an infinite intensification of the stimulus and an infinite increase in the response when the challenge is successfully met? Or do we reach a point beyond which increasing severity produces diminishing returns? And, if we go beyond this point, do we reach a further point at which the challenge becomes so severe that the possibility of responding to it successfully disappears? In that case the law would be that 'the most stimulating challenge is to be found in a mean between a deficiency of severity and an excess of it.'

Is there such a thing as an excessive challenge? We have not yet encountered an example of such, and there are several extreme cases of the operation of challenge-and-response which we have not yet mentioned. We have not yet cited the case of Venice — a city, built on piles driven into the mud banks of a salt lagoon, which has surpassed in wealth and power and glory all the cities built on *terra firma* in the fertile plain of the Po; nor Holland — a country which has been actually salvaged from the sea, but yet has distinguished herself in history far above any other parcel of ground of equal area in the North European plain; nor Switzerland, saddled with her portentous load of mountains. It might seem that the three hardest pieces of ground in Western Europe have stimulated their inhabitants to attain, along different lines, the highest level of social achievement that has as yet been attained by any peoples of Western Christendom.

But there are other considerations. Extreme in degree though these three challenges are, they are limited in range to only one of the two realms which constitute the environment of any society. They are challenges of difficult ground, no doubt, but on the human side — blows, pressures and penalizations — the severity of this physical situation has been not a challenge but a relief; it has shielded them from human ordeals to which their neighbours were exposed.

From Arnold J. Toynbee, *A Study of History*, ed. D. C. Somervell, Oxford University Press, 1947, Vol. I. Selection reprinted by permission of the publisher.

Two Types of Cultures
Ruth Benedict

The basic contrast between the Pueblos and the other cultures of North America is the contrast that is named and described by Nietzsche in his studies of Greek tragedy. He discusses two diametrically opposed ways of arriving at the values of existence. The Dionysian pursues them through 'the annihilation of the ordinary bounds and limits of existence'; he seeks to attain in his most valued moments escape from the boundaries imposed upon him by his five senses, to break through into another order of experience. The desire of the Dionysian, in personal experience or in ritual, is to press through it toward a certain psychological state, to achieve excess. The closest analogy to the emotions he seeks is drunkenness, and he values the illuminations of frenzy. With Blake, he believes 'the path of excess leads to the palace of wisdom.' The Apollonian distrusts all this, and has often little idea of the nature of such experiences. He finds means to outlaw them from his conscious life. He 'knows but one law, measure in the Hellenic sense.' He keeps the middle of the road, stays within the known map, does not meddle with disruptive psychological states. In Nietzsche's fine phrase, even in the exaltation of the dance he 'remains what he is, and retains his civic name.'

The Southwest Pueblos are Apollonian. Not all of Nietzsche's discussion of the contrast between Apollonian and Dionysian applies to the contrast between the Pueblos and the surrounding peoples. The fragments I have quoted are faithful descriptions, but there were refinements of the types in Greece that do not occur among the Indians of the Southwest, and among these latter, again, there are refinements that did not occur in Greece. It is with no thought of equating the civilization of Greece with that of aboriginal America that I use, in describing the cultural configurations of the latter, terms borrowed from the culture of Greece. I use them because they are categories that bring clearly to the fore the major qualities that differentiate Pueblo culture from those of other American Indians, not because all the attitudes that are found in Greece are found also in aboriginal America.

From *Patterns of Culture* by Ruth Benedict. Copyright 1934 by Ruth Benedict. Copyright © renewed 1961 by Ruth Valentine. Reprinted by permission of Houghton Mifflin Company.

ANALYSIS AND INTERPRETATION OF THE READINGS

1. What, according to Bernard Lewis, is "recovered history," and what are its pitfalls?
2. What is Toynbee's explanation of the fact that some civilizations have developed in seemingly unfavorable environments?

CHAPTER 2

Mesopotamian Civilization

CHRONOLOGY

Write in the blank next to each epoch or item the correct dates selected from the list below. All dates are B.C.

- 1792–1750
- 3200–2000
- 705–681
- 1450–1300
- c. 3200
- c. 2000–c. 1600
- 539
- 1300–612

Sumerian era __3200-2000__

Beginning of wheeled transportation __3200__

Old Babylonian era __c. 2000-c. 1600__

Reign of Hammurabi __1792-1750__

Height of Hittite power __1450-1300__

Period of Assyrian ascendancy __1300-612__

Reign of Sennacherib __705-681__

Fall of Babylon to the Persians __539__

IDENTIFICATIONS

Below are a number of items with which you should be familiar after reading Chapter 2. In each blank write the term — an individual, a people, a place, or a thing — described.

1. Akkadian warrior, called "the Great," who conquered Sumeria

   __Sargon__

2. Most advanced in astronomy of all ancient Mesopotamian peoples

3. Founders of civilization in the Tigris-Euphrates valley

4. Most militaristic people of ancient Mesopotamia

5. First people to learn the process of multiplication and division and the extraction of square and cube roots

6. New Babylonian king who conquered Jerusalem

7. Assyrian king memorable for his large library at Nineveh

8. People who invented the lunar calendar

   __Sumerians__

9. Major Babylonian contribution to world literature

10. Sumerian terraced tower surmounted by a shrine

    __Ziggurat__

11. Wedge-shaped writing on clay tablets

    __Cuneiform__

12. Babylonian promulgator of a famous ancient legal code

7

You should also be able to identify the following:

"Hanging Gardens"
Semitic language group
Indo-European language group
Amorites

"King of Justice"
duodecimal system
Medes
Kassites

STUDY QUESTIONS

1. What is the justification for the assertion: "History begins at Sumer"?
2. Identify the three major Sumerian contributions to the course of civilization.
3. Trace the steps in the development of writing by the Sumerians.
4. Show how religious concepts evolved from the Sumerians through the Old Babylonians to the Chaldeans.
5. Describe the characteristics of Sumerian temple architecture. What purposes other than religious did the temples serve?
6. What classes comprised Sumerian society? How free were the "free farmers"?
7. What were the causes of the Sumerian economic decline around 2000 B.C.?
8. What were the two chief differences between the cultures of the Sumerian and the Old Babylonian eras?
9. Describe the character of justice embodied in the Code of Hammurabi. To whom did the term "man" apply in the code?
10. How do you account for the seemingly unfair provisions of Hammurabi's Code? What is the lasting importance of this ancient document?
11. What philosophical or dictatorial principles are embodied in the *Gilgamesh* epic?
12. What changes in religion came under the Old Babylonians?
13. "The Old Babylonians were the most accomplished arithmeticians in antiquity." Explain.
14. What superior military techniques were employed by the Kassites and Hittites?
15. Why was the discovery of ancient Hittite civilization important? What early misjudgments were made about it?
16. How important was the use of iron for the Hittites?
17. Point out the distinctive features of Assyrian civilization at its height. To what extent were the Assyrians indebted to earlier Mesopotamian cultures?
18. What part did "frightfulness" play in Assyrian society and government policy? How did this affect the Assyrians' ultimate fate?
19. Describe the city of Babylon under the New Babylonians.
20. How do you account for the development of astrology by the New Babylonians? What valuable by-products did this pseudo-science yield?
21. Why were the Hebrews heavily indebted to Mesopotamian civilization?

PROBLEMS

1. Read the first five chapters of the Book of Daniel in the Old Testament and comment on the picture you derive of Nebuchadnezzar and the Chaldeans. Why were Daniel's gifts so peculiarly appealing to his captors?
2. In what ways was Mesopotamian civilization adequate to meet human needs and in what ways was it deficient?
3. What "lessons" do you think modern nations might draw from the history of the Mesopotamian peoples?
4. Trace the growth of Assyria from a small independent state to a great empire.
5. Study the forms of Assyrian art and evaluate its quality.
6. Compare the mathematical achievements of the Mesopotamians with those of ancient Greeks.
7. Read the *Epic of Gilgamesh* to discover what light it throws upon Babylonian culture and value judgments.

GEOGRAPHICAL IDENTIFICATIONS

Tigris River	Sumer	Akkad
Euphrates River	Ur	Lagash
Nineveh	Persian Gulf	Assur
Babylon	Chaldean empire	Hattusas
Syria		

THE CODE OF HAMMURABI:
Sundry Enactments

If a son strike his father, they shall cut off his fingers.

If a man destroy the eye of another man, they shall destroy his eye.

If one break a man's bone, they shall break his bone.

If one destroy the eye of a freeman or break the bone of a freeman, he shall pay one mana of silver.

If one destroy the eye of a man's slave or break a bone of a man's slave he shall pay one-half his price.

If a man knock out a tooth of a man of his own rank, they shall knock out his tooth.

If one knock out a tooth of a freeman, he shall pay one-third mana of silver.

If a man strike the person of a man . . . who is his superior, he shall receive sixty strokes with an ox-tail whip in public.

If a man strike another man of his own rank, he shall pay one mana of silver. . . .

If a man strike another man in a quarrel and wound him, he shall swear: "I struck him without intent," and he shall be responsible for the physician. . . .

If a physician operate on a man for a severe wound . . . with a bronze lancet and save the man's life; or if he open an abscess . . . of a man with a bronze lancet and save that man's eye, he shall receive ten shekels of silver. . . .

If he be a freeman, he shall receive five shekels.

If it be a man's slave, the owner of the slave shall give two shekels of silver to the physician.

If a physician operate on a man for a severe wound with a bronze lancet and cause the man's death; or open an abscess . . . of a man with a bronze lancet and destroy the man's eye, they shall cut off his fingers.

If a physician operate on a slave of a freeman for a severe wound with a bronze lancet and cause his death, he shall restore a slave of equal value. . . .

If a builder build a house for a man and do not make its construction firm and the house which he has built collapse and cause the death of the owner of the house, that builder shall be put to death.

From R. F. Harper, *The Code of Hammurabi, King of Babylon.*

THE SOCIAL ORDER IN ASSYRIA:
As Revealed in Letters

In the two following letters we see officials taking an oath, and can observe the hierarchical structure of official society, while the second letter stresses the importance attached to this particular ceremony.

(1) 'To the king my lord, from his servant Ishtar-shum-eresh. Health to the king my lord, and may Nabu and Marduk bless him. The scribes, the diviners, the magicians, the doctors, the observers of the flight of birds, the palace officials who dwell in the city have taken an oath to the gods on the sixteenth day of Nisan: now they can take an oath to the king.'

(2) 'To the king my master from his servant Kaptia. Health to the king my master. Regarding the matter of the oaths of Babylon about which the king wrote to me, I was not present, for the king's letter only reached me after I and my brothers had left for the country of Arashi on a tour of inspection, and I could not reach Babylon in time for the taking of the oaths. On my journey I met the great chamberlain of the palace. When he had led me to Uruk in the presence of your gods, I should have been able to receive the oaths sworn to the king my master. But I had not full confidence in these oaths sworn privately, and I thought: "Let the soldiers with their sons, and their wives as well as their gods, swear the oaths which are due to the king: but I will accept them according to the formula laid down in the letter from the king, when the Elders shall come to swear their oaths to the king my lord."

Finally, here is an astonishing letter from some high official, whose name we do not know, to King Sennacherib, who had reversed the laws governing the succession by nominating his favourite younger son Ashurbanipal to the throne of Assyria, and his elder son to the throne of Babylon.

'What had never been done even in heaven, the king, my lord, hath brought to pass on earth, and hath made us witnesses of it. Thou hast robed one of thy sons in the royal robes and hast named him as ruler of Assyria, and hast named thy elder son to succeed to the throne of Babylon. What the king my lord hath done for his son is not for the good of Assyria. Surely, O King, Ashur hath granted thee power, from the rising to the setting of the sun, and, as touches thy dear children, thy heart may well be content. None the less, the lord my king has conceived an evil plan, and thou hast therein been weak . . .'

Compare this with the following letter from a citizen of Babylon who had come to lay his complaints before the king and had rapidly been dismissed from the royal presence.

'I am as a dead man, I am faint after the sight of the king my master. When I see the countenance of the king my master, I begin again to live, and, though I am still hungered, I am as though refreshed. When last I was granted an audience of the king, I was overcome with fear, and I could not find words to utter . . .'

This terror of royalty is indeed far removed from the other respectful but undaunted reminder of duly established law. We may well feel baffled by the Assyrian court with its strange mixture of servility and frankness towards the person of the king, which is so marked a feature of the ancient East.

ETHICAL CONCEPTS IN THE SUMERIAN RELIGION
S. N. Kramer

The gods preferred the ethical and moral to the unethical and immoral, according to the Sumerian sages, and practically all the major deities of the Sumerian pantheon are extolled in their hymns as lovers of the good and the just, of truth and righteousness. Indeed, there were several deities who had the supervision of the moral order as their main functions: for example, the sun-god, Utu. Another deity, the Lagashite goddess named Nanshe, also played a significant role in the sphere of man's ethical and moral conduct. She is described in one of her hymns as the goddess.

> Who knows the orphan, who knows the widow,
> Knows the oppression of man over man, is the
>   orphan's mother,
> Nanshe, who cares for the widow,
> Who seeks out (?) justice (?) for the poorest (?).
> The queen brings the refugee to her lap,
> Finds shelter for the weak.

In another passage of this hymn, she is pictured as judging mankind on New Year's Day; by her side are Nidaba, the goddess of writing and accounts, and her husband, Haia, as well as numerous witnesses. The evil human types who suffer her displeasure are

> (People) who walking in transgression reached
>   out with high hand, ... ,
> Who transgress the established norms, violate
>   contracts,
> Who looked with favor on the places of evil,
>   . . . . ,
> Who substituted a small weight for a large
>   weight,
> Who substituted a small measure for a large
>   measure,
> Who having eaten (something not belonging
>   to him) did not say "I have eaten it,"
> Who having drunk, did not say "I have drunk
>   it," . . . . ,
> Who said "I would eat that which is forbidden,"
> Who said "I would drink that which is forbidden."

Nanshe's social conscience is further revealed in lines which read:

> To comfort the orphan, to make disappear the
>   widow,
> To set up a place of destruction for the mighty,
> To turn over the mighty to the weak . . . . ,
> Nanshe searches the heart of the people.

Unfortunately, although the leading deities were assumed to be ethical and moral in their conduct, the fact remained that, in accordance with the world view of the Sumerians, they were also the ones who in the process of establishing civilization had planned evil and falsehood, violence and oppression — in short, all the immoral and unethical modes of human conduct. Thus, for example, among the list of *me's*, the rules and regulations devised by the gods to make the cosmos run smoothly and effectively, there are not only those which regulate "truth," "peace," "goodness," and "justice," but also those which govern "falsehood," "strife," "lamentation," and "fear." Why, then, one might ask, did the gods find it necessary to plan and create sin and evil, suffering and misfortune, which were so pervasive that one Sumerian pessimist could say, "Never has a sinless child been born to his mother"? To judge from our available material, the Sumerian sages, if they asked the question at all, were prepared to admit their ignorance in this respect; the will of the gods and their motives were at times inscrutable. The proper course for a Sumerian Job to pursue was not to argue and complain in face of seemingly unjustifiable misfortune, but to plead and wail, lament and confess, his inevitable sins and failings.

But will the gods give heed to him, a lone and not very effective mortal, even if he prostrates and humbles himself in heartfelt prayer? Probably not, the Sumerian teachers would have answered. As they saw it, gods were like mortal rulers and no doubt had more important things to attend to; and so, as in the case of kings, man must have an intermediary to intercede in his behalf, one whom the gods would be willing to hear and favor. As a result, the Sumerian thinkers contrived and evolved the notion of a personal god, a kind of good angel to each particular individual and family head, his divine father who had begot him, as it were. It was to him, to his personal deity, that the individual sufferer bared his heart in prayer and supplication, and it was through him that he found his salvation.

ANALYSIS AND INTERPRETATION OF THE READINGS

1. What light does the extract from Hammurabi's Code throw on social classes among the old Babylonians?

CHAPTER 3
Egyptian Civilization

CHRONOLOGY

In the blanks, write the appropriate dates from the list below. All dates are B.C.

c. 3100	c. 1750	1151
2770–2200	c. 1560–1087	671
2500	c. 2770	525
c. 2050–1786		

_____ Old Kingdom

_____ Assyrian conquest of Egypt

_____ Beginning of Zoser's reign

_____ First unified state in the Nile Valley

_____ Hyksos invasion of Egypt

_____ Middle Kingdom

_____ Persian conquest of Egypt

_____ Death of Ramses III

_____ The New Kingdom (Empire)

IDENTIFICATIONS

You should be able to identify the following:

Memphis	Osiris
Hyksos	Amon-Re
Ahmose	Amenhotep IV (Akhenaton)
ring-money	hieroglyphics
nature myth	Tutankhaton (Tutankhamen)
papyrus	"pi" ratio

Write in the blank below each description the correct item selected from the list below:

Book of the Dead	Plea of the Eloquent Peasant
alphabet	Nefertiti

1. A figure typifying a trend toward naturalism in art.

_____

2. A collection of formulas, inscribed on rolls of papyrus, to guarantee the purchaser's safe entrance into the celestial kingdom.

_____

3. A treatise expounding the policies of an ideal benevolent ruler.

_____

4. A priceless literary tool, little used by its Egyptian inventors.

_____

STUDY QUESTIONS

1. What natural advantages did the Nile Valley have over Mesopotamia as a center for the development of civilization?
2. Why could Herodotus describe Egypt as "the gift of the river"?
3. Discuss briefly the nature of the responsibilities of a pharaoh of the Old Kingdom.
4. What is the evidence that the Old Kingdom, unlike so many ancient states, was a peaceful, nonaggressive community?
5. Why has the Twelfth Dynasty been referred to as a golden age?
6. "The Hyksos conquest contributed strongly to the rise of Egyptian imperialism and to a decline in the character of Egyptian religion." Discuss this statement.
7. Describe the evolution of the Egyptian system of writing. In what respects did it advance beyond the Mesopotamian system?
8. Why was the Egyptian calendar the best in antiquity?
9. Account for the general popularity of the cult of Osiris during the Middle Kingdom.

10. How did Amenhotep IV (Akhenaton) try to offset the debasement of religion under the Empire?

11. Explain the statement that the religion of Amenhotep IV (Akhenaton) was a "qualified monotheism."

12. To what extent and in what directions were the Egyptians scientific? How do you account for the limitations in their intellectual achievements?

13. Why does limestone occupy a prominent place in the history of the twenty-seventh century B.C.?

14. What special features of the "Great Pyramid of Cheops" qualified it to rank as one of the seven wonders of the world?

15. If the extraordinarily arduous construction of the Egyptian pyramids did not rest upon slave labor, how do you account for their accomplishment?

16. During what period were the great Egyptian temples built? Describe their characteristics.

17. How did the sculpture of the Egyptians symbolize their national aspirations?

18. What was the structure of society in Egypt throughout the greater part of its ancient history? What features did Egyptian society have in common with our own and what features were different?

19. How did the position of women differ from that of ancient societies?

20. To what extent was Egyptian art bound by convention? To what extent was it original and individualistic?

21. How do you account for the remarkable longevity of Egyptian civilization?

PROBLEMS

1. Compare and contrast the judicial system under the Old Kingdom with that of the United States.

2. Amenhotep IV (Akhenaton) is generally considered one of the splendid failures in history. Why do you think he failed? To what extent might he be called a success?

3. In what ways was Egyptian civilization superior and in what ways inferior to Mesopotamian civilization?

4. Compare the religions of Egypt and Mesopotamia from the standpoints of ethical concepts, notions of the afterlife, and views of human nature.

5. Despite their great accomplishments in mathematics, medicine, and astronomy, the Egyptians were limited by their very cast of mind from carrying any science very far. Discuss the reasons for this.

6. In the life around you what are the evidences, direct or indirect, of Egyptian achievements?

7. Geography is sometimes said to be the determining factor in a nation's history. To what extent was this true of ancient Egypt?

8. Why is modern Egypt not the center of a great civilization?

GEOGRAPHICAL IDENTIFICATIONS

Nile Delta	Thebes	Nubia
Memphis	Syria	Gizeh
Luxor	Libya	Karnak

AIDS TO AN UNDERSTANDING OF EGYPTIAN CIVILIZATION

Ethical Doctrines of the *Book of the Dead*

. . . I have not done iniquity.
. . . I have not robbed with violence.
. . . I have not done violence to any man.
. . . I have not committed theft.
. . . I have not slain man or woman.
. . . I have not made light the bushel.
. . . I have not acted deceitfully.
. . . I have not purloined the things which belong unto God.
. . . I have not uttered falsehood.
. . . I have not carried away food.
. . . I have not uttered evil words.
. . . I have attacked no man.
. . . I have not killed the beasts, which are the property of God.
. . . I have not acted deceitfully.
. . . I have not laid waste the lands which have been plowed.
. . . I have never pried into matters to make mischief.
. . . I have not set my mouth in motion against any man.
. . . I have not given way to wrath concerning myself without a cause.
. . . I have not defiled the wife of a man.
. . . I have not committed any sin against purity.
. . . I have not struck fear into any man.
. . . I have not encroached upon sacred times and seasons.
. . . I have not been a man of anger.
. . . I have not made myself deaf to the words of right and truth.
. . . I have not stirred up strife.
. . . I have made no man to weep.
. . . I have not committed acts of impurity. . . .
. . . I have not eaten my heart.
. . . I have abused no man.
. . . I have not acted with violence.
. . . I have not judged hastily.
. . . I have not taken vengeance upon the god.
. . . I have not multiplied my speech overmuch.
. . . I have not acted with deceit, and I have not worked wickedness.
. . . I have not uttered curses on the King.
. . . I have not fouled water.
. . . I have not made haughty my voice.
. . . I have not cursed the god.
. . . I have not sought for distinctions.
. . . I have not increased my wealth, except with such things as are justly mine own possessions.
. . . I have not thought scorn of the god who is in my city.

From E. A. Wallis Budge, *The Book of the Dead: The Chapters of Coming Forth by Day.*

The Royal Hymn of Akhenaton

Praise to thee. When thou risest in the horizon, O living Aton, lord of eternity. Obeisance to thy rising in heaven, to illuminate every land, with thy beauty. Thy rays are upon thy beloved son. Thy hand has a myriad of jubilees for the King of Upper and Lower Egypt, . . . thy child who came forth from thy rays. Thou assignest to him thy lifetime and thy years. Thou hearest for him that which is in his heart. He is thy beloved, thou makest him like Aton. When thou risest, eternity is given him; when thou settest, thou givest him everlastingness. Thou begettest him in the morning like thine own forms; ruler of truth, who came forth from eternity, son of Re, wearing his beauty, who offers to him the product of his rays; . . . living in truth, Lord of the Two lands, . . . living forever and ever.

From James Henry Breasted, *Ancient Records of Egypt,* Vol. II.

The King as the Good Shepherd
John A. Wilson

An element in the Egyptian psychology which we have stressed was confidence, a sense of assurance and of special election, which promoted individual assertiveness, a relish of life as it was, and a tolerance for divergences from the most rigid application of the norm. The Egyptian was never introspective and never was rigidly demanding of himself or of others, because he was free from fear. As yet he had been the architect of his own destiny, had achieved a proud, rich, and successful culture, and had survived one period of inner turmoil with a return to the full, round life. This feeling of security and of unimpaired destiny may have been the product of geographic isolation; it may have had its roots in the fertile black soil; it may have been warmed by the good African sun; it may have been intensified by the contrast of the harsh and meager life in the deserts that bordered Egypt. . . . The dogmatic expression of this special providence was the belief that Egypt alone was ruled by a god, that the physical child of the sun-god would govern and protect Egypt throughout eternity. What was there then to fear?

From John A. Wilson, *The Burden of Egypt,* The University of Chicago Press, 1951. Reprinted by permission of the publisher.

ANALYSIS AND INTERPRETATION
OF THE READINGS

1. What differing concepts of deity are reflected in
   the ethical doctrines of the *Book of the Dead*?

CHAPTER
4

The Hebrew and Early Greek Civilizations

CHRONOLOGY

Number the events listed below in their proper chronological order from earliest to latest. Write in the dates (all are B.C.) for the items marked with an asterisk.

_____Chaldean conquest of the Kingdom of Judah*

_____Conquest of Palestine by Alexander the Great

_____Trojan War* (Mycenaean conquest of Troy)

_____Beginning of the Roman protectorate over Palestine

_____Accession of King David*

_____Philistine conquests in Canaan

_____Dark Age in Greek history*

_____Invasion of Greek peninsula by Indo-Europeans

_____Flourishing of Mycenaean civilization

_____End of the United Hebrew Kingdom

IDENTIFICATIONS

You should be familiar with the meaning or role of each of the following persons or terms in relation to Hebrew or early Greek civilization:

Joshua
Samuel
Ark of the Covenant
Judas Maccabeus
diaspora
eschatology
Deuteronomic Code

Abraham
Philistines
Yahweh
National Monolatry
Minos
Michael Ventris
Dorians

STUDY QUESTIONS

1. Explain the origin of the term "Israelite."
2. How did the region called Palestine get its name?
3. How did the Philistine invasions affect the Hebrews' political history?
4. Describe the changes in Hebrew society and economy under Kings David and Solomon.
5. Why did Solomon consider it essential to build a great temple?
6. Identify and characterize each of the four stages in the evolution of the Hebrew religion.
7. Three basic doctrines made up the substance of the teachings of the great prophets Isaiah, Hosea, Amos, and Micah. What were they?
8. What is the real significance of the prophetic revolution in the development of the ancient Hebrew religion?
9. Compare the philosophical points of view of the following books of the Old Testament: Job, Proverbs, Ecclesiastes.
10. What concept of a messiah is set forth in the Book of Daniel?
11. Giving specific examples, explain how the Deuteronomic Code represents an ethical advance over the Code of Hammurabi.
12. "The literature of the Hebrews was the finest produced by any ancient civilization of western Asia." Justify this statement.
13. What is meant by "transcendent theology"? How did its acceptance by the Hebrews affect their view of humanity's relationship with nature?
14. What was the most important "storybook triumph" in the annals of archaeology?
15. In what ways did Minoan society resemble modern Western societies?
16. Minoan art differed considerably from Egyptian and Mesopotamian art. Show how its art suggests the nature of the Minoans' culture.
17. What were the chief characteristics of the Minoan religion?
18. How did Mycenaean civilization differ from the Minoan?
19. What light had the decipherment of "Linear B" thrown on Mycenaean civilization?
20. What is the lasting importance of the Minoan and Mycenaean civilizations?

15

PROBLEMS

1. Compare the portraits of Solomon in I Kings 2–12 and I Chronicles 28–29 and II Chronicles 1–10.
2. Read the Books of Amos and Micah in the Old Testament and answer the following: (a) Where are these prophets from and what is their background? (b) What land is the target of their criticism? (c) What conditions, social and religious, are they deploring? (d) What are their religious and ethical standards?
3. The Book of Job deals with the problem of theodicy, that is, of the origin of evil. Read it and analyze with citations to the text the problem as presented there. Other than his physical rewards, what is the nature of Job's triumph?
4. Read Deuteronomy and sketch the character of the society that Moses demands.
5. Read either Proverbs or Ecclesiastes and analyze with citations to the text the philosophy set forth.
6. Explore further any of the following:
   a. The archaeological discoveries of Heinrich Schliemann or Arthur Evans
   b. Recent developments in Aegean archaeology
   c. Sports in the Minoan culture
   d. Cretan writing and attempts to decipher it
   e. The debt of Crete to Egypt

GEOGRAPHICAL IDENTIFICATIONS

Land of Canaan

Sinai Peninsula

Kingdom of Israel

Kingdom of Judah

Crete

Aegean Sea

Dead Sea

Jordan River

Damascus

Palestine

Knossos

Troy

AIDS TO AN UNDERSTANDING OF THE HEBREW AND EARLY GREEK CIVILIZATIONS

HEBREW PIETY
Psalm 1

Blessed is the man that walketh not in the counsel of the ungodly, nor standeth in the way of sinners, nor sitteth in the seat of the scornful.

But his delight is in the law of the Lord; and in his law doth he meditate day and night.

And he shall be like a tree planted by the rivers of water, that bringeth forth his fruit in his season; his leaf also shall not wither; and whatsoever he doeth shall prosper.

The ungodly are not so: but are like the chaff which the wind driveth away.

Therefore the ungodly shall not stand in the judgment, nor sinners in the congregation of the righteous.

For the Lord knoweth the way of the righteous: but the way of the ungodly shall perish.

THE RELIGION OF THE PROPHETIC REVOLUTION
Amos 5:21-24

I hate, I despise your feast days, and I will not smell in your solemn assemblies.

Though ye offer me burnt offerings and your meat offerings, I will not accept them: neither will I regard the peace offerings of your fat beasts.

Take thou away from me the noise of thy songs; for I will not hear the melody of thy viols.

But let judgment run down as waters, and righteousness as a mighty stream.

HEBREW PHILOSOPHY
Proverbs 10:5-14

He that gathereth in summer is a wise son: but he that sleepeth in harvest is a son that causeth shame.

Blessings are upon the head of the just: but violence covereth the mouth of the wicked.

The memory of the just is blessed: but the name of the wicked shall rot.

The wise in heart will receive commandments: but a prating fool shall fall.

He that walketh uprightly walketh surely: but he that perverteth his ways shall be known.

He that winketh with the eye causeth sorrow: but a prating fool shall fall.

The mouth of a righteous man is a well of life: but violence covereth the mouth of the wicked.

Hatred stirreth up strifes: but love covereth all sins.

In the lips of him that hath understanding wisdom is found: but a rod is for the back of him that is void of understanding.

Wise men lay up knowledge: but the mouth of the foolish is near destruction.

THE BOOK OF JOB
9:1–17

Then Job answered:
"Truly I know that it is so; But how can a man be just before God?

If one wished to contend with him, one could not answer him once in a thousand times.

He is wise in heart, and mighty in strength — who has hardened himself against him, and succeeded? —

He who removes mountains, and they know it not, when he overturns them in his anger;

who shakes the earth out of its place, and its pillars tremble;

who commands the sun, and it does not rise; who seals up the stars;

who alone stretched out the heavens, and trampled the waves of the sea;

who made the Bear and Orion, the Pleiades and the chambers of the south;

who does great things beyond understanding, and marvelous things without number.

Lo, he passes by me, and I see him not; he moves on, but I do not perceive him.

Behold, he snatches away; who can hinder him? Who will say to him, 'What doest thou'?

"God will not turn back his anger; beneath him bowed the helpers of Rahab.

How then can I answer him, choosing my words with him?

Though I am innocent, I cannot answer him; I must appeal for mercy to my accuser.

If I summoned him and he answered me, I would not believe that he was listening to my voice.

For he crushes me with a tempest, and multiplies my wounds without cause.

10:18–22
"Why didst thou bring me forth from the womb?

Would that I had died before any eye had seen me, and were as though I had not been, carried from the womb to the grave.

Are not the days of my life few? Let me alone, that I may find a little comfort before I go whence I shall not return, to the land of gloom and deep darkness, the land of gloom and chaos, where light is as darkness."

19:20-27

My bones cleave to my skin and to my flesh, and I have escaped by the skin of my teeth.

Have pity on me, have pity on me, O you my friends, for the hand of God has touched me!

Why do you, like God, pursue me? Why are you not satisfied with my flesh?

Oh that my words were written! Oh that they were inscribed in a book! Oh that with an iron pen and lead they were graven in the rock for ever!

For I know that my Redeemer lives, and at last he will stand upon the earth;

and after my skin has been thus destroyed, then without my flesh I shall see God, whom I shall see on my side, and my eyes shall behold, and not another. My heart faints within me!

38: 1-20

Then the LORD answered Job out of the whirlwind: "Who is this that darkens counsel by words without knowledge? Gird up your loins like a man, I will question you, and you shall declare to me.

"Where were you when I laid the foundation of the earth? Tell me, if you have understanding. Who determined its measurements — surely you know! Or who stretched the line upon it? On what were its bases sunk, or who laid its cornerstone, when the morning stars sang together, and all the sons of God shouted for joy?

"Or who shut in the sea with doors, when it burst forth from the womb; when I made clouds its garment and thick darkness its swaddling band, and prescribed bounds for it, and set bars and doors, and said, 'Thus far shall you come and no farther, and here shall your proud waves be stayed'?

"Have you commanded the morning since your days began, and caused the dawn to know its place, that it might take hold of the skirts of the earth, and the wicked be shaken out of it?

It is changed like clay under the seal, and it is dyed like a garment. From the wicked their light is withheld, and their uplifted arm is broken.

"Have you entered into the springs of the sea, or walked in the recesses of the deep? Have the gates of death been revealed to you, or have you seen the gates of deep darkness? Have you comprehended the expanse of the earth? Declare, if you know all this.

"Where is the way to the dwelling of light, and where is the place of darkness, that you may take it to its territory and that you may discern the paths to its home?

42:1-6

Then Job answered the Lord: "I know that thou canst do all things, and that no purpose of thine can be thwarted.

'Who is this that hides counsel without knowledge?' Therefore I have uttered what I did not understand, things too wonderful for me, which I did not know.

'Hear, and I will speak; I will question you, and you declare to me.' I had heard of thee by the hearing of the ear, but now my eye sees thee; therefore I despise myself, and repent in dust and ashes."

THE MYCENAEANS AS A GREEK DYNASTY
John Chadwick

One fact stands out at once as of major consequence: the Mycenaeans were Greeks. Schliemann, when he excavated the first grave circle at Mycenae, had no doubt that he had unearthed a Greek dynasty, and in his famous telegram to the king of Greece claimed to have looked upon the face of one of the king's ancestors. But more academic judges were not so certain, and at one time theories of foreign domination were invoked to account for the precocious brilliance of the Mycenaeans at such a remove from the historical Greeks. The proof that the language of their accounts was Greek might be thought to have settled all controversy on this score; but much ingenuity has been expended on attempts to circumvent the implications of this evidence. The language of accounts is not always that of their writers: an Indian business house may find it convenient to keep its accounts in English; a medieval king of England may have had his secretaries write in Latin. But in all such cases which I know of, the language in question is a dominant literary language, and the language replaced by it a local one with restricted currency and often no adequate orthography. If Greek were adopted by foreigners as a written language, as it was in Hellenistic Egypt, then this implies that Greek was already a dominant literary language: a conclusion which on the available evidence is absurd.

Even this does not answer two theories which have been put forward: either that the preserved tablets were written by Greek scribes in Greek at the behest of foreign rulers; or that they were written by foreign scribes in Greek for Greek rulers. The best refutation of these theories is the existence in the tablets of large numbers of transparently Greek personal names, and these are not stratified but belong equally to all classes of society. For instance, a person of the highest standing at Pylos is named *E-ke-ra$_2$-wo*, which appears to be a well-known type of Greek name *Ekhelawon*; at the other end of the social scale a smith has the delightful name *Mnasiwergos* "Mindful-of-his-work" and a goat-herd has the common name *Philaios*.

Many names of course are much harder to interpret as Greek, and some are certainly foreign; but the presence of an element foreign in origin, if not still in speech, does not contradict the positive evidence that Greeks were widely spread throughout society, and we can feel sure that the Mycenaeans were at least predominantly Greek. The 700 years or so between the coming of the Greeks and the Pylos tablets are time enough to allow the pre-Hellenic inhabitants to have been absorbed.

The presence of Greeks at Knossos is still something of an embarrassment. Professor Wace and a few other archaeologists had demonstrated the close links between Knossos and the mainland in the period preceding the fall of the Palace there, and even proposed to explain them as due to mainland influence on Crete, and not vice versa. The truth is that the limitations of archaeological research preclude deductions about the languages spoken by the people studied. The physical remains may allow an anthropological classification, but people of a given physical type do not all speak the same language. The study of "cultures," peoples using artifacts of similar type, is the archaeologists' main weapon. (It is this, for instance, which enables us to feel sure that about 1900 B.C. a wave of invaders entered and settled in Greece. But the inference that these were the ancestors of the Greeks is based upon the knowledge that Greek was subsequently spoken in that area, and could not be made without recourse to non-archaeological premises.)

Thus a clear statement from the archaeologists of the date when mainland influence first appears at Knossos is a vain hope. When a half-civilized people conquer a civilized one, they try to absorb and adapt as much as they can of the superior civilization, so, especially if the actual conquest is not accompanied by great destruction, the event may easily escape the archaeologist's spade. There is, however, one piece of evidence, not strictly archaeological, which proves that the Greek domination of Crete was a comparatively recent event: the use of Linear A, apparently down to the early fifteenth century, is an indication that Greek had not then replaced Minoan as the language of accounts; unless Linear A too is Greek, a possibility which none but the most determined enthusiasts will admit.

From John Chadwick, *The Decipherment of Linear B*, Cambridge University Press, 1958. Reprinted by permission of the publisher and the author.

ANALYSIS AND INTERPRETATION OF THE READINGS

1. What do the passages from the Book of Job tell us about the Hebrew concept of a deity?
2. What do the "Linear B" tablets tell us about the relationship of the Mycenaeans to Greek civilization?

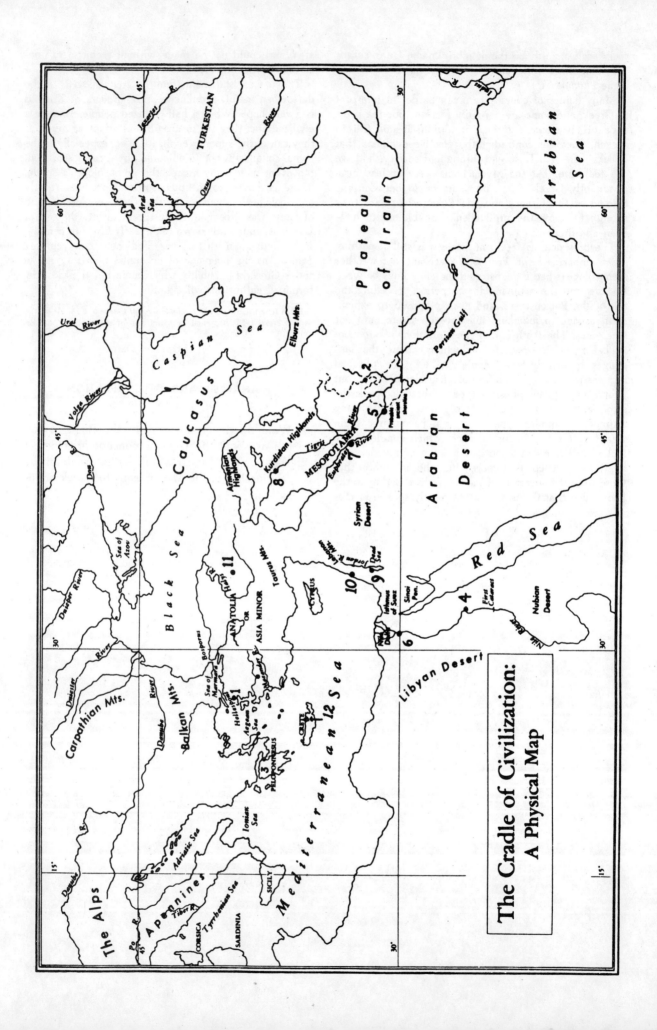

The Cradle of Civilization:
A Physical Map

(Chapters 1–4)
The Dawn of History

MAP WORK

On the map opposite are twelve numbers representing the locations of cities or areas important in the history of the ancient Near East. In the blanks below write the correct number and the name of each place described:

• Assyrian capital which was captured and utterly destroyed in 612 B.C.

_____

• Leading city of Greece about 1600–1200 B.C.

_____

• Capital of the Hittite Empire at its peak.

_____

• Site of Great Pyramid built under Egyptian Old Kingdom.

_____

• Famous target of the Greeks in the *Iliad* and scene of Schliemann's first archaeological discoveries.

_____

• Capital of the Kingdom of Judah which defied the Assyrians but fell to the Chaldeans.

_____

• City whose local deity, Amon, became Amon-Re, one of the two most important Egyptian deities.

_____

• Capital of the northern Hebrew kingdom.

_____

• Site of the earliest Mesopotamian civilization

_____

• Capital of the Chaldeans, which was turned over to Cyrus "without a battle and without fighting."

_____

• Chief center of Minoan civilization in the second millennium B.C.

_____

CHRONOLOGICAL REVIEW

On the chart opposite, plot and label lines representing the approximate dates of each listed era. For an example, the Old Kingdom of Egypt has been plotted.

	3000 B.C.		2000 B.C.		1000 B.C.		C.E.

Old Kingdom
of Egypt

Middle Kingdom
of Egypt

Hyksos rule
in Egypt

Egyptian New
Kingdom

Minoan
civilization

Old Babylonian
Empire

Hittite
Empire

Kassite rule
in the Tigris-
Euphrates Valley

Hebrew conquest
of Canaan

United Hebrew
Monarchy

Kingdom of
Israel

Kingdom of
Judah

Assyrian
Empire

Chaldean or Neo-
Babylonian Empire

Persian
Empire

Greek Civilization

CHRONOLOGY

Following is a list of events in Greek history with which you should be familiar. Arrange them in the spaces below according to their proper chronological order (earliest to latest) and after each write its date, or, in some cases, its approximate date:

rule of Clisthenes
rise of Greek city-states
Peloponnesian War
period of most active colonization
appointment of Solon as magistrate
Persian Wars
Dark Ages
triumph of Thebes over Sparta
rise of the Sophists
beginning of tragic drama

1._____

2._____

3._____

4._____

5._____

6._____

7._____

8._____

9._____

10._____

IDENTIFICATIONS

You should be able to identify the following:

Iliad	Parthenon
Odyssey	phalanx
helot	polity
ostracism	Symposium
basileus	Lysistrata
demagogue	Nicomachean Ethics

Each of the following descriptions applies to one of the three people named in the brackets after it. In each blank, insert the number of the person described:

_____A member of the pre-Socratic school, he believed that the original material of the universe was water. [1. Thales, 2. Anaximenes, 3. Anaximander]

_____The "father of Athenian democracy," he greatly enlarged both the size of the citizen population and its political powers late in the sixth century B.C. [1. Solon, 2. Hippias, 3. Clisthenes]

_____A teacher in Athens, his dictum, "Man is the measure of all things," contained the essence of the Sophist philosophy. [1. Protagoras, 2. Pericles, 3. Phidias]

_____The father of scientific medicine, he emphasized that every disease has a natural cause. [1. Hippocrates, 2. Thales, 3. Pythagoras]

_____A benevolent tyrant, his son's rule was so oppressive that it was forcefully overthrown. [1. Solon, 2. Pisistratus, 3. Hippias]

_____One of the three greatest Greek tragedians, his *Oedipus* emphasized the universal qualities of human nature. [1. Aeschylus, 2. Sophocles, 3. Euripides]

_____A man who left no writings, but whose teaching that universally valid knowledge can make man virtuous had a profound effect on later thinkers. [1. Homer, 2. Socrates, 3. Aristotle]

_____An island dweller, this female poet was a lyricist of great sensitivity. [1. Helen, 2. Sappho, 3. the wife of Socrates]

_____A statesman and general, his Funeral Oration extolled Athenian ideals of democracy and "beauty without extravagance." [1. Solon, 2. Clisthenes, 3. Pericles]

_____The formulator of a famous mathematical theorem, he taught the necessity of purification from earthly desire. [1. Thales, 2. Pythagoras, 3. Aristotle]

_____Author of the *Phaedo* and the *Republic*, he taught that ideas exist in eternal forms. [1. Plato, 2. Protagoras, 3. Myron]

_____Sometimes considered the founder of scientific history, he wrote a famous, dispassionate account of the Peloponnesian War. [1. Herodotus, 2. Xerxes, 3. Thucydides]

STUDY QUESTIONS

1. Describe the primitive character of government in Greece during the Dark Ages.
2. What aspects of Greek religion are illustrated in the myth of Persephone and Demeter?
3. In what way did the Greeks seek "to strike a balance between awe of their gods and pride in themselves"?
4. How did the system of writing developed by Greeks of the classical age differ from the earlier one used by the Mycenaeans, and what were its advantages?
5. How did a transformation in Greek military techniques affect the distribution of political power?
6. Point out the essential differences between the Greek city-states and modern states in the concept of citizenship and the role of citizens.
7. Among societies dominated by male warriors, why did the Spartans become the most militarized?
8. Explain the saying that Spartans were "the only people to whom war might give repose."
9. Point out both the similarities and differences between the Spartan and Athenian governments.
10. What environmental factors favored the development of democracy in Athens?
11. Describe the composition and function of each of the following in the Athenian democracy: the assembly, council of 500, magistrates, and generals.
12. What were the causes of the Persian War? Why in its outcome can it be regarded as "one of the most significant in the history of the [Western] world"?
13. Explain how an Athenian confederacy was transformed into an Athenian empire.
14. Describe the results of the Peloponnesian War for Greece.
15. Explain how and why the progress of democracy in Athens, instead of emancipating women, led them more deeply "into the shadows."
16. How did the Athenians attempt to justify the institution of slavery?
17. What factors prompted the Greeks to "invent philosophy"?

18. Cicero said of the Sophists that they "brought philosophy down from heaven to the dwellings of men." What did he mean?
19. Explain why the three most famous Greek philosophers broke with the teachings of the Sophists.
20. Describe the Socratic method of exploring truth. What aspects of reality did Socrates not examine?
21. Contrast the political system envisioned in Plato's *Republic* with the Athenian democracy.
22. How did Aristotle's conception of ultimate reality, of human nature, and of the ideal government differ from those of his teacher Plato?
23. How did Herodotus, "the father of history," view the nature and significance of history?
24. What aspects of classical Greek civilization are reflected in the Homeric epics?
25. In addition to its artistic excellence, why did tragic drama appeal so strongly to Greeks of the classical age?
26. What innovations did Euripides contribute to tragic drama?
27. What are the parallels between classical Greek sculpture and drama? Why did the sculptors avoid realism?
28. The Greeks are often described as humanists. To what extent is the description appropriate, and what were the limitations of their humanism?

PROBLEMS

1. Why did Athenians at the peak of their democratic development turn to imperialism? Is there any parallel in the history of the United States?
2. Why were the Sophists, who were complete relativists, also such intense and democratic humanists?
3. Read a play by Sophocles and another by Euripides and compare their respective attitudes.
4. Investigate further any of the following:
   a. Homeric religion
   b. The nature of Spartan militarism
   c. Greek tactics in the Persian War
   d. Athenian government under Pericles
   e. Thucydides' account of the Peloponnesian War
   f. Socrates' life and teachings
   g. Plato's *Republic*
   h. Aristotle's biology
   i. Greek sculpture
   j. Athenian life in the time of Athens's ascendancy
5. Compare Athenian ideals as described in the Funeral Oration of Pericles (Thucydides, *The Peloponnesian War*) with those of Sparta as described

by Plutarch in his life of Lycurgus (Plutarch, *Lives of Illustrious Men*).

6. Discuss the effects of wars on Greek civilization.

7. Study the philosophy of Plato as contained in *The Republic* and see if you can reconcile it with the ideals of the typical Greek as described by G. L. Dickinson in *The Greek Way of Life*.

8. Trace as many as possible of the elements of Greek civilization to their origins in the civilizations of western Asia.

9. Read the discussion of Euripides in Edith Hamilton, *The Greek Way* (Chap. XIV). Why does she disagree with the dictum that he was the most tragic of the dramatists? Why does she consider him the exponent of "the modern mind"?

10. Defend or attack the statement: "The culture of the Greeks was the first to be based upon the primacy of intellect—upon the supremacy of the spirit of free inquiry. . . . To an extent never before realized, mind was supreme over faith, logic and science over superstition."

GEOGRAPHICAL IDENTIFICATIONS

Attica	Delphi	Samos
Lesbos	Mt. Olympus	Thebes
Miletus	Rhodes	Naxos
Melos	Athens	Cyprus
Thessaly	Sparta	Naples
Macedonia	Laconia	Argos
Thrace	Messenia	Salamis
Marathon	Peloponnesian	
Gulf of Corinth	Peninsula	
Chios	Syracuse	

THE SPARTAN SYSTEM
Plutarch

And this was the reason why he [Lycurgus] forbade them to travel abroad, and go about acquainting themselves with foreign rules of morality, the habits of ill-educated people, and different views of government. Withal he banished from Lacedæmon all strangers who would not give a very good reason for their coming thither; not because he was afraid lest they should inform themselves of and imitate his manner of government (as Thucydides says), or learn any thing to their good; but rather lest they should introduce something contrary to good manners. With strange people, strange words must be admitted; these novelties produce novelties in thought; and on these follow views and feelings whose discordant character destroys the harmony of the state. He was as careful to save his city from the infection of foreign bad habits, as men usually are to prevent the introduction of a pestilence.

Hitherto I, for my part, see no sign of injustice or want of equity in the laws of Lycurgus, though some who admit them to be well contrived to make good soldiers, pronounce them defective in point of justice. The Cryptia, perhaps (if it were one of Lycurgus's ordinances, as Aristotle says it was), gave both him and Plato, too, this opinion alike of the lawgiver and his government. By this ordinance, the magistrates despatched privately some of the ablest of the young men into the country, from time to time, armed only with their daggers, and taking a little necessary provision with them; in the daytime, they hid themselves in out-of-the-way places, and there lay close, but, in the night issued out into the highways, and killed all the Helots they could light upon; sometimes they set upon them by day, as they were at work in the fields, and murdered them. As, also, Thucydides, in his history of the Peloponnesian war, tells us, that a good number of them, after being singled out for their bravery by the Spartans, garlanded, as enfranchised persons, and led about to all the temples in token of honors, shortly after disappeared all of a sudden, being about the number of two thousand; and no man either then or since could give an account how they came by their deaths. And Aristotle, in particular, adds that the ephori, so soon as they were entered into their office, used to declare war against them, that they might be massacred without a breach of religion. It is confessed, on all hands, that the Spartans dealt with them very hardly; for it was a common thing to force them to drink to excess, and to lead them in that condition into their public halls, that the children might see what a sight a drunken man is; they made them to dance low dances, and sing ridiculous songs, forbidding them expressly to meddle with any of a better kind. And accordingly, when the Thebans made their invasion into Laconia, and took a great number of the Helots, they could by no means persuade them to sing the verses of Terpander, Alcman, or Spendon, "For," said they, "the masters do not like it." So that it was truly observed by one, that in Sparta he who was free was most so, and he that was a slave there, the greatest slave in the world. . . .

From Plutarch, *Lives of Illustrious Men* (Lycurgus), A. H. Clough trans.

ATHENIAN IDEALS: As Described by Pericles in his Famous Funeral Oration
Thucydides

Our form of government does not enter into rivalry with the institutions of others. We do not copy our neighbours, but are an example to them. It is true that we are called a democracy, for the administration is in the hands of the many and not of the few. But while the law secures equal justice to all alike in their private disputes, the claim of excellence is also recognised; and when a citizen is in any way distinguished, he is preferred to the public service, not as a matter of privilege, but as the reward of merit. Neither is poverty a bar, but a man may benefit his country whatever be the obscurity of his condition. There is no exclusiveness in our public life, and in our private intercourse we are not suspicious of one another, nor angry with our neighbour if he does what he likes; we do not put on sour looks at him which, though harmless, are not pleasant. While we are thus unconstrained in our private intercourse, a spirit of reverence pervades our public acts; we are prevented from doing wrong by respect for authority and for the laws, having an especial regard to those which are ordained for the protection of the injured as well as to those unwritten laws which bring upon the transgressor of them the reprobation of the general sentiment.

And we have not forgotten to provide for our weary spirits many relaxations from toil; we have regular games and sacrifices throughout the year; at home the style of our life is refined; and the delight which we daily feel in all these things helps to banish melancholy. Because of the greatness of our city the fruits of the whole earth flow in upon us; so that we enjoy the goods of other countries as freely as of our own.

Then, again, our military training is in many respects superior to that of our adversaries. Our city is thrown open to the world, and we never expel a foreigner or prevent him from seeing or learning anything of which the secret if revealed to an enemy might profit him. We rely not upon management or trickery, but upon our own hearts and hands. And in the matter of education, whereas they from early youth are always undergoing laborious exercises which are to make them brave, we live at ease, and yet are equally ready to face the perils which they face. . . .

For we are lovers of the beautiful, yet with economy, and we cultivate the mind without loss of manliness. Wealth we employ, not for talk and ostentation, but when there is a real use for it. To avow poverty with us is no disgrace; the true disgrace is in doing nothing to avoid it. An Athenian citizen does not neglect the state because he takes care of his own household; and even those of us who are engaged in business have a very fair idea of politics. We alone regard a man who takes no interest in public affairs, not as a harmless, but as a useless character; and if few of us are originators, we are all sound judges of a policy. The great impediment to action is, in our opinion, not discussion, but the want of that knowledge which is gained by discussion preparatory to action. For we have a peculiar power of thinking before we act and of acting too, whereas other men are courageous from ignorance but hesitate upon reflection. And they are surely to be esteemed the bravest spirits who, having the clearest sense both of the pains and pleasures of life, do not on that account shrink from danger. In doing good, again, we are unlike others; we make our friends by conferring, not by receiving favours. Now he who confers a favour is the firmer friend, because he would fain by kindness keep alive the memory of an obligation; but the recipient is colder in his feelings, because he knows that in requiting another's generosity he will not be winning gratitude but only paying a debt. We alone do good to our neighbours not upon a calculation of interest, but in the confidence of freedom and in a frank and fearless spirit.

To sum up: I say that Athens is the school of Hellas, and that the individual Athenian in his own person seems to have the power of adapting himself to the most varied forms of action with the utmost versatility and grace. This is no passing and idle word, but truth and fact; and the assertion is verified by the position to which these qualities have raised the state. For in the hour of trial Athens alone among her contemporaries is superior to the report of her. No enemy who comes against her is indignant at the reverses which he sustains at the hands of such a city; no subject complains that his masters are unworthy of him. And we shall assuredly not be without witnesses; there are mighty monuments of our power which will make us the wonder of this and of succeeding ages; we shall not need the praises of Homer or of any other panegyrist whose poetry may please for the moment, although his representation of the facts will not bear the light of day. For we have compelled every land and every sea to open a path for our valour, and have everywhere planted eternal memorials of our friendship and of our enmity. Such is the city for whose sake these men nobly fought and died; they could not bear the thought that she might be taken from them; and every one of us who survives should gladly toil on her behalf.

I have dwelt upon the greatness of Athens because I want to show you that we are contending for a higher prize than those who enjoy none of these privileges, and to establish by manifest proof the merit of these men whom I am now commemorating. Their loftiest praise has been already spoken. For in magnifying the city I have magnified them, and men like them whose virtues made her glorious. And of how few Hellenes can it be said as of them, that their deeds when weighed in the balance have been found equal to their fame! It seems to me that a death such as theirs has been given the true measure of a man's worth; it may be the first revelation of his virtues, but is at any rate their final seal.

From Thucydides, *The Peloponnesian War*, Benjamin Jowett trans.

THE DEATH OF SOCRATES
Plato

You, Simmias and Cebes, and all other men, will depart at some time or other. Me already, as the tragic poet would say, the voice of fate calls. Soon I must drink the poison; and I think that I had better repair to the bath first, in order that the women may not have the trouble of washing my body after I am dead.

When he had done speaking, Crito said: And have you any commands for us, Socrates — anything to say about your children, or any other matter in which we can serve you?

Nothing particular, he said: only, as I have always told you, I would have you look to yourselves; that is a service which you may always be doing to me and mine as well as to yourselves. And you need not make professions; for if you take no thought for yourselves, and walk not according to the precepts which I have given you, not now for the first time, the warmth of your professions will be of no avail.

We will do our best, said Crito. But in what way would you have us bury you?

In any way that you like: only you must get hold of me, and take care that I do not walk away from you. Then he turned to us, and added with a smile: — I can not make Crito believe that I am the same Socrates who has been talking and conducting the argument: he fancies that I am the other Socrates whom he will soon see, a dead body — and he asks, How shall he bury me? And though I have spoken many words in the endeavor to show that when I have drunk the poison I shall leave you and go to the joys of the blessed, — these words of mine, with which I comforted you and myself, have had, as I perceive, no effect upon Crito. And therefore I want you to be surety for me now, as he was surety for me at the trial: but let the promise be of another sort; for he was my surety to the judges that I would remain, but you must be my surety to him that I shall not remain, but go away and depart; and then he will suffer less at my death, and not be grieved when he sees my body being burned or buried. I would not have him sorrow at my hard lot, or say at the burial, Thus we lay out Socrates, or, Thus we follow him to the grave or bury him; for false words are not only evil in themselves, but they infect the soul with evil. Be of good cheer, then, my dear Crito, and say that you are burying my body only, and do with that as is usual, and as you think best.

When he had spoken these words, he arose and went into the bath-chamber with Crito, who bid us wait; and we waited, talking and thinking of the subject of discourse, and also of the greatness of our sorrow; he was like a father of whom we were being bereaved, and we were about to pass the rest of our lives as orphans. When he had taken the bath his children were brought to him — (he had two young sons and an elder one); and the women of his family also came, and he talked to them and gave them a few directions in the presence of Crito; and he then dismissed them and returned to us.

Now the hour of sunset was near, for a good deal of time had passed while he was within. When he came out, he sat down with us again after his bath, but not much was said. Soon the jailer, who was the servant of the eleven, entered and stood by him, saying: — To you, Socrates, whom I know to be the noblest and gentlest and best of all who ever came to this place, I will not impute the angry feelings of other men, who rage and swear at me, when, in obedience to the authorities, I bid them drink the poison — indeed, I am sure that you will not be angry with me; for others, as you are aware, and not I, are the guilty cause. And so fare you well, and try to bear lightly what must needs be; you know my errand. Then bursting into tears he turned away and went out.

Socrates looked at him and said: I return your good wishes, and will do as you bid. Then turning to us, he said, How charming the man is: since I have been in prison he has always been coming to see me, and at times he would talk to me, and was as good as could be to me, and now see how generously he sorrows for me. But we must do as he says, Crito; let the cup be brought, if the poison is prepared: if not, let the attendant prepare some.

Yet, said Crito, the sun is still upon the hill-tops, and many a one has taken the draught late, and after the announcement has been made to him, he has eaten and drunk, and indulged in sensual delights; do not hasten then, there is still time.

Socrates said: Yes, Crito, and they of whom you speak are right in doing thus, for they think that they will gain by the delay; but I am right in not doing thus, for I do not think that I should gain anything by drinking the poison a little later; I should be sparing and saving a life which is already gone; I could only laugh at myself for this. Please then to do as I say, and not to refuse me.

Crito, when he heard this, made a sign to the servant; and the servant went in, and remained for some time, and then returned with the jailer carrying the cup of poison. Socrates said: You, my good friend, who are experienced in these matters, shall give me directions how I am to proceed. The man answered: You have only to walk about until your legs are heavy, and then to lie down, and the poison will act. At the same time he handed the cup to Socrates, who in the easiest and gentlest manner, without the least fear or change of color or feature, looking at the man with all his eyes, Echecrates, as his manner was, took the cup and said: What do you say about making a libation out of this cup to any god? May I, or not? The man answered: We only prepare, Socrates, just so much as we deem enough. I understand, he said: yet I may and must pray to the gods to prosper my journey from this to that other world — may this then, which is my prayer, be granted to me. Then holding the cup to his lips, quite readily and cheerfully he drank off the poison. And hitherto most of us had been able to control our sorrow; but now when we saw him drinking, and saw too that he had finished the draught, we could no longer forbear, and in spite of myself my own tears were flowing fast; so that I covered my face and wept over myself, for certainly I was not weeping over him, but at the thought of my own calamity in having lost such a companion. Nor was I the first, for Crito, when he found himself unable to restrain his tears, had got up and moved away, and I followed; and at that moment, Apollodorus, who had been weeping all the time, broke out into a loud cry which made cowards of us all. Socrates alone retained his calmness: What is this strange outcry? he said. I sent away the women mainly in order that they might not offend in this way, for I have heard that a man should die in peace. Be quiet then, and have patience. When we heard that, we were ashamed, and refrained our tears; and he walked about until, as he said, his legs began to fail, and then he lay on his back, according to the directions, and the man who gave him the poison now and then looked at his feet and legs; and after a while he pressed his foot hard, and asked him if he could feel; and he said, No; and then his leg, and so upwards and upwards, and showed us that he was cold and stiff. And he felt then himself and said: When the poison reaches the heart, that will be the end. He was beginning to grow cold about the groin, when he uncovered his face, for he had covered himself up, and said (they were his last words) — he said: Crito, I owe a cock to Asclepius; will you remember to pay the debt? The debt shall be paid, said Crito; is there anything else? There was no answer to this question; but in a minute or two a movement was heard, and the attendants uncovered him; his eyes were set, and Crito closed his eyes and mouth.

Such was the end, Echecrates, of our friend, whom I may truly call the wisest, and justest, and best of all men whom I have ever known.

From Benjamin Jowett trans., *The Dialogues of Plato* (Phaedo).

PLATO'S IDEAL STATE: The Life of the Guardians
Plato

Then now let us consider what will be their way of life, if they are to realize our idea of them. In the first place, none of them should have any property of his own beyond what is absolutely necessary; neither should they have a private house or store closed against any one who has a mind to enter; their provisions should be only such as are required by trained warriors, who are men of temperance and courage; they should agree to receive from the citizens a fixed rate of pay, enough to meet the expenses of the year and no more; and they will go to mess and live together like soldiers in a camp. Gold and silver we will tell them that they have from God; the diviner metal is within them, and they have therefore no need of the dross which is current among them, and ought not to pollute the divine by any such earthly admixture; for that commoner metal has been the source of many unholy deeds, but their own is undefiled. And they alone of all the citizens may not touch or handle silver or gold, or be under the same roof with them, or wear them, or drink from them. And this will be their salvation, and they will be the saviors of the State. But should they ever acquire homes or lands or moneys of their own, they will become housekeepers and husbandmen instead of guardians, enemies and tyrants instead of allies of the other citizens; hating and being hated, plotting and being plotted against, they will pass their whole life in much greater terror of internal than of external enemies, and the hour of ruin, both to themselves and to the rest of the State, will be at hand. For all which reasons may we not say that thus shall our State be ordered, and that these shall be the regulations appointed by us for our guardians concerning their houses and all other matters?

Yes, said Glaucon. . . .

. . .

I said: *Until philosophers are kings, or the kings and princes of this world have the spirit and power of philosophy, and political greatness and wisdom meet in one, and those commoner natures who pursue either to the exclusion of the other are compelled to stand aside, cities will never have rest from their evils, — no, nor the human race, as I believe, — and then only will this our State have a possibility of life and behold the light of day.*

From Benjamin Jowett trans., *The Dialogues of Plato* (Republic).

THE GREEK IDEA OF TRAGEDY
Edith Hamilton

The great tragic artists of the world are four, and three of them are Greek. It is in tragedy that the pre-eminence of the Greeks can be seen most clearly. Except for Shakespeare, the great three, Æschylus, Sophocles, Euripides, stand alone. Tragedy is an achievement peculiarly Greek. They were the first to perceive it and they lifted it to its supreme height. Nor is it a matter that directly touches only the great artists who wrote tragedies; it concerns the entire people as well, who felt the appeal of the tragic to such a degree that they would gather thirty thousand strong to see a performance. In tragedy the Greek genius penetrated farthest and it is the revelation of what was most profound in them.

The special characteristic of the Greeks was their power to see the world clearly and at the same time as beautiful. Because they were able to do this, they produced art distinguished from all other art by an absence of struggle, marked by a calm and serenity which is theirs alone. There is, it seems to assure us, a region where beauty is truth, truth beauty. To it their artists would lead us, illumining life's dark confusions by gleams fitful indeed and wavering compared with the fixed light of religious faith, but by some magic of their own, satisfying, affording a vision of something inconclusive and yet of incalculable significance. Of all the great poets this is true, but truest of the tragic poets, for the reason that in them the power of poetry confronts the inexplicable.

Tragedy was a Greek creation because in Greece thought was free. Men were thinking more and more deeply about human life, and beginning to perceive more and more clearly that it was bound up with evil and that injustice was of the nature of things. And then, one day, this knowledge of something irremediably wrong in the world came to a poet with his poet's power to see beauty in the truth of human life, and the first tragedy was written.

From Edith Hamilton, *The Greek Way*, W. W. Norton & Company, Inc., 1958. Reprinted by permission of the publisher.

THE ORIGINS OF GREECE AND THE ILLUSIONS OF AFROCENTRISTS
Mary Lefkowitz

Now, classicists in the late modern world have more than enough grounds for paranoia. We are reminded daily that our subject is useless, irrelevant, boring—all the things that, in our opinion, it is not. But now a new set of charges has been added. Not only students, but also the many academic acolytes of Martin Bernal's influential theories about "the Afroasiatic roots of Western civilization," and Bernal himself, ask us to acknowledge that we have been racists and liars, the perpetrators of a vast intellectual and cultural cover-up, or at the very least the suppressors of an African past that, until our students and our colleagues began to mention it, we had ourselves known nothing about.

Had our teachers deceived us, and their teachers deceived them? Classicists should be perfectly willing to ask themselves these questions, because we know, at least as well as our critics, that much of our so-called knowledge of the past is based on educated guesswork and sensible conjectures. In my own lifetime I have seen many histories and many textbooks rewritten to take account of new finds. Before the Mycenaean "Linear B" syllabary was deciphered in 1952, many scholars believed that people who lived in Greece and Crete between the sixteenth and twelfth centuries B.C. spoke a language other than Greek. When the tablets written in Linear B script were deciphered, however, it became clear that Greek had been spoken in settlements such as Mycenae and Knossos. That is, the world described by Homer was, in some basic sense, real. . . .

Until very recently, moreover, the Greek alphabet was regarded as a relatively late invention, coming into general use only after the beginning of the eighth century B.C. Now Semiticists insist that the shape of the letters shows that the Greek alphabet was modeled on the characters of a much earlier version of the Phoenician syllabary, perhaps from the tenth century B.C., perhaps even earlier.

If classicists managed to get all these things wrong, isn't it possible that they have ignored Egyptian and African elements in Greek culture? . . .

The question of Greek origins has been broached again, and become a subject of passionate popular discussion, with the publication of the first two volumes of Martin Bernal's *Black Athena: The Afroasiatic Roots of Classical Civilization*. Unlike most of his Afrocentric admirers, Bernal can read hieroglyphics and Greek, and he knows other ancient languages; and though his field is political science, he seems at home in the chronological and geographical complexities of the ancient Mediterranean. . . .

As Bernal's discussion, notes, and bibliography testify, he has read widely and thought strenuously about the Mediteranean as a whole, if not exactly

with an open mind, at least without giving priority to the Greeks, as classically trained scholars tend to do. Still, his assessment of the evidence for the Egyptian contribution starts from the unproven premise that European scholars have distorted the evidence, documentary and archaeological. His first volume, subtitled "The Fabrication of Ancient Greece," is a kind of historiographical prelude to the subject, in which he attacks the nineteenth-century notion that the Greeks were Aryans from the north. Bernal proposes to return from the "Aryan Model" to the "Ancient Model," that is, to Herodotus's notion that the Greeks derived their religion and possibly other important customs from the east, and from Egypt in particular. . . .

Nobody would deny that the Egyptians had a notable influence on Greek religion and art. On the basis of the most scrupulous scholarly evaluation of the present evidence, however, nobody should claim that the Greeks stole their best or their most significant ideas from the Egyptians, or from anyone else. Certainly, and fortunately, they did not copy their system of government from the Egyptians. We need only to look at the remains of public buildings. The pharaohs built the pyramids for themselves, mainly with slave labor. The Athenians voted to build the Parthenon for the use of all the citizens.

From Mary Lefkowitz, "Not out of Africa," *The New Republic*, February 10, 1992. Reprinted by permission of *The New Republic*, © 1992, The New Republic, Inc.

ANALYSIS AND INTERPRETATION OF THE READINGS

1. Was it really true that in Sparta, "he who was free was most so, and he that was a slave there, the greatest slave in the world"?

2. What proofs does Pericles offer, in his Funeral Oration, of the greatness of Athens? Do you think these proofs are valid?

3. Why did Socrates appear so willing to drink the hemlock?

4. Do you think that Plato actually believed his ideal state could become a reality?

5. Would Egyptologists agree with Lefkowitz's assumption that the pyramids were built mainly with slave labor?

CHAPTER 6

The Hellenistic Civilization

CHRONOLOGY

c. 600	323
559	301
490	30
338	

Selecting from the above list, write in the blanks provided the correct date for each of the following (all dates are B.C.):

Death of Alexander 323

Battle of Ipsus _____

Zoroaster c. 600

Completion of Roman
conquest of Hellenistic territory 30

Battle of Chaeronea _____

Battle of Marathon 490

Accession of Cyrus to Persian throne 559

IDENTIFICATIONS

The people of the Hellenistic Age most interesting to us now were its intellectuals, its writers, philosophers, and scientists. In the blanks below, write the name of the appropriate individual selected from the following list:

Carneades	~~Archimedes~~	Epicurus
Theocritus	Erasistratus	Ptolemy
Diogenes	Herophilus	Polybius
Menander	Eratosthenes	~~Aristarchus~~
~~Euclid~~	Zeno	

1. "Hellenistic Copernicus"

   Aristarchus

2. Peer of Thucydides

   _____

3. Leading Skeptic

   Carneades

4. Exponent of Cynic philosophy

   Diogenes

5. Greatest geographer of his age

   Eratosthenes

6. Athenian comic playwright

   Menander

7. Author of *Elements of Geometry*

   Euclid

8. Greatest anatomist of antiquity

   Herophilus

9. Founder of the Stoic philosophy

   Zeno

10. Recognized the brain as the seat of human intelligence

    Herophilus

11. Author of the *Almagest*

    Ptolemy

12. Discoverer of specific gravity

Archimedes

13. Founder of a materialist philosophy that affirmed pleasure as the highest good

Epicurus

14. Founder of physiology

_____

15. Pastoral poet of the third century B.C.

Theocritus

You should be able to define or explain each of the following:

magi	Achaean League
Avesta	the Laocoön
Aetolian League	satrap
eschatology	Hellenistic cosmopolitanism
Orphic cult	eclecticism

STUDY QUESTIONS

1. In what sense was Zoroaster the first real theologian in history?
2. Explain the basic teachings of Zoroastrianism. How was it both a universal and a personal religion?
3. Point out the parallels between Zoroastrianism, Judaism, and Christianity.
4. What were the enlightened aspects of Persian imperial rule?
5. Illustrate the eclectic character of Persian culture by describing its architecture.
6. Explain why Philip, ruler of semibarbarous Macedon, was able to conquer the more civilized cities of Greece.
7. In what ways and by what means did Alexander lay the foundations of Hellenistic civilization? In what respects did he break with Greek traditions and ideals?
8. To what extent should the Hellenistic civilization be considered as distinct from the Hellenic rather than a further development of it? What elements of continuity were there between the two civilizations?
9. How did the dominant political pattern of the Hellenistic Age differ from Hellenic political institutions or traditions?
10. Evaluate critically the economic conditions in the Hellenistic Age.
11. How do you explain the rapid growth of cities in spite of the fact that agriculture remained the chief source of wealth?
12. Do you agree that the Stoic philosophy was one of the noblest products of the Hellenistic Age? If so, why?
13. In what ways were Epicureanism and Stoicism alike and in what ways different?
14. How did the Epicurean philosophy differ from that of the Cynics and that of the Skeptics?
15. Contrast the popular religions of the Hellenistic Age with the civic-oriented religion of the Greeks.
16. Which genres of Hellenistic literature most clearly exhibit a penchant for escapism?
17. Characterize Hellenistic sculpture.
18. Why did science flower during the Hellenistic Age?
19. What are the apparent similarities between the Hellenistic Age and our own? What significant differences can be noted?

PROBLEMS

1. Compare the organization of Greece under the Achaean and Aetolian Leagues with that of the United States under the Articles of Confederation.
2. During Hellenistic times, did sculpture retrogress or progress from Greek standards?
3. Read Plutarch's life of Alexander and assess the validity of the notion that "history is the lengthened shadow of a great man."
4. Explain the importance of the Hellenistic Age as a period in world history.
5. Compare the science, literature, and art of the Hellenistic Age with those of the Hellenic Greeks. How do you account for the differences?
6. Compare the philosophy and religion of the Hellenistic Age with those of the Hellenic Greeks. How do you account for the differences?
7. Read W. W. Tarn, *Alexander the Great*, or a more recent biography such as Peter Green, *Alexander of Macedon*, and assess the validity of Alexander's title "the Great."
8. Investigate any of the following aspects of Hellenistic civilization:
   cities and city life
   medical science and practice
   the spread of Mithraism and other mystery cults
   economic trends

GEOGRAPHICAL IDENTIFICATIONS

Alexander's empire

Seleucid empire

Kingdom of the Ptolemies

Indus River

Red Sea

Persian Gulf

Macedonia

"Royal Road"

Bactria

Alexandria

Asia Minor

Cyprus

Syracuse

Pergamon

Halys River

Sardis

Persepolis

Ephesus

THE LAST DAYS OF ALEXANDER
Plutarch

When once Alexander had given way to fears of supernatural influence, his mind grew so disturbed and so easily alarmed, that if the least unusual or extraordinary thing happened, he thought it a prodigy or a presage, and his court was thronged with diviners and priests whose business was to sacrifice and purify and foretell the future. So miserable a thing is incredulity and contempt of divine power on the one hand, and so miserable, also, superstition on the other, which like water, where the level has been lowered, flowing in and never stopping, fills the mind with slavish fears and follies, as now in Alexander's case. But upon some answers which were brought him from the oracle concerning Hephæstion, he laid aside his sorrow, and fell again to sacrificing and drinking; and having given Nearchus a splendid entertainment, after he had bathed as was his custom, just as he was going to bed, at Medius's request he went to supper with him. Here he drank all the next day, and was attacked with a fever, which seized him, not as some write, after he had drunk of the bowl of Hercules; nor was he taken with any sudden pain in his back, as if he had been struck with a lance, for these are the inventions of some authors who thought it their duty to make the last scene of so great an action as tragical and moving as they could. Aristobulus tells us, that in the rage of his fever and a violent thirst, he took a draught of wine, upon which he fell into delirium, and died on the thirtieth of the month Dæsius.

But the journals give the following record. On the eighteenth of the month, he slept in the bathing-room on account of his fever. The next day he bathed and removed into his chamber, and spent his time in playing at dice with Medius. In the evening he bathed and sacrificed, and ate freely, and had the fever on him through the night. On the twentieth, after the usual sacrifices and bathing, he lay in the bathing-room and heard Nearchus's narrative of his voyage, and the observations he had made in the great sea. The twenty-first he passed in the same manner, his fever still increasing, and suffered much during the night. The next day the fever was very violent, and he had himself removed and his bed set by the great bath, and discoursed with his principal officers about finding fit men to fill up the vacant places in the army. On the twenty-fourth he was much worse, and was carried out of his bed to assist at the sacrifices, and gave order that the general officers should wait within the court, whilst the inferior officers kept watch without doors. On the twenty-fifth he was removed to his palace on the other side

the river, where he slept a little, but his fever did not abate, and when the generals came into his chamber, he was speechless, and continued so the following day. The Macedonians, therefore, supposing he was dead, came with great clamors to the gates, and menaced his friends so that they were forced to admit them, and let them all pass through unarmed along by his bedside. The same day Python and Seleucus were despatched to the temple of Serapis to inquire if they should bring Alexander thither, and were answered by the god, that they should not remove him. On the twenty-eighth, in the evening, he died. This account is most of it word for word as it is written in the diary.

From Plutarch, *Lives of Illustrious Men* (Alexander), A. H. Clough trans.

THE STOIC PHILOSOPHY: As Described by Diogenes Laërtius

The first instinct which the animal has is the impulse to self-preservation with which nature endows it at the outset. The first possession which every animal acquires is its own organic unity and the perception thereof. If this were not so, nature must either have estranged from itself the creature which she has made or left it utterly indifferent to itself, neither of which assumptions is tenable. The only alternative is that she should have designed the creature to love itself. For in this way it repels what harms it and welcomes what benefits it. It is not true, as some say, that the first instinct of animals is toward pleasure. For pleasure, if it is an end at all, is a concomitant of later growth which follows when the nature of the animal in and by itself has sought and found what is appropriate to it. Under like circumstances animals sport and gambol and plants grow luxuriant. Nature has made no absolute severance between plants and animals: in her contrivance of plants she leaves out impulse and sensation, while certain processes go on in us as they do in plants. But when animals have been further endowed with instinct, by whose aid they go in search of the things which benefit them, then to be governed by nature means for them to be governed by instinct. When rational animals are endowed with reason, in token of more complete superiority, in them life in accordance with nature is rightly understood to mean life in accordance with reason. For reason is like a craftsman shaping impulse and desire. Hence Zeno's definition of the end is to live in conformity with nature, which means to live a life of virtue, since it is to virtue that nature leads. On the other hand, a virtuous life is a life which conforms to our experience of the course of nature, our human natures being but parts of universal nature. Thus the end is a life which follows nature, whereby is meant not only our own nature, but the nature of the universe, a life wherein we do nothing that is forbidden by the universal law, *i.e.*, by right reason, which pervades all things and is identical with Zeus, the guide and governor of the universe. The virtue of the happy man, his even flow of life, is realised only when in all the actions he does his individual genius is in harmony with the will of the ruler of the universe. Virtue is a disposition conformable to reason, desirable in and for itself and not because of any hope or fear or any external motive. And well-being depends on virtue, on virtue alone, since the virtuous soul is adapted to secure harmony in the whole of life. When reason in the animal is perverted, this is due to one of two causes, either to the persuasive force of external things or to the bad instruction of those surrounding it. The instincts which nature implants are unperverted.

From R. D. Hicks, *Stoic and Epicurean*, Charles Scribner's Sons, 1910.

The Fear of Freedom
E. R. Dodds

Despite its lack of political freedom, the society of the third century B.C. was in many ways the nearest approach to an "open" society that the world had yet seen, and nearer than any that would be seen again until very modern times. The traditions and institutions of the old "closed" society were of course still there and still influential: the incorporation of a city-state in one or other of the Hellenistic kingdoms did not cause it to lose its moral importance overnight. But though the city was there, its walls, as someone has put it, were down: its institutions stood exposed to rational criticism; its traditional ways of life were increasingly penetrated and modified by a cosmopolitan culture. For the first time in Greek history, it mattered little where a man had been born or what his ancestry was: of the men who dominated Athenian intellectual life in this age, Aristotle and Theophrastus, Zeno, Cleanthes, and Chrysippus were all of them foreigners; only Epicurus was of Athenian stock, though by birth a colonial.

And along with this levelling out of local determinants, this freedom of movement in space, there went an analogous levelling out of temporal determinants, a new freedom for the mind to travel backwards in time and choose at will from the past experience of men those elements which it could best assimilate and exploit. The individual began consciously to *use* the tradition, instead of being used by it. This is most obvious in the Hellenistic poets, whose position in this respect was like that of poets and artists today. . . .

Certainly it is in this age that the Greek pride in human reason attains its most confident expression. We should reject, says Aristotle, the old rule of life that counselled humility, bidding man think in mortal terms, for man has within him a divine thing, the intellect, and so far as he can live on that level of experience, he can live as though he were not mortal. The founder of Stoicism went further still: for Zeno, man's intellect was not merely akin to God, it *was* God, a portion of the divine substance in its pure or active state. And although Epicurus made no such claim, he yet held that by constant meditation on the truths of philosophy one could live "like a god among men." . . .

It would be unwise to assume that . . . attempts to purge the tradition had much effect on popular belief. As Epicurus said, "the things which I know, the multitude disapproves, and of what the multitude approves, I know nothing." Nor is it easy for us to know what the multitude approved in Epicurus' time. Then as now, the ordinary man became articulate about such things only, as a rule, upon his tombstone — and not always even there. Extant tombstones of the Hellenistic Age are less reticent than those of an earlier time, and suggest, for what they are worth, that the traditional belief in Hades is slowly fading, and begins to be replaced either by explicit denial of any Afterlife or else by vague hopes that the deceased has gone to some better world — "to the Isles of the Blessed," "to the gods," or even "to the eternal Kosmos." . . .

I do not want to give a false impression of a complex situation by oversimplifying it. Public worship of the city gods of course continued; it was an accepted part of public life, an accepted expression of civic patriotism. But it would, I think, be broadly true to say of it what has been said of Christianity in our own time, that it had become "more or less a social routine, without influence on goals of living." On the other hand, the progressive decay of tradition set the religious man free to choose his own gods, very much as it set the poet free to choose his own style; and the anonymity and loneliness of life in the great new cities, where the individual felt himself a cipher, may have enforced on many the sense of need for some divine friend and helper. . . .

Looking at the picture as a whole, an intelligent observer in or about the year 200 B.C. might well have predicted that within a few generations the disintegration of the inherited structure would be complete, and that the perfect Age of Reason would follow. He would, however, have been quite wrong on both points. . . . It would have surprised our imaginary Greek rationalists to learn that half a millennium after his death Athena would still be receiving the periodic gift of a new dress from her grateful people; that bulls would still be sacrificed in Megara to heroes killed in the Persian Wars eight hundred years earlier; that ancient taboos concerned with ritual purity would still be rigidly maintained in many places. For the *vis inertiae* that keeps this sort of thing going — what Matthew Arnold once called "the extreme slowness of things" — no rationalist ever makes sufficient allowance. Gods withdraw, but their rituals live on, and no one except a few intellectuals notices that they have ceased to mean anything. . . .

The paralysis of scientific thought in general may very well account for the boredom and restlessness of the intellectuals, but what it does not so well account for is the new attitude of the masses. The vast majority of those who turned to astrology or magic, the vast majority of the devotees of Mithraism or Christianity, were evidently not the sort of people to whom the stagnation of science was a *direct* and conscious concern; and I find it hard to be certain that their religious outlook would have been fundamentally different even if some scientist had changed their economic lives by inventing the steam engine.

If future historians are to reach a more complete explanation of what happened, I think that, without ignoring either the intellectual or the economic factor, they will have to take account of another sort of motive, less conscious and less tidily rational. Behind the acceptance of astral determinism there lay, among other things, the fear of freedom — the unconscious flight from the heavy burden of individual choice which an open society lays upon its members. If such a motive is accepted as a *vera causa* (and there is pretty strong evidence that it is a *vera causa* today), we may suspect its operation in a good many places. We may suspect it in the hardening of philosophical speculation into quasi-religious dogma which provided the individual with an unchanging rule of life; in the dread of inconvenient research expressed even by a Cleanthes or an Epicurus; later, and on a more popular level, in the demand for a prophet or a scripture; and more generally, in the pathetic reverence for the written word characteristic of late Roman and mediaeval times — a readiness, as Nock puts it, "to accept statements because they were in books, or even because they were said to be in books."

When a people has travelled as far towards the open society as the Greeks had by the third century B.C., such a retreat does not happen quickly or uniformly. Nor is it painless for the individual. For the refusal of responsibility in any sphere there is always a price to be paid, usually in the form of neurosis. And we may find collateral evidence that the fear of freedom is not a mere phrase in the increase of irrational anxieties and the striking manifestations of neurotic guilt-feeling observable in the later stages of the retreat. These things were not new in the religious experience of the Greeks: we encounter them in studying the Archaic Age. But the centuries of rationalism had weakened their social influence and thus, indirectly, their power over the individual. Now they show themselves in new forms and with a new intensity. . . . The presence of a diffused anxiety among the masses shows itself clearly, not only in the reviving dread of postmortem punishments but in the more immediate terrors revealed by extant prayers and amulets. Pagan and Christian alike prayed in the later Imperial Age for protection against invisible perils — against the evil eye and daemonic possession, against "the deceiving demon" or "the headless dog." One amu-

let promises protection "against every malice of a frightening dream or of beings in the air"; a second, "against enemies, accusers, robbers, terrors, and apparitions in dreams"; a third — a Christian one — against "unclean spirits" hiding under your bed or in the rafters or even in the rubbish-pit. The Return of the Irrational was, as may be seen from these few examples, pretty complete.

From E. R. Dodds, *The Greeks and the Irrational,* University of California Press, 1951. Reprinted by permission of the publisher.

THE HELLENIZATION OF THE NEAR EAST
Moses Hadas

When imperialist historians speak of their nation's armies "liberating" the regions they conquer and bringing them the blessings of civilization we are entitled to remain skeptical. . . . But of the peoples newly subjected to hellenization it may be said that they welcomed the innovations, despite, or it may be because of, the fact that they were themselves heirs to venerable civilizations. Because they were they had much to give the Greeks in return, but by far the stronger current ran from west to east. The western influences affected the upper classes directly, whereas the slighter influence from the east touched mainly the lower classes, whence it forced its way up into respectable Greek society only gradually. And so far from resisting hellenism the upper classes, in the Near if not the Middle East, welcomed it with open arms.

The language of the Greek city, and the official language in all the dominions of the Successors, was Greek. In the beginning natives may have learned it out of necessity, for the uses of commerce or government, or by the compulsion of snobbery, but they continued to use it out of choice, and it soon became at least a second vernacular among a considerable proportion of the population. Upper-class natives must of course have known their native vernaculars, but they spoke to each other in Greek and were literate only in Greek. The use of a new language is not only a sign manifest that a new culture is being accepted but a key to the culture as a whole. We shall see that even books written by natives as propaganda for native values and intended mainly for a native audience were written in Greek, and that even books written in native languages were affected, in form and content, by Greek models.

Some native languages did of course survive, to become the basis for vernaculars in the Near East today, and it is interesting to see to what degree religion was a factor in the survival. The clearest case is hieroglyphic, which Egyptian priests continued to use though they understood it very imperfectly. On the other hand, Egypt was traditionally literate as well as conservative, and there continued to be lower-class Egyptians who could write demotic. In a remote place like Palmyra Aramaic continued to be an official language. But Syriac was able to produce a religious literature in the early centuries of Christianity because it had served as a sub-literary vehicle for religion in the preceding period. Neither would Hebrew have survived but for religious motivations. Aramaic, not Hebrew, was the vernacular, and even before the coming of the Greeks Hebrew had something of the position of Latin in the Middle Ages as the language of Scripture and religion. That position it could retain even if Greek became the vernacular; it was only after the fall of Jerusalem in A.D. 70 and the rise of Christianity that the study of Greek was frowned upon on religious grounds.

In the pre-Christian period literary and other remains of the Jews afford abundant, and for our purposes highly relevant, evidence for the spread of Greek. The Bible was translated into Greek not, as Aristeas alleges in the beginning of his book, as a literary curiosity to be deposited in Ptolemy Philadelphus' library, but, as the end of the book indicates, for the use of a Jewish community who could receive their Scriptures in no other way. It is very doubtful that so devout a man as Philo knew any Hebrew or even Aramaic at all; certainly he makes the phrasing of the Septuagint the basis for his exegesis. Passages of prayer or psalmody which occur in such Greek books as III and IV Maccabees and the Wisdom of Solomon shows similarities with Septuagint phraseology even when they are not quotations, and it has been thought that such passages are therefore translations of Hebrew originals. A more probable explanation is that "Septuagint Greek" had become normal for devotional compositions and that they were written in that language — just as a twentieth-century minister will use the style of the King James Bible for a prayer of his own composition. St. Paul did not receive Greek as part of his enlightenment on the road to Damascus; he must have learned the Greek poets he quotes (and expected his Jewish auditors to know) when he was a faithful Jew.

For the diaspora, then, which came to be more numerous than the population of Palestine, it is plain that Greek was the vernacular and that public worship was conducted in that language. But we know that Greek was a familiar language in Palestine itself. At a relatively early period we find evidence that classical Greek literature was known in Palestine, and the rabbinic writings of the later period contain a high proportion of Greek loan words. When the anti-humanist trend was at its strongest a new and more literal Greek version of the Bible was made, that called Aquila's, in order to reduce the possibilities of latitudinarian interpretation. When Paul addressed a Jerusalem crowd in Hebrew (Acts 22.2) they were pleased; apparently they expected him to speak in Greek and would have understood him if he had done so; in the diaspora Paul did address Jewish congregations in Greek. It would be very strange if the Jewish literature written in Greek in Alexandria and Antioch were not read and even emulated in Palestine.

The most forcible evidence that Greek had become the vernacular comes from epigraphy. Inscriptions in languages other than Greek are extremely rare in hellenized areas, and this is true not only of official inscriptions but even of grave inscriptions, and even in the case of quite humble burials. And it is fully as true of Jewish as of other burials, not only in Alexandria and Rome but in Palestine itself, and during the entire span of Greek and Roman sway. A city like Tiberias, which was a great center for rabbinic study, has yielded very numerous Greek inscriptions and very few Hebrew. Greek inscriptions, along with Greek decoration, appear in the ruins of synagogues, and the directional signs in the temple were in Greek.

Adoption of Greek architectural forms certainly caused a revision in ritual practices to approach Greek modes of worship, and even among the Jews. Mosaic and other Greek decoration, sometimes with distinctly pagan themes, has been discovered in synagogues, significantly in such as came to some catastrophic end, like those in Galilee or in Dura-Europus. On the basis of rabbinic literature it had been firmly believed that such decoration was impossible; but the literature was crystallized after the anti-humanist tendency had become a condition of survival. It is easy to imagine that before the crises which called forth official prohibitions the Jews, like other native peoples, would be attracted by the pomp and elegance of the Greek temples and forms of worship and so far as possible emulate them. It is not unlikely that Greek music was also influential. Certainly the Church adapted Greek musical forms; the best key for studying ancient Greek music today are the chants of the Russian Orthodox Church.

From Moses Hadas, *Hellenistic Culture-Fusion and Diffusion*, Columbia University Press, 1959. Reprinted by permission of Rachel Hadas.

ANALYSIS AND INTERPRETATION OF THE READINGS

1. Why should a man so powerful and successful as Alexander have fallen a victim of superstition?
2. To what extent was Stoicism fatalistic?
3. What is the relationship of reason and instinct, according to the Stoics?
4. According to E. R. Dodds, what accounted for the weakening of rationalism in the late Hellenistic period?

CHAPTER 7 | Roman Civilization

CHRONOLOGY

Sometime around the year_____a group of Italic people founded Rome on the Tiber River. After a period of subjection to Etruscan rule during the_____century, the Romans conquered neighboring peoples until by the year_____ they had subdued the entire Italian peninsula. Expansion led to further expansion, the most famous example of which came about through the Punic Wars. The first of these struggles was launched in _____, but the long intermittent contest was not over until the destruction of Carthage in _____. As early as_____, Rome had become a republic, the early history of which was marked by a contest for control of the state between the patricians and plebeians. Notable triumphs of the latter class occurred in_____when the office of tribune was created, and in_____ when the Law of the Twelve Tables was set down. With the passage of a law granting full legislative powers to the assembly in_____, the plebeians achieved, at least nominally, their final victory. Conquest of the Mediterranean rim brought more troubles to the Republic. Attempted agrarian reforms by the Gracchi in the_____and_____ decades of the second century B.C. failed; the nation drifted into one-man rule. Among those who exercised it were Marius, who, first elected consul in_____, served six more terms until his death in_____, and Sulla, dictator on behalf of the patrician Senate from_____to_____. But it was Julius Caesar who between the time he crossed the Rubicon in_____and his assassination in_____, effectively ended the Republic. His grandnephew and heir, Augustus, established the Principate or Early Empire in _____, which brought both Roman culture and territorial expansion to their highest points and maintained relative peace for_____centuries. The death of the "good emperor" Marcus Aurelius, in_____, ushered in a period of crisis and civil war with fatal results for Roman civilization, although strong rule was reimposed in_____.

IDENTIFICATIONS

Fill in each blank below with the appropriate term.

1. The first written Roman law, it was set down on tablets of wood.

_____

2. Among the branches or divisions of Roman law, this classification was held to be the law common to all men of whatever nation.

_____

3. A judicial official, he defined the law and instructed the judges in a particular suit.

_____

4. Originally named for their capacity to provide their own cavalry equipment, these men became rich property owners in the late Republic.

_____

5. A plebeian official, he was meant by his veto to protect the citizens against unlawful acts of the patricians.

_____

6. The work of a great poet of the Augustan age, this epic poem celebrated the founding of Rome, her imperial triumphs, and glorious destiny.

_____

7. Although honored as Augustus, he preferred this simple title:

_____

Fill in each blank below with the name of the individual described

1. Killed in a conflict with the conservative aristocrats, this tribune had sought to limit the amount of land any citizen might hold.

_____

2. This general terrorized the Italian peninsula for sixteen years and outfought the Roman armies but in the end lost the war.

_____

3. An orator and philosopher, he affirmed the natural law as a legal principle.

_____

4. A slave gladiator, he led a rebellion that ravaged southern Italy for two years.

_____

5. This general nicknamed "the Delayer" won victory for Rome in the Second Punic War.

_____

6. A gullible encyclopedist, this "scientist" put together a famous and misleading *Natural History* in the first century C.E.

_____

7. A brilliant and ironic historian of the first century C.E., he sought not merely to record the past but to indict the present.

_____

8. The founder of a mystical philosophy, he taught that the universe is a series of emanations from God.

_____

9. The leading Roman exponent of Epicurean philosophy, he was also a majestic poet.

_____

10. An emperor in the late second century C.E., he was also a famous Stoic.

_____

STUDY QUESTIONS

Circle the correct number or numbers in each of the following multiple-choice questions. Where none of the choices is correct, write the proper answer in the space provided at the end of each question.

1. The founders of Rome were (1) Etruscans from Asia Minor; (2) Greek colonists who had earlier settled in southern Italy; (3) Italic people who were descended from Indo-European invaders; (4)_____

_____

_____

2. The early Roman Senate was (1) an elected body; (2) appointed by the king; (3) composed of the heads of clans; (4)_____

_____

_____

3. The old Roman king (1) was an absolute monarch unrestrained by law; (2) exercised patriarchal authority with powers limited by custom; (3) could best be described as a strong constitutional monarch; (4)_____

4. The Romans were brought into direct contact with Greek culture through (1) the Punic Wars; (2) their conquest of the Etruscans; (3) their conquest of southern Italy; (4)————

————

————

5. The overthrow of the Roman monarchy brought several political changes. Among them were (1) a quick settlement of the ancient differences between patricians and plebeians; (2) the substitution of two elected consuls for the king; (3) the establishment of the office of dictator in times of crisis; (4)————

————

————

6. The plebeians of the early Republic were (1) conquered peoples of Italy; (2) small farmers and craftsmen; (3) an urban proletariat; (4)

————

————

7. In religion (1) the Romans early developed a highly ethical set of beliefs; (2) Rome took over the Greek religion intact; (3) the Romans clearly showed the worldly, practical nature of their character; (4)————

————

————

8. The final conquest of Carthage by Rome (1) led directly to further Roman expansion both to the east and to the west; (2) contributed to the decline of the small farmer; (3) brought an era of peace and prosperity for the next hundred years; (4) ————

————

9. The revision of the Roman calendar on the Egyptian model was enacted by (1) Augustus Caesar; (2) Marcus Aurelius; (3) Pompey; (4)

————

————

10. Cicero (1) borrowed heavily from Stoicism; (2) leaned strongly, as did many other Romans, towards Epicureanism; (3) strongly influenced European medieval and Renaissance writers through his eloquent Latin prose; (4)————

————

Study Questions

You should be able to answer the following:

1. "Both Greek and Roman civilizations originally developed in peninsulas with similar climates, yet the natural features of Italy contributed toward making Roman the inferior culture of the two." Discuss this statement.
2. Which aspects of Roman society or culture were derived from the Etruscans? Which from the Greeks?
3. Tradition says that the overthrow of the Roman monarchy in the sixth century B.C. was a revolt against a foreign oppressor. What other and more important factors contributed to that revolution? What were its results?
4. Why were the political victories of the plebeians in the early Republic largely illusory?
5. What were the causes of the rapid growth of slavery in Roman society? How did the institution of slavery in Rome differ from that in Greece?
6. Compare the religion of the Romans with that of the Greeks in their conceptions of deity and of the role of the individual.
7. How did Rome's victory in the Punic Wars contribute to fatal defects in Roman civilization?
8. What factors in Roman society inhibited industrialization?
9. How did Cicero's political philosophy differ from that of the earlier Stoics?
10. Why did Stoicism have a stronger appeal to Romans than Epicureanism?
11. In what way was natural law a concept superior to civil law?

12. How did the status of Roman women change during the period between the Punic Wars and the early Empire?
13. "The narrow conservatism of [the Roman] upper classes was a fatal hindrance to the health of the state." Illustrate this from the history of the last century of the Republic.
14. "For all their achievements in engineering, the Romans acomplished little in science." Justify this assertion.
15. How did the Roman attitude toward manual labor contribute to the decline of Roman culture?
16. In what ways did Roman architecture and sculpture reflect Roman ideals and personality traits?
17. Aside from consolidating Octavian's power, what was the significance of his victory over Antony and Cleopatra in 31 B.C.?
18. Explain the statement: "Roman history is the real beginning of Western history as we know it."

PROBLEMS

1. Do you agree with the authors that the Roman influence on the modern world is usually over-rated?
2. The art and architecture of a people usually reveal a great deal about their aspirations, ideals, and character. With this in mind compare Roman art and architecture with any of the following: (a) Egyptian, (b) Minoan, (c) Assyrian, (d) Hellenic.
3. "Even without political problems the Roman Empire would probably have been fated to extinction for economic reasons." Discuss the validity of this statement.
4. Read the *Meditations* of Marcus Aurelius and compare with Hellenistic Stoicism.
5. Compare in as many ways as you can Ancient Rome and the United States. (See Guglielmo Ferrero, *Ancient Rome and Modern America*.) What factors account for the differences?

6. Attempt to determine the extent of Etruscan influence upon Roman society and culture.
7. Machiavelli (*Discourses on Livy*, I, 37) asserted that the Gracchan agrarian reforms and the dissension which they led to were a prime cause of the decline of the Roman Republic. Do you agree?
8. In assessing the causes of Rome's decline, compare Toynbee's discussion (A *Study of History*, D. C. Somervell ed., Vol. I, Part IV: "The Breakdown of Civilizations") with Rostovtzev, *History of the Ancient World*, Vol. II, Chap. XXV: "Causes of the Decline of Ancient Civilization."
9. How was Roman civilization modified by contact with other peoples? Were these contacts beneficial or detrimental to Rome?
10. Why were Roman achievements so outstanding in the field of law?
11. How do you account for the fact that the Romans made little advancement in science despite the fact that the vast contribution of Hellenistic science was at their disposal?
12. What do you think were the chief demerits of the civilization of ancient Rome?
13. Ortega y Gasset in *The Revolt of the Masses* (Chap. 14) identifies Julius Caesar as one of the two "really clear heads" of the ancient world. In the light of Roman history and of later European history evaluate Ortega's judgment.

GEOGRAPHICAL IDENTIFICATIONS

Gaul	Tiber River	Naples
Carthage (city)	Sicily	Syria
Dacia	Rome	Illyria
Rhine River	Athens	Actium
Danube River	Rubicon River	Macedon
Strait of Gibraltar	Adriatic Sea	Asia Minor

A ROMAN OF THE OLD SCHOOL: As Described by Plutarch

Ten years after his consulship, Cato stood for the office of censor, which was indeed the summit of all honor, and in a manner the highest step in civil affairs; for besides all other power, it had also that of an inquisition into every one's life and manners. For the Romans thought that no marriage or rearing of children, nay, no feast or drinking-bout ought to be permitted according to every one's appetite or fancy, without being examined and inquired into; being indeed of opinion, that a man's character was much sooner perceived in things of this sort than in what is done publicly and in open day. They chose, therefore, two persons, one out of the patricians, the other out of the commons, who were to watch, correct, and punish, if any one ran too much into voluptuousness, or transgressed the usual manner of life of his country; and these they called Censors. They had power to take away a horse, or expel out of the senate any one who lived intemperately and out of order. It was also their business to take an estimate of what every one was worth, and to put down in registers everybody's birth and quality; besides many other prerogatives. And therefore the chief nobility opposed his pretensions to it. Jealousy prompted the patricians, who thought that it would be a stain to everybody's nobility, if men of no original honor should rise to the highest dignity and power; while others conscious of their own evil practices, and of the violation of the laws and customs of their country, were afraid of the austerity of the man; which, in an office of such great power, was likely to prove most uncompromising and severe. And so, consulting among themselves, they brought forward seven candidates in opposition to him, who sedulously set themselves to court the people's favor by fair promises, as though what they wished for was indulgent and easy government. Cato, on the contrary, promising no such mildness, but plainly threatening evil livers, from the very hustings openly declared himself, and exclaiming, that the city needed a great and thorough purgation, called upon the people, if they were wise, not to choose the gentlest, but the roughest of physicians; such a one, he said, he was, and Valerius Flaccus, one of the patricians, another; together with him, he doubted not but he should do something worth the while, and that, by cutting to pieces and burning like a hydra, all luxury and voluptuousness. He added, too, that he saw all the rest endeavoring after the office with ill intent, because they were afraid of those who would exercise it justly, as they ought. And so truly great and so worthy of great men to be its leaders was, it would seem, the Roman people, that they did not fear the severity and grim countenance of Cato, but rejecting those smooth promisers who were ready to do all things to ingratiate themselves, they took him, together with Flaccus; obeying his recommendations not as though he were a candidate, but as if he had had the actual power of commanding and governing already.

From Plutarch, *Lives of Illustrious Men* (Marcus Cato), A. H. Clough trans.

THE LAW OF THE TWELVE TABLES

TABLE IV: *Concerning the Rights of a Father and of Marriage*

LAW I

A father shall have the right of life and death over his son born in lawful marriage, and shall also have the power to render him independent, after he has been sold three times.*

LAW II

If a father sells his son three times, the latter shall be free from paternal authority.

LAW III

A father shall immediately put to death a son recently born, who is a monster, or who has a form different from that of members of the human race.

LAW IV

When a woman brings forth a son within the next ten months after the death of her husband, he shall be born in lawful marriage, and shall be the legal heir of his estate.

• • •

* This privilege, the *patria potestas*, enjoyed by Roman fathers, was a relic of the patriarchal authority originally asserted by a man over his household, including the members of his immediate family, his slaves, and other dependents. Derived from ancient custom, it continued to exist for centuries after Rome had attained an exalted rank in the scale of civilization. . . .
A marked peculiarity of this relation was what was known as the *unitas personae*, under which a father and his son subject to his control were, by means of a legal fiction, held to be but a single person in law. Hence, when the father died, the son at once succeeded him. . . . Despite the *unitas personae*, the child was strictly not a person but a thing. . . . The father was authorized to make any disposition of his offspring that he chose; he could scourge, maim, imprison, torture, or execute them at his pleasure. Nor was this right infrequently or sparingly exercised; the Roman annals are full of instances where sons were inhumanly treated and put to death by their fathers.

TABLE VII: *Concerning Crimes*

LAW IV

If anyone who has arrived at puberty, secretly, and by night, destroys or cuts and appropriates to his own use, the crop of another, which the owner of the land has laboriously obtained by plowing and the cultivation of the soil, he shall be sacrificed to Ceres, and hung.

If he is under the age of puberty, and not yet old enough to be accountable, he shall be scourged, in the discretion of the Praetor, and shall make good the loss by paying double its amount.

LAW V

Anyone who turns cattle on the land of another, for the purpose of pasture, shall surrender the cattle, by way of reparation.

LAW VI

Anyone who, knowingly and maliciously, burns a building, or a heap of grain left near a building, after having been placed in chains and scourged, shall be put to death by fire. If, however, he caused the damage by accident, and without malice, he shall make it good; or, if he has not the means to do so, he shall receive a lighter punishment.

LAW VII

When a person, in any way, causes an injury to another which is not serious, he shall be punished with a fine of twenty *asses*.

LAW VIII

When anyone publicly abuses another in a loud voice, or writes a poem for the purpose of insulting him, or rendering him infamous, he shall be beaten with a rod until he dies.

LAW IX

When anyone breaks a member of another, and is unwilling to come to make a settlement with him, he shall be punished by the law of retaliation.

From S. P. Scott, *The Civil Law*, The Central Trust Company, Cincinnati, 1932, Vol. I. Reprinted by permission of the Samuel P. Scott Trust and the Jefferson Medical College of Philadelphia.

LATER ROMAN LAW: The Commentaries of Gaius on the Institutes of the Civil Law

In conclusion, it should be noted that, as it is provided by the *Lex Ælia Sentia* that slaves who have been manumitted for the purpose of defrauding a patron, or creditors, do not become free; for the Senate, at the suggestion of the Divine Hadrian, decreed that this rule should also apply to foreigners, while the other provisions of the same law do not apply to them.

There is another division with reference to the law of persons, for some persons are their own masters, and some are subject to the authority of others.

Again, of those persons who are subject to the authority of another, some are in his power, others are in his hand, and others are considered his property.

Let us now consider those that are subject to the authority of another, for, when we ascertain who they are, we shall then understand what persons are their own masters.

In the first place, let us examine those who are in the power of another.

Slaves are in the power of their masters, and this power is acknowledged by the Law of Nations, for we know that among all nations alike the master has the power of life and death over his slaves, and whatever property is acquired by a slave is acquired by his master.

At the present time, however, neither Roman citizens nor any other persons who are under the empire of the Roman people are permitted to employ excessive or causeless severity against their slaves; for by a constitution of the Most Holy Emperor Antoninus anyone who kills his slave, without good reason, is not less liable than one who kills the slave of another; and the excessive harshness of masters is restrained by another constitution of the same Emperor; for he, having been consulted by certain governors of provinces with reference to slaves who flee for refuge to the temples of the Gods or the statues of the Emperor,* ordered that if the cruelty of masters appeared to be intolerable, they should be compelled to sell their slaves; and in both cases he acted justly, for we should not make a bad use of our rights, in accordance with which principle the administration of their own property is forbidden to spendthrifts.

But, as among Roman citizens, a double ownership may exist (for a slave is understood to be subject to bonitarian or quiritarian right or to belong to both these classes) so we merely say that a slave is in the power of his owner if he forms part of his property by bonitarian right, even if at the same time he may not belong to him by quiritarian right; for anyone who has the bare quiritarian right in a slave is not understood to have him in his power.

In like manner, our children whom we have begotten in lawful marriage are under our control. This right is peculiar to Roman citizens, for there are hardly any other men who have such authority over their children a we have, and this the Divine Hadrian stated in the Edict which he published with reference to persons who petitioned for Roman citizenship for themselves and for their children, for he said: "It does not escape my

----

* The right of asylum, derived by Rome from Greece, did not attach to all temples, or Imperial statues, but only to such as long continued custom had invested with that privilege, of which debtors, slaves, and violators of the law constantly availed themselves. The clergy, after the introduction of Christianity, being well aware of the financial and political advantages which would accrue to them by the perpetuation of this practice, encouraged and confirmed it, until the abuse of the right of sanctuary, through the immunity enjoyed by notorious criminals, became one of the worst scandals of medieval times.

knowledge that the Galatians hold that children are in the power of their parents."

Roman citizens are understood to have contracted marriage according to the Civil Law and to have the children begotten by them in their power if they marry Roman citizens, or even Latins or foreigners whom they have the right to marry; for the result of legal marriage is that the children follow the condition of the father and not only are Roman citizens by birth, but also become subject to paternal authority.

Therefore, certain veterans are usually granted permission by the Imperial Constitutions to contract civil marriage with those Latin or foreign women whom they first marry after their discharge, and the children born of such unions become Roman citizens by birth, and are subject to the authority of their fathers.

Marriage, however, cannot take place with persons of servile condition.

Nor are we permitted to marry any free woman, as we should refrain from contracting matrimony with certain ones of this class.

From S. P. Scott, *The Civil Law,* The Central Trust Company, Cincinnati, 1932, Vol. I. Reprinted by permission of the Samuel P. Scott Trust and the Jefferson Medical College of Philadelphia.

Late Roman Stoicism: As Exemplified by The Philosophy of Marcus Aurelius

What then is that which is able to conduct a man? One thing and only one, philosophy. But this consists in keeping the daemon within a man free from violence and unharmed, superior to pains and pleasures, doing nothing without a purpose, nor yet falsely and with hypocrisy, not feeling the need of another man's doing or not doing anything; and besides, accepting all that happens, and all that is allotted, as coming from thence, wherever it is, from whence he himself came; and, finally, waiting for death with a cheerful mind, as being nothing else than a dissolution of the elements of which every living being is compounded. But if there is no harm to the elements themselves in each continually changing into another, why should a man have any apprehension about the change and dissolution of all the elements? For it is according to nature, and nothing is evil which is according to nature.

• • •

Does another do me wrong? Let him look to it. He has his own disposition, his own activity. I now have what the universal nature wills me to have; and I do what my nature now wills me to do.

Let the part of thy soul which leads and governs be undisturbed by the movements in the flesh, whether of pleasure or of pain; and let it not unite with them, but let it circumscribe itself and limit those affects to their parts. But when these affects rise up to the mind by virtue of that other sympathy that naturally exists in a body which is all one, then thou must not strive to resist the sensation, for it is natural: but let not the ruling part of itself add to the sensation the opinion that it is either good or bad.

Live with the gods. And he does live with the gods who constantly shows to them that his own soul is satisfied with that which is assigned to him, and that it does all that the daemon wishes, which Zeus hath given to every man for his guardian and guide, a portion of himself. And this is every man's understanding and reason.

• • •

As thou intendest to live when thou art gone out . . . so it is in thy power to live here. But if men do not permit thee, then get away out of life, yet so as if thou wert suffering no harm. The house is smoky, and I quit it. Why dost thou think that this is any trouble? But so long as nothing of the kind drives me out, I remain, am free, and no man shall hinder me from doing what I choose; and I choose to do what is according to the nature of the rational and social animal.

• • •

Soon, very soon, thou wilt be ashes, or a skeleton, and either a name or not even a name; but name is sound and echo. And the things which are much valued in life are empty and rotten and trifling, and [like] little dogs biting one another, and little children quarrelling, laughing, and then straightway weeping. But fidelity and modesty and justice and truth are fled

Up to Olympus from the wide-spread earth.
HESIOD, *Works, etc.,* v. 197.

What then is there which still detains thee here? if the objects of sense are easily changed and never stand still, and the organs of perception are dull and easily receive false impressions; and the poor soul itself is an exhalation from blood. But to have good repute amidst such a world as this is an empty thing. Why then dost thou not wait in tranquillity for thy end, whether it is extinction or removal to another state? And until that time comes, what is sufficient? Why, what else than to venerate the gods and bless them, and to do good to men, and to practise tolerance and self-restraint. . . .

From George Long trans., *The Thoughts of the Emperor Marcus Aurelius.*

Two Roman Virtues
Harold Mattingly

Pietas is the most Roman of all the virtues and the most difficult for the modern mind to understand. There is no single English word that will cover all her meanings. "Piety" corresponds roughly if not exactly to a part, "pity" to another part. Where the word pietas is used in its widest sense, "goodness" is our nearest English equivalent. Pietas implies readiness to act rightly in all cases where obligation exists, and often expresses the reciprocal relationship between two parties. To the Roman she was the cardinal virtue; the scrupulous care for covenanted duties was to him more valuable than romantic devotion or chivalrous generosity. Duty is owed first of all to the gods. This is piety in the religious sense, never quite excluded by other shades of meaning, for duty to the gods can be held to include in itself all minor duties. Duty to parents, children, and kindred comes very close after. The good man must not be wanting in proper respect for his closest natural ties. There is a special Pietas applicable to dependents and clients, for between them and the patron there exists a relationship governed by exact laws. Towards others, strangers at home or abroad, Pietas does not at first extend, for they are outside the covenant; but the stranger at home may be admitted to clientship, the enemy abroad to grace, and Pietas, now very near in meaning to "pity," pleads for his admission. A contemporary, hearing the story of Dido betrayed by Aeneas, curls the lip at a hero who can behave so meanly. But Dido herself never calls Aeneas, her faithless lover, "impius," and the Roman could pity Dido without blaming Aeneas as we do. It mattered to him much more than it does to us that Aeneas had deliberately refrained from binding himself by the ties to which pietas is attached. If he could in any sense be termed "impius," it would be for his ingratitude to his benefactress rather than for his cruelty to his love. A virtue so wide in scope as pietas was admirably suited to sum up the character of a virtuous emperor and the Romans honored Antoninus Pius much as Englishmen honored Victoria "the Good." Something was lost, when the title Pius, combined with Felix, was stereotyped as part of the imperial style and the emperor could begin at once to enjoy a reputation without first earning it.

Libertas is a virtue that interests us most closely today. She seems to us the vital spirit of any state that is worth living and dying for. Under the Roman Empire her range was sadly limited. Even the best of emperors could not pretend that he could offer liberty in the old sense, and it was not every emperor who cared to remember that he was but the trustee for the rights of his subjects. Trajan, on one occasion when he called in the old republican coinage, reissued a number of types as his own restorations, and by his choice emphasized the fact that the Empire was the direct descendant of the free Republic. He honored even the memory of Brutus the "liberator," one of the murderers of Julius Caesar. But the old constitution, if not dead, was changed out of all recognition. The people no longer elected the magistrates — that right had passed to the senate — and even the senate was in fact terribly weak when faced with the immense powers concentrated in the hands of the emperor. Liberty, in the purely political sense, hardly existed. So far as the word still had meaning, liberty looked to the personal rights of the citizen which a good emperor would still respect — the right to freedom from wanton interference by the police or arbitrary and unnecessary increases of taxation. When the possession of Empire was in doubt, both parties naturally made their appeal to Libertas. The pretender would claim to be championing Libertas against a tyrant. The reigning emperor, if he succeeded in overthrowing the usurper, might boast of "Libertas Restituta," constitutionalism asserted against revolution. By a curious turn of thought, assisted by verbal similarity, Libertas was often associated with Liberalitas. The emperor's free spirit showed itself in freeness in giving. One of the chief advantages of Libertas to our plain Roman was his share in the imperial largesses. Caracalla's extension of Roman citizenship over the whole Empire was naturally celebrated under the same title.

From Harold Mattingly, *The Man in the Roman Street*, W. W. Norton & Company, Inc., 1966. Reprinted by permission of the publisher.

ANALYSIS AND INTERPRETATION OF THE READINGS

1. Why was Cato, despite his severity, chosen Censor by the pleasure-loving Romans?
2. Do you consider that the law of the Romans showed an advance over the law of the Mesopotamian peoples and of the ancient Hebrews? Explain.
3. Compare the philosophy of Marcus Aurelius with the teachings of Jesus in the Sermon on the Mount (Matthew 5 and 6).

Christianity and the Transformation of the Roman World

CHRONOLOGY

Write the correct date or dates in the blank preceding each of the events listed below.

_____Death of St. Augustine

_____Founding of Constantinople

_____Reign of Diocletian

_____Execution of Boethius

_____Council of Nicaea

_____Edict of Toleration by Galerius

_____Assumption of title "King of Rome" by a German chieftain

_____Sack of Rome by Visigoths

_____Life of St. Benedict (approximate)

_____Battle of Adrianople

IDENTIFICATIONS

In each blank below write the correct term or title.

1. Tradition and theory that justifies papal authority.

_____

2. Christian sect which believed that Christ was inferior to God the Father and not coeternal with Him.

_____

3. A bishop who ruled over any of several of the oldest and largest Christian communities, such as Antioch, Alexandria, and Constantinople.

_____

4. Autobiography of a famous theologian who held Church office in Africa.

_____

5. Name given to St. Jerome's Latin translation of the Bible.

_____

6. A famous book joining classical and Christian ideals, whose author was put to death by the ruler he had served.

_____

7. A bishop of a large city whose authority extended over the clergy of an entire province.

_____

8. A lasting achievement of Justinian which includes "the most important lawbook that the world has ever seen."

_____

9. A Germanic people that established a kingdom in northwest Africa and sacked Rome in 455.

_____

10. Major work of a great Church father incorporating a philosophy of history predominant throughout the Middle Ages.

_____

Write in the blanks the names of the various persons described below.

1. Roman emperor who named his capital after himself and made the throne hereditary.

_____

2. Fourth-century ascetic who laid down a set of rules for a monastic order widely followed in eastern Christendom.

_____

3. Native of Tarsus who proclaimed Christianity a universal religion and greatly extended its early character.

_____

4. Roman aristocrat and polished Latinist whose writings forged a link between ancient Greek thinkers and the Middle Ages.

_____

5. Monastic figure who did more than any other to establish the Benedictine monasteries as centers of learning.

_____

6. Last ruler of a united Roman Empire, cruel in vengeance but surnamed "the Great."

_____

7. Archbishop of Milan who humbled this same Roman emperor.

_____

8. Roman emperor who, after trying vainly to exterminate Christianity, issued an edict of toleration.

_____

9. Extreme ascetic who spent nearly forty years on the top of a pillar.

_____

10. Founder of western monasticism whose rule was almost universally used in Latin Christendom.

_____

11. Bishop of Hippo and greatest of the Latin Church fathers whose writings have been held in esteem by both Roman Catholics and Protestants.

_____

12. Ostrogothic conqueror who gave Italy an intelligent and progressive rule in contrast to many native Roman emperors.

_____

STUDY QUESTIONS

1. Describe the political structure of the Roman Empire as reorganized by Diocletian. By what means did he strengthen the empire? In what significant ways did he change its character?
2. Explain this comment on Diocletian's regime: "It was almost as if the defeat of Antony and Cleopatra at Actium was now being avenged."
3. Explain the relationship between the growth of bureaucracy during the third and fourth centuries and the widening gap between rich and poor.
4. What were the fundamentals of Jesus' teachings?
5. Describe the contributions of Paul to Christianity.
6. How did conditions in the Roman world during the third century aid the growth of Christianity?
7. What factors helped Christianity triumph over other contemporary competing religions?
8. How did the role of the Christian clergy differ from that of the clergy of most earlier religions?
9. How did doctrinal disputes within the Church contribute to separation between East and West? How did they affect relations between church and state?
10. Describe the attitude or role of each of the following emperors in relation to Christianity: Constantine, Julian, Theodosius ("the Great"), and Valentinian III.

11. Describe the development of Christian organization down to 400 C.E. and explain its importance in the context of a collapsing Roman Empire.

12. What were the chief causes of the rise of Christian asceticism in the third and fourth centuries?

13. What were the differences between the dominant rules of eastern and western monasticism?

14. What were the major contributions of Benedictine monasticism to Western civilization?

15. Discuss the effects of the Germanic invasions in the West. Why was the East much less affected?

16. How did St. Augustine defend the doctrine of predestination? What did he mean by the "City of God"?

17. What changes were made in Christianity as a result of the work of the Church fathers?

18. What elements of classical or pagan culture were carried over into the culture of the Middle Ages? By what means?

19. How does the Justinian Code reflect changes in the philosophy of Roman law between the third and sixth centuries C.E.? What did the Code contribute to modern legal or political theory?

20. Why was Justinian's attempt to reconquer the West a failure in spite of military victories?

PROBLEMS

1. Read any two of the synoptic Gospels (Matthew, Mark, or Luke) and compare the accounts of the life of Jesus.

2. Read some of the major epistles of St. Paul and consider what they reveal about the nature of early Christianity.

3. Investigate further any of the following:
   a. Early monasticism
   b. The Arian controversy
   c. The rise of papal supremacy in the Western Church

4. Compare and contrast the teachings of Jesus with those of the Hebrew prophets.

5. Compare the teachings of the Apostle Paul and St. Augustine. What teachings of St. Augustine have been carried over into modern Christianity?

6. Examine the relationship between early Christianity and competing salvationist cults such as Mithraism and Gnosticism.

GEOGRAPHICAL IDENTIFICATIONS

Lombardy	Nicaea	Syria
Rome	Constantinople	Milan
Adrianople	Antioch	Hippo
Nicomedia	Alexandria	Tarsus
Judea	Split	Thessalonica
Nazareth	Jersualem	

AIDS TO AN UNDERSTANDING OF CHRISTIANITY AND THE TRANSFORMATION OF THE ROMAN WORLD

EARLY CHRISTIANITY: The Sermon on the Mount

And seeing the multitudes, he went up into a mountain: and when he was set, his disciples came unto him:

And he opened his mouth, and taught them, saying,

Blessed are the poor in spirit: for theirs is the kingdom of heaven.

Blessed are they that mourn: for they shall be comforted.

Blessed are the meek: for they shall inherit the earth.

Blessed are they which do hunger and thirst after righteousness: for they shall be filled.

Blessed are the merciful: for they shall obtain mercy.

Blessed are the pure in heart: for they shall see God.

Blessed are the peacemakers: for they shall be called the children of God.

Blessed are they which are persecuted for righteousness' sake: for theirs is the kingdom of heaven.

Blessed are ye, when men shall revile you, and persecute you, and shall say all manner of evil against you falsely, for my sake.

Rejoice, and be exceeding glad: for great is your reward in heaven: for so persecuted they the prophets which were before you.

Ye are the salt of the earth: but if the salt have lost his savour, wherewith shall it be salted? it is thenceforth good for nothing, but to be cast out, and to be trodden under foot of men.

Ye are the light of the world. A city that is set on a hill cannot be hid.

Neither do men light a candle, and put it under a bushel, but on a candlestick; and it giveth light unto all that are in the house.

Let your light so shine before men, that they may see your good works, and glorify your Father which is in heaven.

Think not that I am come to destroy the law, or the prophets: I am not come to destroy, but to fulfil.

For verily I say unto you, Till heaven and earth pass, one jot or one tittle shall in no wise pass from the law, till all be fulfilled.

Whosoever therefore shall break one of these least commandments, and shall teach men so, he shall be called the least in the kingdom of heaven: but whosoever shall do and teach them, the same shall be called great in the kingdom of heaven.

For I say unto you, That except your righteousness shall exceed the righteousness of the scribes and Pharisees, ye shall in no case enter into the kingdom of heaven.

Ye have heard that it was said by them of old time, Thou shalt not kill; and whosoever shall kill shall be in danger of the judgment:

But I say unto you, That whosoever is angry with his brother without a cause shall be in danger of the judgment: and whosoever shall say to his brother, Raca, shall be in danger of the council: but whosoever shall say, Thou fool, shall be in danger of hell fire.

Therefore if thou bring thy gift to the altar, and there rememberest that thy brother hath aught against thee;

Leave there thy gift before the altar, and go thy way; first be reconciled to thy brother, and then come and offer thy gift.

Agree with thine adversary quickly, while thou art in the way with him; lest at any time the adversary deliver thee to the judge, and the judge deliver thee to the officer, and thou be cast into prison.

Verily I say unto thee, Thou shalt by no means come out thence, till thou hast paid the uttermost farthing.

Ye have heard that it was said by them of old time, Thou shalt not commit adultery:

But I say unto you, That whosoever looketh on a woman to lust after her hath committed adultery with her already in his heart.

And if thy right eye offend thee, pluck it out, and cast it from thee: for it is profitable for thee that one of thy members should perish, and not that thy whole body should be cast into hell.

And if thy right hand offend thee, cut it off, and cast it from thee: for it is profitable for thee that one of thy members should perish, and not that thy whole body should be cast into hell.

It hath been said, Whosoever shall put away his wife, let him give her a writing of divorcement:

But I say unto you, That whosoever shall put away his wife, saving for the cause of fornication, causeth her to commit adultery: and whosoever shall marry her that is divorced committeth adultery.

Again, ye have heard that it hath been said by them of old time, Thou shalt not forswear thyself, but shalt perform unto the Lord thine oaths:

But I say unto you, Swear not at all; neither by heaven; for it is God's throne:

Nor by the earth; for it is his footstool: neither by Jerusalem; for it is the city of the great King.

Neither shalt thou swear by thy head, because thou canst not make one hair white or black.

But let your communication be, Yea, yea; Nay, nay: for whatsoever is more than these cometh of evil.

Ye have heard that it hath been said, An eye for an eye, and a tooth for a tooth:

But I say unto you, That ye resist not evil: but whosoever shall smite thee on thy right cheek, turn to him the other also.

And if any man will sue thee at the law, and take away thy coat, let him have thy cloak also.

And whosoever shall compel thee to go a mile, go with him twain.

Give to him that asketh thee, and from him that would borrow of thee turn not thou away.

Ye have heard that it hath been said, Thou shalt love thy neighbour and hate thine enemy.

But I say unto you, Love your enemies, bless them that curse you, do good to them that hate you, and pray for them which despitefully use you, and persecute you;

That ye may be the children of your Father which is in heaven: for he maketh his sun to rise on the evil and on the good, and sendeth rain on the just and on the unjust.

For if ye love them which love you, what reward have ye? do not even the publicans the same?

And if ye salute your brethren only, what do ye more than others? do not even the publicans so?

Be ye therefore perfect, even as your Father which is in heaven is perfect.

° ° °

No man can serve two masters: for either he will hate the one, and love the other; or else he will hold to the one, and despise the other. Ye cannot serve God and mammon.

Therefore I say unto you, Take no thought for your life, what ye shall eat, or what ye shall drink; nor yet for your body, what ye shall put on. Is not the life more than meat, and the body than raiment?

Behold the fowls of the air: for they sow not, neither do they reap, nor gather into barns; yet your heavenly Father feedeth them. Are ye not much better than they?

Which of you by taking thought can add one cubit unto his stature?

And why take ye thought for raiment? Consider the lilies of the field, how they grow; they toil not, neither do they spin:

And yet I say unto you, That even Solomon in all his glory was not arrayed like one of these.

Wherefore, if God so clothe the grass of the field, which to day is, and to morrow is cast into the oven, shall he not much more clothe you, O ye of little faith?

Therefore take no thought, saying, What shall we eat? or, What shall we drink? or, Wherewithal shall we be clothed?

(For after all these things do the Gentiles seek:) for your heavenly Father knoweth that ye have need of all these things.

But seek ye first the kingdom of God, and his righteousness; and all these things shall be added unto you.

Take therefore no thought for the morrow: for the morrow shall take thought for the things of itself. Sufficient unto the day is the evil thereof.

Matthew 5; 6:24-34

EARLY CHRISTIANITY: The Theology of the Apostle Paul

And we know that all things work together for good to them that love God, to them who are the called according to his purpose.

For whom he did foreknow, he also did predestinate to be conformed to the image of his Son, that he might be the firstborn among many brethren.

Moreover, whom he did predestinate, them he also called: and whom he called, them he also justified: and whom he justified, them he also glorified.

What shall we then say to these things? If God be for us, who can be against us?

He that spared not his own Son, but delivered him up for us all, how shall he not with him also freely give us all things?

Who shall lay any thing to the charge of God's elect? It is God that justifieth.

Who is he that condemneth? It is Christ that died, yea rather, that is risen again, who is even at the right hand of God, who also maketh intercession for us.

Who shall separate us from the love of Christ? shall tribulation, or distress, or persecution, or famine, or nakedness, or peril, or sword?

As it is written, For thy sake we are killed all the day long; we are accounted as sheep for the slaughter.

Nay, in all these things we are more than conquerors through him that loved us.

For I am persuaded, that neither death, nor life, nor angels, nor principalities, nor powers, nor things present, nor things to come,

Nor height, nor depth, nor any other creature, shall be able to separate us from the love of God, which is in Christ Jesus our Lord.

° ° °

What shall we say then? Is there unrighteousness with God? God forbid.

For he saith to Moses, I will have mercy on whom I will have mercy, and I will have compassion on whom I will have compassion.

So then it is not of him that willeth, nor of him that runneth, but of God that sheweth mercy.

For the Scripture saith unto Pharaoh, Even for this same purpose have I raised thee up, that I might shew my power in thee, and that my name might be declared throughout all the earth.

Therefore hath he mercy on whom he will have mercy, and whom he will he hardeneth.

Thou wilt say then unto me, Why doth he yet find fault? For who hath resisted his will?

Nay but, O man, who art thou that repliest against God? Shall the thing formed say to him that formed it, Why hast thou made me thus?

Hath not the potter power over the clay, of the same lump to make one vessel unto honour, and another unto dishonour?

Romans 8:28-39; 9:14-21

EARLY CHRISTIANITY: Paul's Political Theory

Let every soul be subject unto the higher powers. For there is no power but of God: the powers that be are ordained of God.

Whosoever therefore resisteth the power, resisteth the ordinance of God: and they that resist shall receive to themselves damnation.

For rulers are not a terror to good works, but to the evil. Wilt thou then not be afraid of the power? do that which is good, and thou shalt have praise of the same:

For he is the minister of God to thee for good. But if thou do that which is evil, be afraid; for he beareth not the sword in vain: for he is the minister of God, a revenger to execute wrath upon him that doeth evil.

Wherefore ye must needs be subject, not only for wrath, but also for conscience' sake.

For, for this cause pay ye tribute also: for they are God's ministers, attending continually upon this very thing.

Render therefore to all their dues: tribute to whom tribute is due; custom to whom custom; fear to whom fear; honour to whom honour.

Owe no man any thing, but to love one another: for he that loveth another hath fulfilled the law.

———

Romans 13:1-8

EARLY CHRISTIANITY: Excerpts from the Rule of St. Benedict

Concerning obedience. The first grade of humility is obedience without delay. This becomes those who, on account of the holy service which they have professed, or on account of the fear of hell or the glory of eternal life consider nothing dearer to them than Christ: so that, so soon as anything is commanded by their superior, they may not know how to suffer delay in doing it, even as if it were a divine command. Concerning whom the Lord said: "As soon as he heard of me he obeyed me." And again he said to the learned men: "He who heareth you heareth me." Therefore let all such, straightway leaving their own affairs and giving up their own will, with unoccupied hands and leaving incomplete what they were doing — the foot of obedience being foremost, — follow with their deeds the voice of him who orders. And, as it were, in the same moment, let the aforesaid command of the master and the perfected work of the disciple — both together in the swiftness of the fear of God, — be called into being by those who are possessed with a desire of advancing to eternal life. And therefore let them seize the narrow way of which the Lord says: "Narrow is the way which leadeth unto life." Thus, not living according to their own judgment nor obeying their own desires and pleasures, but walking under another's judgment and command, passing their time in monasteries, let them desire an abbot to rule over them. Without doubt all such

live up to that precept of the Lord in which he says: "I am not come to do my own will but the will of him that sent me." . . .

Concerning silence. Let us do as the prophet says: "I said, I will take heed to my ways that I sin not with my tongue, I have kept my mouth with a bridle: I was dumb with silence, I held my peace even from good; and my sorrow was stirred." Here the prophet shows that if one ought at times, for the sake of silence, to refrain from good sayings; how much more, as a punishment for sin, ought one to cease from evil words. . . . And therefore, if anything is to be asked of the prior, let it be asked with all humility and subjection of reverence; lest one seem to speak more than is fitting. Scurrilities, however, or idle words and those exciting laughter, we condemn in all places with a lasting prohibition: nor do we permit a disciple to open his mouth for such sayings.

Concerning humility. . . . The sixth grade of humility is, that monk be contented with all lowliness or extremity, and consider himself, with regard to everything which is enjoined on him, as a poor and unworthy workman; saying to himself with the prophet: "I was reduced to nothing and was ignorant; I was made as the cattle before thee, and I am always with thee." The seventh grade of humility is, not only that he, with his tongue, pronounce himself viler and more worthless than all; but that he also believe it in the innermost workings of his heart; humbling himself and saying with the prophet, etc. . . . The eighth degree of humility is that a monk do nothing except what the common rule of the monastery, or the example of his elders, urges him to do. The ninth degree of humility is that a monk restrain his tongue from speaking; and, keeping silence, do not speak until he is spoken to. The tenth grade of humility is that he be not ready, and easily inclined, to laugh. . . . The eleventh grade of humility is that a monk, when he speaks, speak slowly and without laughter, humbly with gravity, using few and reasonable words; and that he be not loud of voice. . . . The twelfth grade of humility is that a monk, shall not only with his heart but also with his body, always show humility to all who see him: that is, when at work, in the oratory, in the monastery, in the garden, on the road, in the fields. And everywhere, sitting or walking or standing, let him always be with head inclined, his looks fixed upon the ground; remembering every hour that he is guilty of his sins. . . .

• • •

Whether the monks should have any thing of their own. More than any thing else is this special vice to be cut off root and branch from the monastery, that one should presume to give or receive anything without the order of the abbot, or should have anything of his own. He should have absolutely not anything: neither a book, nor tablets, nor a pen — nothing at all. — For indeed it is not allowed to the monks to have their own bodies or wills in their own power. But all things necessary they must expect from the Father of the monastery; nor is it allowable to have anything which the abbot did not give or permit. All things shall be common to all, as it is written: "Let not any man presume or call anything his own." But if any one shall have been discovered delighting in this most evil vice: being warned once and again, if he do not amend, let him be subjected to punishment.

From E. F. Henderson, *Select Historical Documents of the Middle Ages*, G. Bell and Sons, Ltd., 1925.

ANALYSIS AND INTERPRETATION OF THE READINGS

1. What doctrines of the Apostle Paul do you not find explicit in the teachings of Jesus?
2. Is the political theory of Paul more reconcilable with democracy or with absolutism?
3. Is the Rule of St. Benedict an example of primitive communism? Explain your answer.
4. Does the Rule incorporate an extreme and uncompromising asceticism?
5. Can you see any reasons why the Benedictine Rule became the standard for the monks of Latin Christendom?

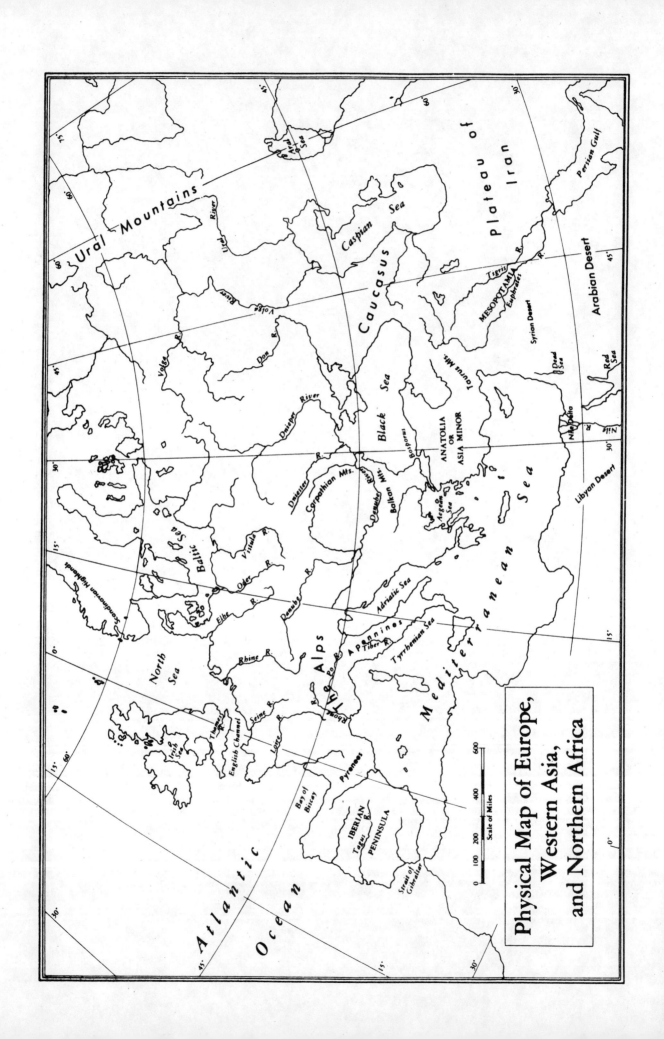

Physical Map of Europe,
Western Asia,
and Northern Africa

Ural Mountains

Aral Sea

Caspian Sea

Plateau of Iran

Persian Gulf

Ural River

Volga River

Don R.

Caucasus

Arabian Desert

Tigris R.

Euphrates R.

MESOPOTAMIA

Syrian Desert

45°

Dnieper River

Black Sea

Taurus Mts.

Dead Sea

Red Sea

30°

Carpathian Mts.

Dniester R.

Pruth R.

Danube Mts.

Bosporus

ANATOLIA
OR
ASIA MINOR

Nile Delta

Nile R.

Libyan Desert

Balkan Mts.

Aegean Sea

Scandinavian Highlands

Baltic Sea

Vistula R.

Oder R.

Elbe R.

Danube R.

Adriatic Sea

Mediterranean Sea

Tyrrhenian Sea

North Sea

Rhine R.

The Alps

Apennines

Po R.

Tiber R.

Rhone R.

Thames R.

Seine R.

Loire R.

English Channel

Irish Sea

Bay of Biscay

Pyrenees

IBERIAN
PENINSULA

Tagus R.

Strait of Gibraltar

Atlantic Ocean

Scale of Miles
0   100   200   400   600

(Chapters 5–8)
The Classical Civilizations of Greece and Rome

MAP WORK

On the map opposite, outline the borders of the Empire of Alexander the Great and the Roman Empire at the period of its greatest expansion (98–117 C.E.)

CHRONOLOGICAL REVIEW

In the blanks at the left number the events below in their correct chronological sequence from earliest to latest.

_____Beginning of the Peloponnesian War

_____Macedonian conquest of Greece

_____Death of Tiberius Gracchus

_____Reforms of Solon

_____Death of Socrates

_____Reign of Augustus

_____Death of Boethius

_____Sack of Rome by Visigoths

_____*Corpus Juris Civilis*

_____Theban conquest of Sparta

_____Founding of Rome

_____Death of Pericles

_____Caesar's march on Rome

_____Death of Marcus Aurelius

_____Battle of Ipsus

_____Beginning of the Punic Wars

_____Reforms of Clisthenes

_____Establishment of the Roman Republic

_____Death of Alexander

_____Publication of the Law of the Twelve Tables

_____Beginnings of Greek city-states

_____Roman destruction of Carthage

_____Greek-Persian wars

_____Founding of Constantinople

CHAPTER 9

Rome's Three Heirs: The Byzantine, Islamic, and Early Medieval Western Worlds

CHRONOLOGY

Number the events listed below in their correct chronological sequence from earliest to latest.

_____Separation of Greek and Roman branches of the Church

_____The *Hijrah* (Hegira)

_____Coronation of Charlemagne as Emperor

_____Beginning of the Umayyad caliphate

_____Beginning of Iconoclastic movement

_____Death of Muhammad

_____Beginning of Abbasid caliphate

_____Destruction of Baghdad by Mongols

_____Accession to papacy of St. Gregory the Great

_____Battle of Tours

_____Fall of Constantinople to the Ottoman Turks

_____Battle of Manzikert

_____Crusaders' capture of Constantinople

_____Accession of Pepin the Short

IDENTIFICATIONS

You should be familiar with the following:

Kabah
Shiites
caliph
Bedouins
Koran
ulama
alchemy
Arabian Nights

Beowulf
"Book of Kells"
Seljuk Turks
Quraish (tribe)
mayor of the palace
Sufis
faylasufs

In the blanks below write the name of the person described:

1. A Persian poet who wrote the *Rubaiyat*.

_____

2. An emperor whose successful defense of Constantinople against the Arabs ranks as one of the most significant battles in European history.

_____

3. An emperor who paved the way for his state's downfall by appealing to the West for help against the Turks.

_____

4. A Russian ruler who, by accepting baptism by a Byzantine missionary, provided a strong bastion for Eastern Orthodox Christianity.

_____

5. An Abbasid caliph of regal splendor who sent an elephant as a gift to Charlemagne.

_____

6. An Islamic philosopher known as "the Commentator" by Western medieval writers, whom he greatly influenced by his interpretation of Aristotle.

_____

7. The greatest clinical physician of the medieval world, who first discovered the real nature of smallpox.

_____

8. The Prophet's son-in-law, who posthumously became identified with a militant Muslim minority.

_____

9. Discoverer of the contagious nature of tuberculosis, whose chief work, the *Canon,* was regarded as a medical authority until the seventeenth century.

_____

10. An eighth-century emperor who provoked a famous religious controversy.

_____

11. A brutal Frankish chieftain who founded the Merovingian dynasty.

_____

12. A Church father who wrote a life of St. Benedict and worked to strengthen papal authority.

_____

13. A military figure nicknamed "the Hammer" and reputed to be the second founder of the Frankish state.

_____

14. A leader of the English Benedictines who aided the accession of the Carolingian dynasty.

_____

15. An Anglo-Saxon Benedictine who wrote a remarkable Latin *History of the English Church.*

_____

16. A princess whose writings testify to a high educational level among Byzantine women.

_____

STUDY QUESTIONS

1. Why is it difficult to date the beginning of the Byzantine Empire? What is the justification for choosing the accession of the emperor Heraclius as a starting point?
2. Why was Byzantine history marked by intrigues and palace revolts?
3. How did changes in agriculture and the farming classes affect the welfare of the Byzantine state?
4. Explain the issues in the Iconoclastic Controversy. What were its results?
5. What significant differences in religious trends and emphases can you detect between the Byzantine and Roman churches?
6. Remembering the constant difficulties it was in, how do you account for the long life of the Byzantine Empire?
7. "The structural design of Santa Sophia was something altogether new in the history of architecture." Explain the meaning of this statement.
8. What consequences have followed the Russian assertion that Moscow was "the third Rome"?
9. In what ways was Byzantine civilization superior to that of western Europe, and through what channels did Byzantium, both in its own day and later, influence the West?
10. What are the main doctrines of the religion of Islam?
11. What factors other than religion account for the rapidity and extent of the Arab conquests?
12. Judaism, Christianity, and Islam, the three great Semitic religions, are closely related. What are the main points of difference among them?
13. Explain: "the Umayyad caliphate appears to some extent like a Byzantine successor state."
14. In what ways was early and medieval Islamic society more progressive than the norm? What limitations were there in its democratic or equalitarian aspects?
15. What were the major elements of Islamic philosophy?
16. What were the leading Islamic accomplishments in science and medicine?
17. What, for the West, has been "the legacy of Islam"?
18. What did Gregory the Great add to the work of the earlier Latin Church fathers?
19. How did papal ambition and the spread of Benedictine monasticism contribute to the growth of Frankish power and the Carolingian accession?

20. Why does Charlemagne rank as one of the most important rulers of the medieval period?
21. What was the nature of the "Carolingian Renaissance"? What were its limitations?
22. In spite of a generally low level of civilization in western Europe at the end of the tenth century, what had been accomplished that held promise of a brighter future?

2. In what respects are Islam and Christianity contradictory? In what respects are they similar?
3. Read *History of the Franks* by Bishop Gregory of Tours and try to account for the churchman's complacent attitude toward the crimes of King Clovis.

PROBLEMS

1. Investigate further any of the following:
   a. The migration of the Slavs
   b. The architecture of Santa Sophia
   c. The Judaic-Christian roots of Islam
   d. Arabic science
   e. The legacy of Islam to the West
   f. The split between the Eastern and Western Churches
   g. The coronation of Charlemagne
   h. The reign of Alfred the Great

GEOGRAPHICAL IDENTIFICATIONS

Mecca	Manzikert
Medina	Gibraltar
Damascus	Antioch
Venice	Ctesiphon
Baghdad	Thessalonica
Byzantium	Pyrenees Mountains
Ravenna	Yathrib
Bukhara	Mosul
Nicaea	Trebizond
Cordova	Iraq
Toledo	Tours

LIFE IN THE BYZANTINE EMPIRE
Steven Runciman

Already by the Fifth Century the population of Constantinople, excluding its suburbs, must have numbered about a million persons, and it remained roughly at that level till the Latin conquest, after which it declined rapidly, to be well under a hundred thousand in 1453. The area of the City was even greater than such a population would justify. The base of the triangle on which it stood was some five miles across, where the land-walls built by Theodosius II stretched across in a double line from the Marmora to the Golden Horn, pierced by eleven gates, the military alternating with the civil. From either end the sea-walls ran for some seven miles each before they met at the blunted apex on the Bosphorus. Within the walls were various crowded towns and villages separated by orchards and parks. Like Old Rome, Constantinople could boast of seven hills. These rose steeply over the Bosphorus and the Golden Horn, but from the Sea of Marmora the slopes were gentler and the lay-out more spacious.

* * *

The smartest shopping district lay inland. Along the central ridge from the entrance of the Palace and the Hippodrome for two miles there ran westward the street called Mesê, the Central Street, a wide street with arcades on either side, passing through two forums — open spaces decorated with statues — the Forum of Constantine, close to the Palace, and the larger Forum of Theodosius, and finally branching into two main roads, the one going through the Forums of the Bull and of Arcadius to Studium and the Golden Gate and the Gate of Pegæ, the other past the Church of the Holy Apostles to Blachernæ and the Charisian Gate. Along the arcades of the Mesê Street were the more important shops, arranged in groups according to their wares — the goldsmiths and next to them the silversmiths, the clothiers, the furniture-makers and so on. The richest of all were near the Palace, at the Baths of Zeuxippus. There were the silk emporia in the great bazaar known as the House of Lights because its windows were illuminated by night.

There was no particular fashionable residential district. Palaces, hovels and tenements all jostled together. The houses of the rich were built in the old Roman manner, two stories high, presenting a blank exterior and facing inward round a courtyard, sometimes covered in, and usually adorned with a fountain and any exotic ornament that fancy might suggest. Poorer houses were constructed with balconies or windows overhanging the street, from which the idler ladies of the household could watch their neighbours' daily life. The residential streets had mostly been built by private contractors, but a law of Zeno's attempted to introduce some order. Streets had to be 12 feet wide, and balconies might not extend to within 10 feet of the opposite wall and must be 15 feet above the ground. Outside staircases were forbidden, and where the streets had already been built less than 22 feet wide windows for prospect were not allowed, only gratings for ventilation. This law remained the basic charter of Byzantine town-planning. There were strict regulations about drainage. All the drains led carefully to the sea, and no one, except an Imperial personage, could be buried within the City. Medical officers in each parish gave further attention to the public health.

* * *

The poor of Constantinople lived in great squalor, their slums jostling against the palaces of the rich, but they were perhaps better off than the poor of most nations. The Circus, their one recreation, was open to them free. The distribution of free bread had been stopped by Heraclius, but free food was still provided for men that undertook work for the State, such as keeping parks and aqueducts in repair or helping in the State bakeries. It was the Quæstor's business to see that the destitute were thus given useful work and that there was no unemployment. To further this, no one was allowed to enter the City except on authorised business. There were, moreover, alms-houses and hospitals for the old and infirm, founded usually by the Emperor or some noble and attached to and managed by a monastery or convent. We possess the title-deeds of several of the foundations of the Comneni. For the children of the poor there were the State orphanages. The Orphanotrophus, the official in charge of the orphanages, had early become an important member of the State hierarchy, with enormous sums under his control. Under the Iconoclasts the Church for a while captured the management of the orphanages, but the Macedonian Emperors restored it to the civil powers and enhanced the position of the Orphanotrophus. The biggest orphanage was in the precincts of the Great Palace. An earthquake destroyed it in Romanus III's reign, but Alexius I refounded it, forgetting the cares of State as he watched over the children.

With all these charitable institutions there was probably very little actual starvation. It is noticeable that when the populace rose up in riot, it was never prompted by anarchical or communistic desires. The rabble might wish to depose an oppressive minister or destroy hated foreigners, but it never sought to alter the structure of society. Indeed, it was to rescue the purple Imperial blood from the overboldness of some usurper that the People most often gave expression to its basic sovereignty.

From Steven Runciman, *Byzantine Civilization*, Edward Arnold and Company, 1933. Reprinted by permission of the publisher.

THE MUSLIM FAITH: Excerpts from the Koran

SURA XXXV: *The Creator, or the Angels*

In the Name of God, the Compassionate, the Merciful.

Praise be to God, Maker of the Heavens and of the Earth! Who employeth the ANGELS as envoys, having two and three and four pairs of wings: He addeth to his creature what He will! Truly God hath power over all things.

The Mercy which God layeth open for man no one can withhold; and what He withholdeth, none can afterwards send forth. And He is the Mighty, the Wise.

O men! bear in mind the favour of God towards you. Is there a creator other than God who nourisheth you out of heaven and earth? There is no God but He! How then are ye turned aside from Him?

If they treat thee as an impostor, then before thee have apostles been treated as impostors — But to God shall all things return.

O men! verily the promise of God is true: let not then the present life deceive you with vain hopes: and let not the Deceiver deceive you as to God.

Yes, Satan is your foe. For a foe then hold him. He summoneth his followers only to become inmates of the flame.

The unbelievers, — for them a terrible punishment! — But believers and doers of good works, for them is mercy, and a great reward!

Shall he, the evil of whose deeds are so tricked out to him that he deemeth them good, be treated like him who seeth things aright? Verily God misleadeth whom He will, and guideth whom He will. Spend not thy soul in sighs for them: verily God knoweth their doings.

It is God who sendeth forth the winds which raise the clouds aloft; then drive We them on to some land dead from drought, and give life thereby to the earth after its death. So shall be the Resurrection.

If any one desireth greatness, greatness is wholly with God. The good word riseth up to Him, and the righteous deed doth He exalt. But a severe punishment awaiteth the plotters of evil things; and the plots of such will be in vain.

Moreover God created you of dust — then of the germs of life — then made you two sexes and no female conceiveth or bringeth forth without his knowledge; and the aged ageth not, nor is aught minished from man's age, but in accordance with the Book. An easy thing truly is this to God.

Nor are the two seas alike: the one is fresh, sweet, pleasant for drink, and the other salt, bitter; yet from both ye eat fresh fish, and take forth for yourselves ornaments to wear; and thou seest the ships cleaving the waters that ye may go in quest of his bounties; and haply ye will be thankful.

He causeth the night to enter in upon the day, and the day to enter in upon the night; and He hath given laws to the sun and to the moon, so that each journeyeth to its appointed goal: This is God your Lord: All power is his: But the gods whom ye call on beside Him have no power over the husk of a date-stone!

• • •

SURA LVI: *The Inevitable*

In the Name of God, the Compassionate, the Merciful.

Day that shall abase! Day that shall exalt!
When the earth shall be shaken with a shock,
And the mountains shall be crumbled with a crumbling,
And become scattered dust,
And into three bands shall ye be divided;
Then the people of the right hand — how happy the
    people of the right hand!
And the people of the left hand — how wretched the
    people of the left hand!
And they who were foremost on earth — the foremost
    still. [Probably the first to embrace Islam.]
These are they who shall be brought nigh to God,
In gardens of delight;
A crowd from the ancients,
And few from later generations;
On inwrought couches
Reclining on them face to face:
Immortal youths go round about to them
With goblets and ewers and a cup from a fountain;
Their brows ache not from it, nor fails the sense;
And with such fruits as they shall make choice of,
And with flesh of such birds as they shall long for:
And theirs shall be the Houris with large dark eyes like
    close-kept pearls,
A recompense for their labours past.
No vain discourse shall they hear therein, nor charge
    of sin,
But only the cry, "Peace! Peace!"
And the people of the right hand — how happy the
    people of the right hand!
Amid thornless lote-trees
And bananas clad with flowers,
And extended shade,
And flowing waters,
And abundant fruits,
Unfailing, and unforbidden,
And lofty couches.
Verily of a rare creation have We created the Houris,
And We have made them ever virgins,
Dear to their spouses, of equal age with them,
For the people of the right hand,
A crowd from the ancients,
And a crowd from later generations.
But the people of the left hand — how wretched shall be
    the people of the left hand!
Amid pestilential winds and in scalding water,
And the shadow of a black smoke,
Not cooling, and not pleasant.
They truly, ere this, were blessed with worldly goods,
But persisted in heinous wickedness,
And were wont to say,
"When we have died, and become dust and bones,
    shall we indeed be raised?

And our fathers the men of yore?"
Say: Aye, the former and the latter:
Gathered shall they surely be for the time of a known
    day.
Then verily ye, O ye the erring, the imputers of false-
    hood
Shall surely eat of the tree Zakkoum,
And fill your bellies with it,
And thereupon shall ye drink of the boiling water,
And ye shall drink as the thirsty camel drinketh.
This shall be their repast in the day of reckoning!

——————

From J. M. Rodwell trans., *The Koran*.

THE CHARACTER OF ISLAMIC CIVILIZATION
Bernard Lewis

Islam — the offspring of Arabia and the Arabian Prophet — was not only a system of belief and cult. It was also a system of state, society, law, thought and art — a civilisation with religion as its unifying, eventually dominating, factor. From the Hijra onwards Islam meant submission not only to the new faith, but to the community — in practice, to the suzerainty of Medina and the Prophet, later of the Empire and Caliph. Islam was at first Arab citizenship, later the first-class citizenship of the Empire. Its code was the *Shari'a*, the holy law developed by jurists from the Qur'ān and the traditions of the Prophet. The *Shari'a* was not only a normative code of law but also, in its social and political aspects, a pattern of conduct, an ideal towards which men and society must strive. Islam admitted no legislative power since law could emanate only from God through revelation, but customary law and civil legislation, the will of the ruler, survived un-officially with occasional limited recognition from the jurists. The divinely granted Shari'a regulated every aspect of life, not only belief and cult, but also public law, constitutional and international, and private law, criminal and civil. Its ideal character is clearest in its constitutional aspect. According to the Shari'a, the head of the community is the Caliph, an elected vicegerent of God with supreme power in all military, civil and religious matters and with the duty of maintaining in-tact the spiritual and material legacy of the Prophet. The Caliph had no spiritual powers himself. He could not change doctrine, nor create new doctrine; he was supported by no priesthood, but only by the semi-clerical class of the 'Ulamā, the doctors of the divine law whose powers were limited to interpretation. In practice, the Caliph became the puppet of military commanders and political adventurers who, from the ninth century onwards, were the real rulers of Islam. By the eleventh century the Sultan emerged as supreme secular ruler alongside the Caliph, with powers recog-nised *post facto* and reluctantly by the jurists. In the administration of law we see the same contrast. Along-side the Qādi, administering the Holy Law, there were secular courts, the ostensible purpose of which was to deal with matters not falling within the Qādi's jurisdic-tion and to remedy injustices by the use of discretionary powers.

Both these gifts of the Arab, his language and his faith, were of course subject from the earliest times to external influences. There are foreign words even in pre-Islamic poetry and in the Qur'ān, many more in the period of the conquests. Administrative terms from Persian and Greek, theological and religious terms from Hebrew and Syriac, scientific and philosophic terms from Greek show the immense influence of the older civilisations of the area on the new one that was being born. Islamic society of the classical period was a com-plex development incorporating within itself many ele-ments of diverse origin: Christian, Jewish and Zoroas-trian ideas of prophecy, legal religion, eschatology and mysticism, Sasanid and Byzantine administrative and imperial practices. Perhaps the most important was the impact of Hellenism, especially in science, philosophy, art and architecture, and even to some slight extent in literature. So great is the Hellenistic influence that Islam has been described as the third heir alongside Greek and Latin Christendom of the Hellenistic legacy. But the Hellenism of Islam was the later Near Eastern Hellenism, semi-orientalized by Aramaic and Christian influences, the uninterrupted continuation of late an-tiquity rather than a rediscovery, as in the West, of classical Athens.

——————

From Bernard Lewis, *The Arabs in History*, Hutchinson University Library, 1950.

THE NEED TO UNDERSTAND ISLAM
Harvey Cox

Odious Western images of Muhammad and of Islam have a long and embarrassingly honorable lineage. Dante places the prophet in that circle of hell reserved for those stained by the sin he calls *seminator di scandalo e di scisma*. As a schismatic, Muhammad's fitting punishment is to be eternally chopped in half from his chin to his anus, spilling entrails and excre-ment at the door of Satan's stronghold. His loyal dis-ciple Ali, whose sins of division were presumably on a lesser scale, is sliced only "from forelock to chin." There is scandal, too. A few lines later, Dante had Muham-mad send a warning to a contemporary priest whose sect was said to advocate the community of goods and who was also suspected of having a mistress. The ad-monition cautions the errant padre that the same fate awaits him if he does not quickly mend his ways. Al-ready in Dante's classic portrait, we find the image of the Moslem linked with revolting violence, distorted doctrine, a dangerous economic idea, and the tantaliz-ing hint of illicit sensuality.

Nothing much has changed in the 600 years since. Even the current wave of interest in Eastern spirituality among many American Christians has not done much to improve the popular estimate of Islam. It is fashionable now in the West to find something of value in Buddhism or Hinduism, to peruse the *Sutras* or the *Bhagavad Gita*, to attend a lecture by Swami Muktananda or the Dalai Lama, even to try a little yoga or meditation. But Americans in general and Christians in particular seem unable to find much to admire in Islam. As G. H. Hansen observes, with only a modicum of hyperbole, in his book *Militant Islam*, the mental picture most Westerners hold of this faith of 750 million people is one of ". . . strange bearded men with burning eyes, hieratic figures in robes and turbans, blood dripping from the amputated hands and from the striped backs of malefactors, and piles of stones barely concealing the battered bodies of adulterous couples." Lecherous, truculent, irrational, cruel, conniving, excitable, dreaming about lascivious heavens while hypocritically enforcing oppressive legal codes: the stereotype of the Moslem is only partially softened by a Kahlil Gibran who puts it into sentimental doggerel or a Rudolph Valentino who does it with zest and good humor. . . .

The first thing we probably need to recognize is that the principal source of the acrimony underlying the Christian–Moslem relationship is a historical equivalent of sibling rivalry. Christians somehow hate to admit that in many ways their faith stands closer to Islam than to any other world religion. Indeed, that may be the reason Muhammad was viewed for centuries in the West as a charlatan and an imposter. The truth is, theologically speaking at least, both faiths are the offspring of an earlier revelation through the Law and the Prophets to the people of Israel. Both honor the Virgin Mary and Jesus of Nazareth. Both received an enormous early impetus from an apostle — Paul for Christianity and Muhammad for Islam — who translated a particularistic vision into a universal faith. The word "Allah" (used in the core formula of Islam: "There is no God but Allah and Muhammad is his prophet") is not an exclusively Moslem term at all. It is merely the Arabic word for God, and is used by Arabic Christians when they refer to the God of Christian faith.

There is nothing terribly surprising about these similarities since Muhammad, whose preaching mission did not begin until he reached forty, was subjected to considerable influence from Christianity during his formative years and may have come close — according to some scholars — to becoming an Abyssinian Christian. As Arend van Leeuwen points out in his thoughtful treatment of Islam in *Christianity in World History*, "The truth is that when Islam was still in the initial stages of its development, there was nothing likely to prevent the new movement from being accepted as a peculiar version of Arabian Christianity." Maybe the traditional Christian uneasiness with Islam is that it

seems just a little *too* similar. We sense the same aversion we might feel toward a twin brother who looks more like us than we want him to and whose habits remind us of some of the things we like least in ourselves.

The metaphor of a brother, or perhaps a cousin, is entirely germane. Muhammad considered himself to be in a direct line with the great biblical prophets and with Jesus. The title he preferred for himself was *al-nabi al-ummi*, the "prophet of the nations" (or of the "gentiles"). He believed he was living proof that the God who had called and used previous prophets such as Abraham and Job, neither of whom was Jewish, could do the same thing again. Later on, Moslem theologians liked to trace the genealogy of Muhammad back to Hagar, the bondwoman spouse of Abraham. The Old Testament story says that Hagar's giving birth to Ishmael stirred up such jealousy between her and Sarah, Abraham's first wife and the mother of Isaac, that Sarah persuaded Abraham to banish the bondwoman and her child into the desert. There Hagar gave up hope and left the child under a shrub to die. But God heard the child's weeping, created a well of water in the desert to save them both, and promised Hagar that from her son also, as from Isaac, He would "create a great nation." According to the symbolism of this old saga, the Jews and the Arabs (and by extension all Moslems) are the common offspring of Abraham (called "Ibrahim" in Arabic). This makes Christians and Moslems cousins, at least by legendary lineage.

The similarity between Christians and Moslems does not stop with religious genealogy. The actual elements of the Koran's message — faith, fasting, alms, prayer, and pilgrimage — all have Christian analogues. Despite its firm refusal to recognize any divine being except God (which is the basis for its rejection of Christ's divinity), Islam appears sometimes to be a pastiche of elements from disparate forms of Christianity molded into a potent unity. Take the Calvinist emphasis on faith in an omnipotent deity, the pietistic cultivation of daily personal prayer, the medieval teaching on charity, the folk-Catholic fascination with pilgrimage, and the monastic practice of fasting, and you have all the essential ingredients of Islam. All, that is, except the confluence of forces which, through the personality of Muhammad and the movement he set off, joined these elements in the white heat of history and fused them into a coherent faith of compelling attractiveness.

Like Paul, who said his apostleship was to both Jews and gentiles, Muhammad believed his mission was twofold. He felt called by God to bring the law and the Gospel to the heretofore neglected peoples of Arabia. But he also felt he had a mission *to* those very peoples — Christians and Jews (whom he called "peoples of the book") — *from* whom the original message of salvation had come. In one important respect, therefore, Muhammad's mission was different from St. Paul's. Since Muhammad carried on his preaching in the early decades of the seventh century, he not only had to deal with a Judaism he considered corrupted (as Paul had too); he also had to face an even more corrupted form of Christianity. Fortunately for St. Paul, since the Christian movement was only a decade or so old when he lived, he had to cope only with a few legalizers and gnostics. The infant Church had not yet tasted the corruption that comes, perhaps inevitably, from power and longevity. From a certain Christian perspective, Muhammad was as much a reformer as an apostle. A prophet of the gentiles, he also saw himself as a purifier of the faith of all the "people of the book," Christians and Jews, calling them away from the ornate and decadent versions of the faith they had fallen into and back to its simple essence, at least as he understood it. There is always something of this urge to simplify, to return *ad fontes*, in any reformer. And Muhammad was no exception.

No one should minimize the fact that in any genuine conversation between Christians and Moslems certain real differences in theology and practice will have to be faced, what scholars often call "rival truth claims." But such conflicting assertions can be properly understood only against the flesh-and-blood history that has somehow made them rivals. Religious teachings do not inhabit a realm apart. They mean what they do to people because of the coloration given to them by long historical experience. Therefore a previous question has to be asked. It is this: If Christianity and Islam share such common roots and, despite real differences, some striking similarities, why have they grown so bitter toward each other over the centuries? Why did the average white American feel less sympathetic to Islam than to any other world religion even *before* our current flap with the ayatollahs?

The explanation for this hostility is not a pretty story. Its major lineaments can be indicated with the names of three figures who symbolize its most critical stages. The first is Alexander the Great, whose career corresponds to what might be called the prehistory of Christianity. The second is Constantine the Great, who exemplifies its early period. The third is Pope Urban II, who expresses its classical phase, one of the most formative in the Christian–Moslem interaction.

Christopher Dawson, the late Roman Catholic cultural historian, once remarked that "Muhammad is the Orient's answer to Alexander the Great." At first this sounds like one of those wonderfully sweeping but highly improbable aphorisms. Muhammad, after all, lived and preached a full thousand years after Alexander. The prodigious Macedonian disciple of Aristotle conquered everything between Greece and northern India before he was thirty-three and spread the culture and values of Hellenism wherever his soldiers trod. But a thousand years is not a long time when one is dealing with cultural domination and the backlash it ultimately elicits. This is what Dawson had in mind.

Alexander did more than conquer everything before

him. Unlike previous conquerors, who sought mainly booty and tribute, he wanted to convert his colonized peoples into Hellenists. Alexander's conquest mixed military, political, and religious power. It was obviously going to require a comparable fusion of elements to throw off his conquest. After a thousand years that response finally came. It was Islam.

When the Islamic response to Roman–Hellenistic domination exploded in the early seventh century, the entire world was stunned by its vitality. In retrospect, however, we can understand its religious ideology in large measure as a reverse mirror image of what it was overthrowing. Take its rejection of the divinity of Christ, for example. Alexander had allowed himself to be viewed as a divine being, a god-emperor, and this ideology persisted through centuries of European culture in one form or another. The Koran's strenuous insistence that there was only one God, and its rejection of all semidivine beings, must be seen at least in part as a rejection of the political use of Christology to sacralize various forms of human rule.

The Moslem rejection of the divinity of Christ is not just simpleminded monotheistic stubbornness. It began as "political theology." For the Arabians, living on what were then the outskirts of the Eastern Empire, it marked a rejection not only of the non-Semitic categories in which the doctrine of Christ's divinity were elaborated in the Church councils (the "being of one substance with the Father") but also of the political hierarchy the doctrine helped to sanctify, especially in the Byzantine environment. When the Pantocrator Christ began to sacralize an empire in which the Arabians were the underdogs, their refusal of the doctrine made perfect sense. Alexander the Great had created the cultural imperium for which Christianity eventually supplied the sacred ideology. The Islamic revolt against this system was a revolt not against the Gospel as they understood it but against what Christianity had come to be. Islam's implacable insistence on one God not only freed thousands of people from their fear of the evil jinns and united the feuding tribes of Arabia (and later a vast part of the known world); it also served as a counterideology to the political function that Christian trinitarianism was beginning to serve. No "rival truth claim" debate between Christians and Moslems can begin until this history is recognized.

Islam began as a liberation theology, but, like Christianity, which had a comparable beginning, it could not resist the wiles of worldly power. As in the case of most successful liberation movements, Islam incorporated many of the cultural and political characteristics of its enemies. Though Muhammad was hounded out of Mecca by its local power elites, one hundred years after his death a glittering capital for the new Islamic empire was founded at Baghdad, the "Constantinople of Islam." Moslems became imperialists themselves, although in most instances they allowed Christians and Jews to practice their faiths. Forced conversions were rare. Above all, Moslems became the supreme masters and cultivators of the very Greek wisdom that had been imposed on them by Alexander. They became devout disciples of the same Aristotle whose zealous pupil had set out to spread his master's learning in their lands a millennium before. It was the Arabs, after all, who brought Aristotle back to the West and eventually to the cluttered desk of Thomas Aquinas. At its height, Islamic culture vastly outshone that of the Christian West, which most Moslems more or less accurately regarded as a barren outpost. But at the same time, the original liberating impulse of Islam had begun to run out. Today, paradoxically, this very spoiling by success may provide a needed bridge between Christians and Moslems, since Christians have experienced the same sad, familiar story in their own history.

Muhammad's judgment on the Christianity of his day is one of the great ironies of history. This Christianity, which began in the life of a Palestinian Jew who was executed because he was viewed as a threat to the Roman Empire and to the Hellenistically inclined rulers of his colonized nation, was seen a few centuries later by Muhammad, the prophet of another downtrodden nation, as the religious sanction for his own people's domination. What is remarkable about Muhammad is not that he rejected current theories about the divinity of Christ but that he did *not* reject Jesus himself. Rather he tried, from his own vantage point, to bypass the caricature of the Gospel which imperial Christianity had elaborated and to reclaim the faith of a people much like his own who had once looked to Allah for justice and mercy.

Jesus, then, is another vital link between the two faiths. To this day, Jesus holds a central place in Islamic teaching and is sometimes even depicted as a kind of supreme exemplar of what is meant by "submission to God" (the meaning of the word "Islam").

In popular Islamic belief, Jesus often occupies an even more important position. Thus many Moslems believe that when the long awaited "Twelfth Iman," whose name is *al-Mahdi*, finally appears to usher in the reign of justice on earth (*not* in the sky, incidentally), he will either be accompanied by Jesus or will turn out to be the same one whose "coming in Glory" the Christian creeds confess. Obviously there is much to discuss here between these two "Jesus traditions," if the ground can be cleared of spiteful stereotypes and the sibling rivalry can be held at bay.

Both Christianity and Islam began as visions of captive peoples who yearned for deliverance and caught a glimpse of hope in the promise of God. The two can understand each other only when both begin to acknowledge these common roots, step out of the long shadow of Alexander the Great, and try to learn from each other what has gone so terribly wrong over the years of their common history.

From Harvey Cox, "Understanding Islam—No More Holy Wars," *The Atlantic Monthly*, January 1981. Reprinted by permission of the author.

ANALYSIS AND INTERPRETATION OF THE READINGS

1. Was the Byzantine conception of popular sovereignty similar to the modern conception?
2. What resemblances do you find between the doctrines of the Koran and the doctrines of the Old and New Testament?
3. Explain Cox's quotation from Christopher Dawson: "Muhammad is the Orient's answer to Alexander the Great."

CHAPTER 10

The High Middle Ages (1050–1300): Economic, Social, and Political Institutions

CHRONOLOGY

In the blanks below, write the following events in their correct chronological order: Norman conquest of England; Battle of Las Navas de Tolosa; Accession of Hugh Capet to the French throne; Accession of Philip Augustus; Battle of Legnano; signing of Magna Carta; Death of Philip IV ("the Fair"); Henry IV's humiliation at Canossa; first European windmills.

_____

_____

_____

_____

_____

_____

_____

_____

IDENTIFICATIONS

You should be familiar with the following terms:

trade fairs
three-field system
journeyman
"Holy Roman Empire"
communes (Italian)

baron
grand jury
Capetian dynasty
Ile-de-France
Hohenstaufen

And the following people:

Eleanor of Aquitaine
Otto the great
Frederick Barbarossa
Thomas Becket

Blanche of Castille
Gregory VII
Frederick II
St. Louis (France)

In the space provided after each, define the following terms:

manorialism_____

_____

_____

vassal_____

_____

knight_____

_____

fief_____

_____

_____

craft guild_____

_____

_____

merchant guild_____

_____

_____

itinerant judges_____

_____

_____

_____

serf_____

_____

_____

baillis_____

_____

_____

lord's demesne_____

_____

_____

_____

STUDY QUESTIONS

1. What were the causes of the "agricultural revolution" in northern and western Europe? Why did it not occur earlier than the High Middle Ages?
2. How was the increased use of horses related to greater agricultural productivity? How did the greater use of iron help?
3. What were the demographic effects of the agricultural revolution?
4. Explain the origin of the medieval European manor. How did it differ from the old Roman landed estate?
5. Explain this statement: "the entire manorial system emphasized communal enterprise and solidarity."
6. How did medieval serfdom differ from Roman slavery?
7. What were the causes of the decline of serfdom in the thirteenth century?

8. How did the nobility benefit from the agricultural revolution, even after the emancipation of their serfs?
9. What is the original and literal meaning of "chivalry"?
10. How did the life style and social attitudes of the nobility change during the High Middle Ages?
11. "Whereas the Romans were really only interested in land *communications*, medieval people, starting in the eleventh century, concentrated on land *transport*." Explain.
12. Account for the growth of European towns in the twelfth and thirteenth centuries. What was the "symbiotic relationship" between towns and countryside?
13. How did medieval guilds differ from modern trade unions?
14. How did the growth of a merchant class affect prevailing attitudes toward moneylending and profit?
15. Summarize the effects of the revival of trade in western Europe.
16. Germany, in 1050 the most centralized European territory, by 1300 was the most hopelessly fragmented. Explain how this came about.
17. How did the emperor Frederick II, in spite of his brilliance and energy, contribute to the misfortunes of both Italy and Germany?
18. Define political feudalism as it existed in western medieval Europe. In view of its decentralized character, how could it nevertheless contribute to the growth of stable governments?
19. How did William the Conqueror aid the development of a national monarchy in England?
20. What developments in the judiciary mark the reign of Henry II as one of the most momentous in all of English history?
21. Why was Henry II's reign more successful than those of his two sons?
22. Explain why Magna Carta was basically a feudal document rather than "a charter of liberties for the common man." What principles of value for the future did it embody?
23. What was the origin of the English Parliament? How did its composition change and its importance grow under Edward I?
24. Why did the Capetians have more difficulty in strengthening the monarchy in France than did the Norman rulers in England? How were they able to overcome these difficulties?

PROBLEMS

1. Investigate further any of the following:
   a. The development of agricultural technology during the High Middle Ages

b. Social and domestic life of the feudal nobility
c. The personality and deeds of Frederick II of Hohenstaufen
d. The thirteenth-century origins of the English Parliament
e. Medieval craft guilds
2. Compare the life of the medieval peasant with that of the modern workingman. In what respects was the life of the former superior? In what respects inferior?
3. Describe the chief differences between feudalism as a system of government and the modern state.
4. What factors operated during the High Middle Ages to bring into existence the nation-state?
5. Trace the development of Anglo-American democratic institutions in the high-medieval age.
6. Discuss the effects upon civilization of the growth of cities.
7. Debate — pro or con — this proposition: The rise of national monarchies was essential to the development of modern civilization.

GEOGRAPHICAL IDENTIFICATIONS

Normandy
Flanders
Lübeck
Bruges
Urals
Paris
Milan
Naples
Cologne
Berlin
Swabia
Munich
Florence
Palermo
Pisa

Venice
Genoa
Ghent
Lorraine
Freiburg
Champagne
Hastings
Granada
Aragon
Castille
Bologna
Palermo
Seine River
Rhine River
Elbe River

CEREMONIAL RELATIONSHIP BETWEEN LORD AND VASSAL

Through the whole remaining part of the day those who had been previously enfeoffed by the most pious Count Charles did homage to the [new] count, taking up now again their fiefs and offices and whatever they had before rightfully and legitimately obtained. On Thursday, the seventh of April, homages were again made to the count, being completed in the following order of faith and security.

First they did their homage thus. The count asked the vassal if he were willing to become completely his man, and the other replied, "I am willing"; and with hands clasped, placed between the hands of the count, they were bound together by a kiss. Secondly, he who had done homage gave his fealty to the representative of the count in these words, "I promise on my faith that I will in future be faithful to Count William, and will observe my homage to him completely against all persons, in good faith and without deceit." And, thirdly, he took his oath to this upon the relics of the saints. Afterward the count, with a little rod which he held in his hand, gave investitures to all who by this agreement had given their security and accompanying oath.

From J. H. Robinson, *Readings in European History*, Vol. I.

THE EMANCIPATION OF A SERF

To all the faithful of Christ to whom the present writing shall come, Richard, by the divine permission abbot of Peterborough and of the Convent of the same place, eternal greeting in the Lord:

Let all know that we have manumitted and liberated from all yoke of servitude William, the son of Richard of Wythington, whom previously we have held as our born bondman, with his whole progeny and all his chattels, so that neither we nor our successors shall be able to require or exact any right or claim in the said William, his progeny, or his chattels. But the same William, with his whole progeny and all his chattels, shall remain free and quit and without disturbance, exaction, or any claim on the part of us or our successors by reason of any servitude forever.

We will, moreover, and concede that he and his heirs shall hold the messuages, land, rents, and meadows in Wythington which his ancestors held from us and our predecessors, by giving and performing the fine which is called *merchet* for giving his daughter in marriage,

and tallage from year to year according to our will, — that he shall have and hold these for the future from us and our successors freely, quietly, peacefully, and hereditarily, by paying to us and our successors yearly 40s. sterling, at the four terms of the year, namely: at St. John the Baptist's day 10s., at Michaelmas 10s., at Christmas 10s., and at Easter 10s., for all service, exaction, custom, and secular demand; saving to us, nevertheless, attendance at our court of Castre every three weeks, wardship, and relief, and outside service of our lord the king, when they shall happen.

And if it shall happen that the said William or his heirs shall die at any time without an heir, the said messuage, land, rents, and meadows with their appurtenances shall return fully and completely to us and our successors. Nor will it be allowed to the said William or his heirs to give, sell, alienate, mortgage, or encumber in any way, the said messuage, land, rents, meadows, or any part of them, by which the said messuage, land, rents, and meadows should not return to us and our successors in the form declared above. And if this should occur later, their deed shall be declared null, and what is thus alienated shall come to us and our successors. . . .

Given at Borough, for the love of Lord Robert of good memory, once abbot, our predecessor and maternal uncle of the said William, and at the instance of the good man, Brother Hugh of Mutton, relative of the said abbot Robert, A.D. 1278, on the eve of Pentecost.

From J. H. Robinson, *Readings in European History*, Vol. I.

↓ Read

SIGNIFICANT PROVISIONS OF MAGNA CARTA

No *scutage* or aid shall be imposed in our kingdom, unless by the common council of our kingdom, except to redeem our person, and to make our eldest son a knight, and once to marry our eldest daughter; and for this there shall only be paid a reasonable aid.

And the city of London shall have all its ancient liberties and free customs, as well by land as by water.

Furthermore, we will and grant that all other cities and boroughs, and towns, and ports, shall have all their liberties and free customs; and shall have the common council of the kingdom concerning the assessment of their aids, except in the three cases aforesaid.

And for the assessing of scutages we shall cause to be summoned the archbishops, bishops, abbots, earls, and great barons of the realm, singly by our letters.

And furthermore, we shall cause to be summoned in

general by our sheriffs and bailiffs, all others who hold of us in chief, at a certain day, that is to say, forty days (before their meeting) at least, to a certain place; and in all letters of such summons, we will declare the cause of the summons.

And summons being thus made, the business shall proceed on the day appointed, according to the advice of such as shall be present, although all that were summoned come not.

We will not for the future grant to any one, that he may take aid of his own free-tenants, unless to redeem his body; and to make his eldest son a knight, and once to marry his eldest daughter; and for this there shall only be paid a reasonable aid.

• • •

A free man shall not be amerced for a small fault, but according to the degree of the fault; and for a great crime, in proportion to the heinousness of it, saving to him his contenement, and after the same manner a merchant, saving to him his merchandise.

And a villain shall be amerced after the same manner, saving to him his wainage, if he falls under our mercy; and none of the aforesaid amerciaments shall be assessed, but by the oath of honest men of the neighbourhood.

• • •

No constable or bailiff of ours shall take corn or other chattels of any man, unless he presently gives him money for it, or hath respite of payment from the seller.

No constables shall distrein any knight to give money for castle-guard, if he himself shall do it in his own person, or by another able man, in case he shall be hindered by any reasonable cause.

And if we shall lead him, or if we shall send him into the army, he shall be free from castle-guard, for the time he shall be in the army, by our command.

No sheriff or bailiff of ours, or any other, shall take horses or carts of any for carriage.

Neither shall We or our officers or others, take any man's timber for our castles, or other uses, unless by the consent of the owner of the timber.

• • •

No freeman shall be taken, or imprisoned, or disscis'd, or outlaw'd, or banished, or any ways destroyed; nor will we pass upon him, or commit him to prison, unless by the legal judgment of his peers, or by the law of the land.

We will sell to no man, we will deny no man, nor defer right or justice.

All merchants shall have safe and secure conduct to go out of, and come into England; and to stay there, and to pass, as well by land as by water; to buy and sell by the ancient and allowed customs, without any evil tolls, except in time of war, or when they shall be of any nation in war with us.

And if there shall be found any such in our land in the beginning of a war, they shall be attached, without damage to their bodies or goods, until it may be known

unto us, or our chief justiciary, how our merchants be treated in the nation at war with us: and if ours be safe there, they shall be safe in our land.

• • •

If any one hath been dispossessed, or deprived by us without the legal judgment of his peers, of his lands, castles, liberties or right, we will forthwith restore them to him; and if any dispute arises upon this head, let the matter be decided by the five and twenty barons hereafter mentioned, for the preservation of the peace.

As for those things, of which any person has, without the legal judgment of his peers, been dispossessed or deprived, either by King Henry our father, or our brother King Richard, and which we have in our hands, or are possessed by others, and we are bound to warrant and make good, we shall have a respite, till the term usually allowed the croises; excepting those things about which there is a suit depending, or whereof an inquest hath been made by our order, before we undertook the crusade. But when we return from our pilgrimage, or if we do not perform it, we will immediately cause full justice to be administered therein.

• • •

And whereas, for the honour of God, and the amendment of our kingdom, and for quieting the discord that has arisen between Us and our barons, we have granted all the things aforesaid; willing to render them firm and lasting, we do given and grant our subjects the following security; namely, that the barons may choose five and twenty barons of the kingdom, whom they think convenient, who shall take care, with all their might, to hold and observe, and cause to be observed, the peace and liberties we have granted them, and by this our present Charter confirmed. . . .

———

From John Fairburn ed., *Magna Charta, the Bill of Rights; with the Petition of Right . . .*

THE NATURE OF MEDIEVAL TRADE: *Two Examples*

[1]

Genoa, July 24, [1215]

I, Arnulf of Basel, promise you, Enrico Medico, to import for you into Genoa four *centenaria* of good and fine glass, of the best and finest for making mirrors that I can find in Germany and from the best furnace; and I promise to deliver and consign it to your possession or to that of your accredited messenger by the next [feast of] All Saints, under penalty of the double, all my goods being pledged, etc. And I am doing this for you in consideration of £3 Genoese which you are obligated to give me for each *centenarium*. Furthermore, I, the aforesaid Enrico, promise you at that time to accept said glass personally or through my messenger and to give said price to you or your accredited messenger peacefully and without causing trouble. Otherwise, I promise you, making the stipulation, the penalty of the double, all my goods being pledged, etc. Witnesses: Guglielmo Provenzale, dealer in spices; Giovanni d'Usignolo; and Nicoloso, dealer in spices. Done in Genoa in the home of Enrico di Negro and his kin, July 24, between terce and nones.

[2]

[Siena, April, 1445]

Before you, magnificent and powerful lords, our most particular lords, premising the humble recommendations, etc.

It is related with due reverence by your most faithful servants, Vitale, son of Maestro Allegro of Imola, Jew, and Stefano di Giovanni of Ragusa, that they have heard through report that in some parts of your district there are certain mountains which have veins of every kind of metal; and for that reason they have come to your city and wish to mine in said mountains. They would like to ask by singular grace to be allowed to mine in the territory of Montieri, that is, in the village of Boccheggiano and in the village of Roccastrada, with these pacts, conditions, and procedures: that where they begin to mine no other person be allowed to mine within a mile from them for a period of twenty-five years; and if it should happen that two years pass without their mining anything, then this grace is to be understood to be null and void; and they offer forever to give your Commune out of anything they mine or find one part out of twelve. Also, in regard to everything they mine — that is, gold, silver, and any other metal — they promise your Commune that they will have it melted and refined by artisans living in your town, that is, by goldsmiths; and if [the goldsmiths] themselves wish to do this, they promise

not to send [the metal] to others, that is, outside your city. Also, [they promise] that they will have it all struck in the mint of your Commune.

Also we wish to be allowed to use any water in the said localities and to erect there any building [needed] to work the said metal, and to be allowed to cut wood without detriment or damage to any of your communities or to private persons, [since] this grace is not to be understood to be detrimental in any part to them.

And this they would like to ask by grace of your lordships, to whom they ever recommend themselves, whom may God preserve as they wish. Praise be to God.

From Robert S. Lopez and Irving W. Raymond (eds.), *Medieval Trade in the Mediterranean World*, Columbia University Records of Civilization, Sources, and Studies, Columbia University Press. Reprinted by permission of the publisher.

ANALYSIS AND INTERPRETATION OF THE READINGS

1. What improvement in status did manumission bring to a serf?
2. Do you get the impression that William had been in abject poverty during his period of serfdom?
3. What particular abuses or unjust practices did King John promise to renounce?
4. Did Magna Carta offer any benefits to the nonfeudal elements of the population? If so, in which clauses?
5. Study carefully the first seven clauses quoted. Just what financial limitations did they put upon the king? Did these clauses really incorporate the principle of "no taxation without representation," as was alleged in later times?

The High Middle Ages (1050–1300): Religious and Intellectual Developments

CHRONOLOGY

Write the correct date or dates in the blank after each of the following events:

Founding of monastery of Cluny_____

Council of Clermont_____

Concordat of Worms_____

Death of St. Bernard of Clairvaux_____

Pontificate of Innocent III_____

Fourth Lateran Council_____

Death of emperor Frederick II of Hohenstaufen_____

Completion of the *Romance of the Rose* by John of Meun_____

Fall of the last of the Crusaders' holdings in the Holy Land_____

First papal jubilee in Rome_____

Death of Dante_____

IDENTIFICATIONS

In the blanks below, write the correct terms taken from the following list:

lay investiture	minnesingers
Cistercians	Papal States
fabliaux	Goliards
canon law	Sicilian Vespers
Fourth Lateran Council	Scholasticism
Sic et Non	Albigensians
primogeniture	Waldensians

_____was the product of a centralized system of Church courts which both enhanced papal prestige and improved legal standards.

_____was the ceremony whereby a churchman had the symbols of office conferred on him by the king or a noble.

The_____were territories near Rome over which popes attempted to establish direct sovereignty.

The_____of 1282 led to a fierce struggle involving the pope, the French king, and the Span-ish house of Aragon.

_____was a rule of inheritance that dis-advantaged younger sons.

The_____were a monastic order founded about 1100 who strikingly demonstrated an inten-sified religious zeal.

The_____decreed that sacraments ad-ministered by the Church were indispensable for salvation.

The_____claimed to be Christians but subscribed to the extreme religious dualism of Manichaeism.

In_____Abelard attempted to subject theology to the tools of logic.

The_____were a heretical group orig-inating in southern France who strove for literal imitation of the life of Christ.

_____was a highly intellectual world-view that attempted to reconcile classical pagan philosophy with the Christian faith.

The Latin lyrics of the_____flaunted the ascetic ideals of Christianity.

The_____were coarse but entertaining prose stories written in the vernacular.

The_____were the German equivalent of French troubadours.

Circle the name of the appropriate individual in the following statements. If none of those listed is ap-propriate, write the correct name in the blank space at (d).

A pope who for his reforming zeal and challeng-ing of secular rulers was called a "Holy Satan" was (a) Boniface VIII, (b) Gregory I, (c) Gregory VII, (d)_____

_____

The founder of the order of friars to which St. Thomas Aquinas belonged was (a) St. Dominic, (b) St. Augustine, (c) St. Francis of Assisi, (d)

_____

The pope who forced King John to acknowledge England as a papal fief was (a) Innocent III, (b) Nicholas I, (c) Innocent IV, (d)_____

_____

The first pope to preach a Crusade was (a) Gregory VII, (b) Gregory the Great, (c) Urban II, (d) _____

The leader of a unique Crusade which succeeded through peaceful diplomacy was (a) Frederick Barbarossa, (b) Frederick II, (c) Richard the Lionhearted, (d) _____

The ruler who declared: "As every knee is bowed to Jesus, so all men should obey His Vicar" was (a) Innocent III, (b) Frederick II, (c) John XII, (d) _____

The Byzantine emperor who appealed to the pope for aid against the Seljuk Turks was (a) Leo III, Isaurian, (b) Saladin, (c) Alexius Comnenus, (d) _____

Greatest of the Scholastic philosophers and long-time professor at the University of Paris was (a) Robert Grosseteste, (b) William of Lorris, (c) Gottfried von Strassburg, (d) _____

The translator of Aristotle's *Ethics* and a pioneer in mathematics, astronomy, and optics was (a) Roger Bacon, (b) Abelard, (c) Robert Grosseteste, (d) _____

A gifted, challenging, but highly controversial teacher who clashed with the Church and was convicted of heresy was (a) Heloise, (b) Peter Lombard, (c) Peter Abelard, (d) _____

A leader of the Cluny reform movement who was elected Pope in 1073 took the name of (a) Boniface VIII, (b) Innocent III, (c) Pius IV, (d) _____

The pope whose humiliation by a French king marked a dramatic reversal of the papacy's temporal power was (a) Innocent III, (b) Gregory VII, (c) John XII, (d) _____

STUDY QUESTIONS

1. Why did the founding of the monastery of Cluny represent an important step toward the development of papal power?
2. Explain the significance of the decree on papal elections issued in 1059.
3. What were the contributions of Pope Gregory VII to the rise of the papal monarchy? What was Gregory's conception of "right order in the world"?
4. The investiture struggle was seemingly a quarrel over symbols and ceremony. What were the real underlying issues? How were they settled?

5. What were the goals of Pope Innocent III? To what extent did he reach them? Which of his projects failed disastrously?
6. How did the clash between the popes and various monarchs in the thirteenth and fourteenth centuries ultimately weaken the power of the papacy?
7. What were Urban II's motives in calling the First Crusade?
8. What were the religious causes of the Crusades?
9. In their struggles with secular rulers the popes "overemployed their spiritual weapons." Explain.
10. "While the crusading idea helped build up the papal monarchy, it also helped destroy it." Explain how.
11. Estimate the positive and negative effects of the Crusades on European society and economy.
12. How did the friars differ from regular monks, and how did they enhance the Church's influence?
13. What change in religious beliefs is indicated by the twelfth-century cult of the Virgin Mary, and how did this change affect social attitudes and artistic expression?
14. What is the significance of the new theology of the Eucharist developed in the twelfth century.
15. How do you account for the rise of popular heretical movements in the late twelfth century?
16. What was the relationship between cathedral schools and high-medieval universities?
17. Show how the great medieval universities set the pattern for higher education in the modern Western world. In what ways were they different from modern institutions?
18. How did the life of medieval students differ from that of their modern descendants?
19. To what extent were Grosseteste and Roger Bacon forerunners of modern science?
20. What was St. Thomas Aquinas attempting in writing his *Summaries*? In what way, if any, did his thought differ from that of the early Church father St. Augustine?
21. Why did the acceptance of Aristotle by Scholastic thinkers constitute a philosophical revolution?
22. What were the main types of secular literature in the High Middle Ages? Give examples of each type.
23. How do the ideas and attitudes expressed in the *Divine Comedy* contrast with those of the early Middle Ages?
24. Dante's *Divine Comedy* has been described as a synthesis of high-medieval knowledge and beliefs. In what ways does it also show originality?
25. Point out the differences between the Romanesque and Gothic styles of architecture.

26. In addition to their religious function, what aspects of high-medieval culture are reflected in the great Gothic cathedrals?

PROBLEMS

1. Investigate further any of the following:
   a. The Cluniac reform movement
   b. St. Francis of Assisi
   c. One of the first four Crusades
   d. Medieval science
   e. The Goliard Poets
   f. A major Gothic cathedral (Chartres, Notre Dame of Paris, Amiens, Lincoln, Canterbury, or Cologne, for example)
2. Compare modern universities with their medieval prototypes.
3. Read the chapter entitled "The Virgin and the Dynamo" in Henry Adams, *The Education of Henry Adams* and decide whether it expresses accurately the medieval religious temper.
4. To what extent was medieval Scholasticism a "rationalist" philosophy? Was it an example of rationalism in the modern sense?
5. Which, in your opinion, was a better summation of late medieval ideals and attitudes, Gothic architecture or vernacular literature?

6. Read the *Song of Roland* and explain how it illustrates interests and ideals of high-medieval civilization.
7. What relationship, if any, can you find between the European Crusades and the colonialism of modern times?
8. The Scholastics "had extraordinary faith in the powers of human reason—probably more than we do today." Do you agree or disagree? Substantiate your argument.

GEOGRAPHICAL IDENTIFICATIONS

Cluny	Clairvaux
Assisi	Rouen
Venice	Antioch
Clermont	Chartres
Amiens	Vienna
Aragon	Bologna
Hungary	Provence
Oxford	Naples
Cambridge	Paris
Montpellier	Rheims
Salamanca	Laon
Heidelberg	Lyons
Worms	

AIDS TO AN UNDERSTANDING OF THE HIGH MIDDLE AGES: RELIGIOUS AND INTELLECTUAL DEVELOPMENTS

LATE MEDIEVAL CHRISTIANITY: "On Heresy"
St. Thomas Aquinas

Accordingly there are two ways in which a man may deviate from the rectitude of the Christian faith. First, because he is unwilling to assent to Christ; and such a man has an evil will, so to say, in respect of the very end. This belongs to the species of unbelief in pagans and Jews. Secondly, because, though he intends to assent to Christ, yet he fails in his choice of those things wherein he assents to Christ, because he chooses, not what Christ really taught, but the suggestions of his own mind.

Therefore heresy is a species of unbelief, belonging to those who profess the Christian faith, but corrupt its dogmas.

* * *

... The Apostle says (Tit. iii. 10, 11): *A man that is a heretic, after the first and second admonition, avoid: knowing that he, that is such an one, is subverted.*

I answer that, With regard to heretics two points must be observed: one, on their own side, the other, on the side of the Church. On their own side there is the sin, whereby they deserve not only to be separated from the Church by excommunication, but also to be severed from the world by death. For it is a much graver matter to corrupt the faith which quickens the soul, than to forge money, which supports temporal life. Wherefore if forgers of money and other evil-doers are forthwith condemned to death by the secular authority, much more reason is there for heretics, as soon as they are convicted of heresy, to be not only excommunicated but even put to death.

On the part of the Church, however, there is mercy which looks to the conversion of the wanderer, wherefore she condemns not at once, but *after the first and second admonition,* as the Apostle directs: after that, if he is yet stubborn, the Church no longer hoping for his conversion, looks to the salvation of others, by excommunicating him and separating him from the Church, and furthermore delivers him to the secular tribunal to be exterminated thereby from the world by death. For Jerome commenting on Gal. v. 9, *A little leaven,* says: *Cut off the decayed flesh, expel the mangy sheep from the fold, lest the whole house, the whole paste, the whole body, the whole flock, burn, perish, rot, die. Arius was but one spark in Alexandria, but as that spark was not at once put out, the whole earth was laid waste by its flame.*

From St. Thomas Aquinas, *Summa Theologica,* Vol. II. Reprinted by permission of Benziger Brothers, publishers and copyright owners.

↓ Read
THE STRUGGLE BETWEEN SECULAR AND SPIRITUAL AUTHORITIES: Gregory VII's Conception of the Pope's Prerogatives

Among the letters and decrees of Gregory VII a list of propositions is found which briefly summarizes the claims of the papacy. The purpose of this so-called *Dictatus* is unknown; it was probably drawn up shortly after Gregory's accession and no doubt gives an official statement of the powers which he believed that he rightly possessed. The more important of the twenty-seven propositions contained in the *Dictatus* are given below.

The Roman church was founded by God alone.

The Roman bishop alone is properly called universal.

He alone may depose bishops and reinstate them.

His legate, though of inferior grade, takes precedence, in a council, of all bishops and may render a decision of deposition against them.

He alone may use the insignia of empire.

The pope is the only person whose feet are kissed by all princes.

His title is unique in the world.

He may depose emperors.

No council may be regarded as a general one without his consent.

No book or chapter may be regarded as canonical without his authority.

A decree of his may be annulled by no one; he alone may annul the decrees of all.

He may be judged by no one.

No one shall dare to condemn one who appeals to the papal see.

The Roman church has never erred, nor ever, by the witness of Scripture, shall err to all eternity.

He may not be considered Catholic who does not agree with the Roman church.

The pope may absolve the subjects of the unjust from their allegiance.

From J. H. Robinson, *Readings in European History,* Vol. I.

↓ Read
THE STRUGGLE BETWEEN SECULAR AND SPIRITUAL AUTHORITIES: Henry IV's Violent Reply to Gregory VII

We, forsooth, have endured all this in our anxiety to save the honor of the apostolic see, but thou hast mistaken our humility for fear, and hast, accordingly, ventured to attack the royal power conferred upon us by God, and threatened to divest us of it. As if we had received our kingdom from thee! As if the kingdom and the empire were in thy hands, not in God's! For our Lord Jesus Christ did call us to the kingdom, although he has not called thee to the priesthood: that thou hast attained by the following steps.

By craft abhorrent to the profession of monk, thou hast acquired wealth; by wealth, influence; by influence, arms; by arms, a throne of peace. And from the throne of peace thou hast destroyed peace; thou hast turned subjects against their governors, for thou, who wert not called of God, hast taught that our bishops, truly so called, should be despised. Thou hast put laymen above their priests, allowing them to depose or condemn those whom they themselves had received as teachers from the hand of God through the laying on of bishops' hands.

Thou hast further assailed me also, who, although unworthy of anointing, have nevertheless been anointed to the kingdom, and who, according to the traditions of the holy fathers, am subject to the judgment of God alone, to be deposed upon no charge save that of deviation from the faith, — which God avert! For the holy fathers by their wisdom committed the judgment and deposition of even Julian the Apostate not to themselves but to God alone. Likewise the true pope, Peter, himself exclaims: "Fear God. Honor the king." But thou, who dost not fear God, art dishonoring me, his appointed one. Wherefore, St. Paul, since he spared not an angel of heaven if he should preach other than the gospel, has not excepted thee, who dost teach other doctrine upon earth. For he says, "If any one, whether I, or an angel from heaven, shall preach the gospel other than that which has been preached to you, he shall be damned."

Thou, therefore, damned by this curse and by the judgment of all our bishops and ourselves, come down and relinquish the apostolic chair which thou hast usurped. Let another assume the seat of St. Peter, who will not practice violence under the cloak of religion, but will teach St. Peter's wholesome doctrine. I, Henry, king by the grace of God, together with all our bishops, say unto thee: "Come down, come down, to be damned throughout all eternity!"

From J. H. Robinson, *Readings in European History*, Vol. I.

THE CRUSADES: Pope Urban II's Speech at the Council of Clermont

Although, O sons of God, you have promised more firmly than ever to keep the peace among yourselves and to preserve the rights of the church, there remains still an important work for you to do. Freshly quickened by the divine correction, you must apply the strength of your righteousness to another matter which concerns you as well as God. For your brethren who live in the east are in urgent need of your help, and you must hasten to give them the aid which has often been promised them. For, as the most of you have heard, the Turks and Arabs have attacked them and have conquered the territory of Romania [the Greek empire] as far west as the shore of the Mediterranean and the Hellespont, which is called the Arm of St. George. They have occupied more and more of the lands of those Christians, and have overcome them in seven battles. They have killed and captured many, and have destroyed the churches and devastated the empire. If you permit them to continue thus for awhile with impunity, the faithful of God will be much more widely attacked by them. On this account I, or rather the Lord, beseech you as Christ's heralds to publish this everywhere and to persuade all people of whatever rank, foot-soldiers and knights, poor and rich, to carry aid promptly to those Christians and to destroy that vile race from the lands of our friends. I say this to those who are present, it is meant also for those who are absent. Moreover, Christ commands it.

All who die by the way, whether by land or by sea, or in battle against the pagans, shall have immediate remission of sins. This I grant them through the power of God with which I am invested. O what a disgrace if such a despised and base race, which worships demons, should conquer a people which has the faith of omnipotent God and is made glorious with the name of Christ! With what reproaches will the Lord overwhelm us if you do not aid those who, with us, profess the Christian religion! Let those who have been accustomed unjustly to wage private warfare against the faithful now go against the infidels and end with victory this war which should have been begun long ago. Let those who, for a long time, have been robbers, now become knights. Let those who have been fighting against their brothers and relatives now fight in a proper way against the barbarians. Let those who have been serving as mercenaries for small pay now obtain the eternal reward. Let those who have been wearing themselves out in both body and soul now work for a double honor. Behold! on this side will be the sorrowful and poor, on that, the rich; on this side, the enemies of the Lord, on that, his friends. Let those who go not put off the journey, but rent their lands and collect money for their expenses; and as soon as winter is over and spring comes, let them eagerly set out on the way with God as their guide.

From O. J. Thatcher and E. J. McNeal, *A Source Book for Medieval History.*

LATE MEDIEVAL PHILOSOPHY: The Rationalism of Abelard

Abelard supplies one hundred and fifty-eight problems, carefully balancing the authorities pro and con, and leaves the student to solve each problem as best he may. This doubtless shocked many of his contemporaries. Later scholastic lecturers did not hesitate to muster all possible objections to a particular position, but they always had a solution of their own to propose and defend.

The following will serve as examples of the questions Abelard raised in the *Yea and Nay*:

Should human faith be based upon reason, or no?

Is God one, or no?

Is God a substance, or no?

Does the first Psalm refer to Christ, or no?

Is sin pleasing to God, or no?

Is God the author of evil, or no?

Is God all-powerful, or no?

Can God be resisted, or no?

Has God free will, or no?

Was the first man persuaded to sin by the devil, or no?

Was Adam saved, or no?

Did all the apostles have wives except John, or no?

Are the flesh and blood of Christ in very truth and essence present in the sacrament of the altar, or no?

Do we sometimes sin unwillingly, or no?

Does God punish the same sin both here and in the future, or no?

Is it worse to sin openly than secretly, or no?

From J. H. Robinson, *Readings in European History*, Vol. I.

↓ Read

LATE MEDIEVAL PHILOSOPHY: The Rationalism of St. Thomas Aquinas

Now though the aforesaid truth of the Christian faith surpasses the ability of human reason, nevertheless those things which are naturally instilled in human reason cannot be opposed to this truth. For it is clear that those things which are implanted in reason by nature, are most true, so much so that it is impossible to think them to be false. Nor is it lawful to deem false that which is held by faith, since it is so evidently confirmed by God. Seeing then that the false alone is opposed to the true, as evidently appears if we examine their definitions, it is impossible for the aforesaid truth of faith to be contrary to those principles which reason knows naturally.

Again. The same thing which the disciple's mind receives from its teacher is contained in the knowledge of the teacher, unless he teach insincerely, which it were wicked to say of God. Now the knowledge of naturally known principles is instilled into us by God, since God Himself is the author of our nature. Therefore the divine Wisdom also contains these principles. Consequently whatever is contrary to these principles, is contrary to the divine Wisdom; wherefore it cannot be from God. Therefore those things which are received by faith from divine revelation cannot be contrary to our natural knowledge.

Having shown then that it is not futile to endeavour to prove the existence of God, we may proceed to set forth the reasons whereby both philosophers and Catholic doctors have proved that there is a God. In the first place we shall give the arguments by which Aristotle sets out to prove God's existence: and he aims at proving this from the point of view of movement, in two ways.

The *first way* is as follows. Whatever is in motion is moved by another: and it is clear to the sense that something, the sun for instance, is in motion. Therefore it is set in motion by something else moving it. Now that which moves it is itself either moved or not. If it be not moved, then the point is proved that we must needs postulate an immovable mover: and this we call God. If, however, it be moved, it is moved by another mover. Either, therefore, we must proceed to infinity, or we must come to an immovable mover. But it is not possible to proceed to infinity. Therefore it is necessary to postulate an immovable mover....

The Philosopher proceeds in a *different way* in 2 *Metaph.* to show that it is impossible to proceed to infinity in efficient causes, and that we must come to one first cause, and this we call God. This is how he proceeds. In all efficient causes following in order, the first is the cause of the intermediate cause, and the intermediate is the cause of the ultimate, whether the intermediate be one or several. Now if the cause be removed, that which it causes is removed. Therefore if we remove the first the intermediate cannot be a cause. But if we go on to infinity in efficient causes, no cause will be first. Therefore all the others which are intermediate will be removed. Now this is clearly false. Therefore we must suppose *the existence of a first efficient cause:* and this is God....

Another argument in support of this conclusion is adduced by Damascene from the government of things: and the same reasoning is indicated by the Commentator in 2 *Phys.* It runs as follows. It is impossible for contrary and discordant things to accord in one order always or frequently except by someone's governance, whereby each and all are made to tend to a definite end. Now we see that in the world things of different natures accord in one order, not seldom and fortuitously, but always or for the most part. Therefore it follows that there is *someone by whose providence the world is governed.* And this we call God.

From St. Thomas Aquinas, *Summa contra Gentiles*, trans. by the English Dominican Fathers, Vol. I. Copyright 1924 by Burns, Oates and Washbourne Ltd. Reprinted by permission of Burns & Oates Ltd.

LATE MEDIEVAL PHILOSOPHY: Dante's Universalistic View in *De Monarchia*

As therefore we have already said, there are three doubts, and these doubts suggest three questions, concerning Temporal Monarchy, which in more common speech is called the Empire; and our purpose is, as we have explained, to inquire concerning these questions in their given order, and starting from the first principle which we have just laid down. The first question, then, is whether Temporal Monarchy is necessary for the welfare of the world; and that it is necessary can, I think, be shown by the strongest and most manifest arguments; for nothing, either of reason or of authority, opposes me. Let us first take the authority of the Philosopher in his Politics. There, on his venerable authority, it is said that where a number of things are arranged to attain an end, it behooves one of them to regulate or govern the others, and the others to submit. And it is not only the authority of his illustrious name which makes this worthy of belief, but also reason, instancing particulars. . . .

And as the part is to the whole, so is the order of parts to the order of the whole. The part is to the whole, as to an end and highest good which is aimed at. And, therefore, the order in the parts is to the order in the whole, as it is to the end and highest good aimed at. . . . Therefore we find a double order in the world, namely, the order of the parts in relation to each other, and their order in relation to some one thing which is not a part . . . ; and the order of the parts in relation to the one thing which is not a part is the higher, for it is the end of the other order, and the other exists for the sake of it. Therefore, if the form of this order is found in the units of the mass of mankind, much more may we argue by our syllogism that it is found in mankind considered as a whole; for this latter order, or its form, is better. But it is sufficiently plain [that] this order is found in all the units of the mass of mankind. Therefore it is, or should be, found in the mass considered as a whole. And therefore all the parts that we have mentioned, which are comprised in kingdoms, and the kingdoms themselves ought to be ordered with reference to one Prince or Princedom, that is, with reference to a Monarch or Monarchy.

Again, things are well and at their best with every son when he follows, so far as by his proper nature he can, the footsteps of a perfect father. Mankind is the son of heaven, which is most perfect in all its works; for it is "man and the sun which produce man," according to the second book on Natural Learning. The human race, therefore, is best when it imitates the movements of heaven, so far as human nature allows. And since the whole heaven is regulated with one motion, to wit, that of the *primum mobile*, and by one mover, who is God, in all its parts, movements, and movers (and this human reason readily seizes from science); therefore, if our argument be correct, the human race is at its best state when, both in its movements, and in regard to those who move it, it is regulated by a single Prince, as by the single movement of heaven, and by one law, as by the single motion. Therefore is is evidently necessary for the welfare of the world for there to be a Monarchy, or single Princedom,

which men call the Empire. And this thought did Boethius breathe when he said: "Oh happy race of men, if your hearts are ruled by the love which rules the heaven."

———————

From Dante Alighieri, *De Monarchia*, F. J. Church trans.

LATE MEDIEVAL SCIENCE: The Empiricism of Roger Bacon, from *Opus Majus*

Having laid down fundamental principles of the wisdom of the Latins so far as they are found in language, mathematics, and optics, I now wish to unfold the principles of experimental science, since without experience nothing can be sufficiently known. For there are two modes of acquiring knowledge, namely, by reasoning and experience. Reasoning draws a conclusion and makes us grant the conclusion, but does not make the conclusion certain, nor does it remove doubt so that the mind may rest on the intuition of truth, unless the mind discovers it by the path of experience; since many have the arguments relating to what can be known, but because they lack experience they neglect the arguments, and neither avoid what is harmful nor follow what is good. For if a man who has never seen fire should prove by adequate reasoning that fire burns and injures things and destroys them, his mind would not be satisfied thereby, nor would he avoid fire, until he placed his hand or some combustible substance in the fire, so that he might prove by experience that which reasoning taught. But when he has had actual experience of combustion his mind is made certain and rests in the full light of truth. Therefore reasoning does not suffice, but experience does. . . .

He therefore who wishes to rejoice without doubt in regard to the truths underlying phenomena must know how to devote himself to experiment. For authors write many statements, and people believe them through reasoning which they formulate without experience. Their reasoning is wholly false. For it is generally believed that the diamond cannot be broken except by goat's blood, and philosophers and theologians misuse this idea. But fracture by means of blood of this kind has never been verified, although the effort has been made; and without that blood it can be broken easily. For I have seen this with my own eyes, and this is necessary, because gems cannot be carved except by fragments of this stone. . . . Moreover, it is generally believed that hot water freezes more quickly than cold water in vessels, and the argument in support of this is advanced that contrary is excited by contrary, just like enemies meeting each other. But it is certain that cold water freezes more quickly for any one who makes the experiment. . . .

But experience is of two kinds; one is gained through our external senses, and in this way we gain our experience of those things that are in the heavens by instruments made for this purpose, and of those things here below by means attested by our vision. Things that do not belong in our part of the world we know through other scientists who have had experience of them. As, for example, Aristotle on the authority of Alexander sent two thousand men through different parts of the world to gain experimental knowledge of all things that are on the surface of the earth, as Pliny bears witness in his Natural History. This experience is both human and philosophical, as far as man can act in accordance with the grace given him; but this experience does not suffice him, because it does not give full attestation in regard to things corporeal owing to its difficulty, and does not touch at all on things spiritual. It is necessary, therefore, that the intellect of man should be otherwise aided, and for this reason the holy patriarchs and prophets, who first gave sciences to the world, received illumination within and were not dependent on sense alone. The same is true of many believers since the time of Christ. For the grace of faith illuminates greatly, as also do divine inspirations, not only in things spiritual, but in things corporeal and in the sciences of philosophy; as Ptolemy states in the Centilogium, namely, that there are two roads by which we arrive at the knowledge of facts, one through the experience of philosophy, the other through divine inspiration, which is far the better way, as he says.

From Roger Bacon, *Opus Majus*, R. B. Burke trans., University of Pennsylvania Press. Reprinted by permission of the publisher.

ANALYSIS AND INTERPRETATION OF THE READINGS

1. Did Pope Gregory claim the powers of an absolute monarch over the whole earth?
2. What was the fundamental issue in the quarrel between Henry IV and Gregory VII?
3. Pope Urban II's speech at the Council of Clermont has been described as one of the most effective in the history of oratory. Can you explain why? What varied motives did he appeal to in attempting to arouse his hearers to action?
4. Compare the rationalism of Abelard with that of St. Thomas Aquinas.
5. Were Dante's views on the imperial authority more "modern" than those of the upholders of Papal supremacy?
6. Do you detect any weaknesses in the empiricism of Roger Bacon?

The Later Middle Ages (1300–1500)

CHRONOLOGY

Using the blanks below, arrange the following events in their proper chronological order: union of Aragon and Castile, outbreak of the Black Death in Europe, Battle of Crécy, beginning of the "Babylonian Captivity" of the papacy, accession of the Tudor king Henry VII, death of Boccaccio, the *Jacquerie*, end of the Great Schism, burning of John Hus, death of Ivan the Great, fall of Constantinople, Mongol invasion of the Kievan state.

1346
1305
1358
1415
1485

_____

_____

_____

_____

_____

_____

_____

_____

_____

_____

IDENTIFICATIONS

You should know the meaning and importance of the following terms:

Hanseatic League
"book transfers"
Knights of the Garter
heretics of the Free Spirit

Lollards
Wars of the Roses
Imitation of Christ
nominalism

Council of Constance
Khanate of the
  Golden Horde
Ciompi 1347-1350

Canterbury Tales
Grand Duchy of
  Moscow

You should be able to identify the following persons:

Richard II
Urban VI
Martin V
John Hus
Giotto

Wat Tyler
Clement VII
Master Eckhart
Joan of Arc
Hubert and Jan van Eyck

STUDY QUESTIONS

1. What were the causes of the economic depression that lasted roughly a century and a half in the later Middle Ages?
2. Summarize the effects of the Black Death upon (a) demographic trends, (b) the condition of agriculture, (c) the role of towns and cities.
3. What new business techniques came into operation during the fourteenth and fifteenth centuries?
4. How do you account for the rash of lower-class revolts in the later Middle Ages?
5. How did the English Peasants' Revolt of 1381 differ from the French *Jacquerie* of two decades before? In what ways was the *Ciompi* uprising in Florence, in spite of its failure, still more significant for future history?
6. How do you explain the aristocracy's obsession with luxury and extravagant display during the later Middle Ages?
7. What did the papacy gain in power and why did it at the same time lose respect during the period of residence at Avignon?
8. What caused the Great Schism of 1378–1417? How was it ended?
9. What were the objectives of the conciliar movement within the Church and by what means did the popes defeat it?
10. How do you explain the late-medieval "hunger for the divine"? What divergent forms did it take?

11. Explain the "practical mysticism" of the religious handbook attributed to Thomas à Kempis.

12. Why did John Wyclif's teachings win support among the English aristocracy? In what way did his work anticipate the later Protestant Revolution?

13. Name the major political divisions of Italy around 1450.

14. What were the causes of the Hundred Years' War? How do you explain the spectacular victories of the English armies and also their ultimate defeat?

15. How did the results of the Hundred Years' War strengthen the French monarchy and also promote national unity in England in spite of internal conflict there?

16. Account for the expansion of the Kingdom of Poland in the fourteenth and fifteenth centuries. What factors eventually checked it?

17. List the principal stages in the evolution of the Russian state in the later Middle Ages. What circumstances led to Russia's separation from western Europe?

18. What were the contributions of Ivan III ("the Great") to the Russian imperial tradition?

19. How does William of Ockham's philosophy represent a significant departure from that of St. Thomas Aquinas? Are the differences related to changes in the condition of society during the fourteenth century?

20. If Ockham rejected Aquinas's confidence in human reason, how could he have contributed to the rise of the scientific method?

21. What were the reasons for, and what was the significance of, the growth of literatures in vernacular languages?

22. What qualities entitle Boccaccio's *Decameron* to rank as a landmark in the evolution of European literature?

23. How is naturalism illustrated in late-medieval art?

24. Summarize the technological advances made during the later Middle Ages. Which do you consider the most important and why?

PROBLEMS

1. Investigate further any of the following:
   a. Changes in the techniques of warfare between 1300 and 1500
   b. The English Wars of the Roses
   c. The effects of the Black Death
   d. The conciliar reform movement
   e. The teachings and influence of John Wyclif or of John Hus
   f. The nominalism of William of Ockham
   g. Byzantine influence upon Russian culture and institutions
2. Read Bernard Shaw's play *Saint Joan* and evaluate it as an exposition of political trends and concepts in the later Middle Ages.
3. Compare the *Decameron* with the *Canterbury Tales* as commentaries upon human nature and society.

GEOGRAPHICAL IDENTIFICATIONS

Toulouse	Amalfi
Bremen	Lübeck
Prague	Basel
Genoa	Milan
Burgundy	Bordeaux
Bruges	Florence
Pisa	Avignon
Naples	Castile
Venice	Siena
Kiev	Acquitaine
Volga	Urals
Constance	Lithuania

NATURALISM AS SEEN IN
BOCCACCIO'S *The Decameron*

In the year then of our Lord 1348, there happened at Florence, the finest city in all Italy, a most terrible plague; which, whether owing to the influence of the planets, or that it was sent from God as a just punishment for our sins, had broken out some years before in the Levant; and after passing from place to place, and making incredible havoc all the way, had now reached the west; where, spite of all the means that human foresight could suggest, as keeping the city clear from filth, and excluding all suspected persons; notwithstanding frequent consultations what else was to be done; nor omitting prayers to God in frequent processions: in the spring of the foregoing year, it began to show itself in a sad and wonderful manner; and, different from what it had been in the east, where bleeding from the nose is the fatal prognostic, here there appeared certain tumours in the groin, or under the armpits, some as big as a small apple, others as an egg; and afterwards purple spots in most parts of the body: in some cases large and but few in number, in others less and more numerous, both sorts the usual messengers of death. To the cure of this malady, neither medical knowledge nor the power of drugs was of any effect; whether because the disease was in its own nature mortal, or that the physicians (the number of whom, taking quacks and women pretenders into account, was grown very great) could form no just idea of the cause, nor consequently ground a true method of cure; whichever was the reason, few or none escaped; but they generally died the third day from the first appearance of the symptoms, without a fever or other bad circumstance attending. And the disease, by being communicated from the sick to the well, seemed daily to get ahead, and to rage the more, as fire will do by laying on fresh combustibles. . . .

But I am weary of recounting our late miseries; therefore, passing by everything that I can well omit, I shall only observe, that the city being left almost without inhabitants, it happened one Tuesday in the evening as I was informed by persons of good credit, that seven ladies all in deep mourning, as most proper for that time, had been attending Divine service (being the whole congregation), in new St. Mary's Church: who, as united by the ties either of friendship or relation, and of suitable years; viz., the youngest not less than eighteen, nor the eldest exceeding twenty-eight; so were they all discreet, nobly descended, and perfectly accomplished, both in person and behaviour. I do not mention their names, lest they should be displeased with some things said to have passed in conversation, there being a greater restraint on those diversions now.

. . . And that I may relate therefore all that occurred without confusion, I shall affix names to every one bearing some resemblance to the quality of the person. The eldest then I call Pampinea, the next to her Flammetta, the third Philomena, the fourth Emilia, the fifth Lauretta, the sixth Neiphile, the youngest Eliza: who being got together by chance rather than any appointment, into a corner of the church, and there seated in a ring; and leaving off their devotions, and falling into some discourse together concerning the nature of the times; in a little while Pampinea thus began:

"My dear girls, you have often heard as well as I, that no one is injured, where we only make an honest use of our own reason: now reason tells us that we are to preserve our lives by all possible means and, in some cases, at the expense of the lives of others. And if the laws which regard the good of the community allow this, may not we much rather (and all that mean honestly as we do), without giving offence to any, use the means now in our power for our own preservation. . . . We stay here for no other purpose that I can see, but to observe what numbers come to be buried, or to listen if the monks, who are now reduced to a very few, sing their services at the proper times, or else to show by our habits the greatness of our distress. And if we go from hence, we are saluted with numbers of the dead and sick carried along the streets; or with persons who had been outlawed for their villainies, now facing it out publicly, in defiance of the laws. Or we see the scum of the city enriched with the public calamity, and insulting us with reproachful ballads. Nor is anything talked of but that such an one is dead or dying; and, were any left to mourn, we should hear nothing but lamentations. . . .

Therefore the case is the same, whether we stay here, depart hence, or go home; especially as there are few who are able to go, and have a place to go to, left but ourselves. And those few, I am told, fall into all sorts of debauchery; and even the religious and ladies shut up in monasteries, supposing themselves entitled to equal liberties with others, are as bad as the worst. . . . Wherefore, lest through our own wilfulness or neglect, this calamity, which might have been prevented, should befall us, I should think it best (and I hope you will join with me) for us to quit the town, and avoiding, as we would death itself, the bad example of others, to choose some place of retirement, of which every one of us has more than one, where we may make ourselves innocently merry, without offering the least violence to the dictates of reason and our own consciences. There will our ears be entertained with the warbling of the birds, and our eyes with the verdure of the hills and valleys; with the waving of corn-fields like the sea itself; with trees of a thousand different kinds, and a more open and serene sky which, however overcast, yet affords a far more agreeable prospect than these desolate walls. The air also is pleasanter, and there is greater plenty of everything, attended with fewer inconveniences: for, though people die there as well as here, yet we shall have fewer such objects before us, as the inhabitants are less in number; and on the other part, if I judge right, we desert nobody, but are rather ourselves forsaken. For all our friends, either by death, or endeavouring to avoid it, have left us, as if we in no way belonged to them. As no blame then can ensue by following this advice, and perhaps sickness and death by not doing so, I would have us take our maids, and everything we may be supposed to want, and to remove every day to a different place, taking all the diversions in the meantime which the seasons will permit; and there continue, unless death should interpose, till we see what end Providence designs for these things."

[And so the ladies, in company with some gentlemen bent upon the same purpose, took refuge in a villa outside Florence, where they amused themselves by telling tales — the tales which make up the remainder of *The Decameron*.]

From Giovanni Boccaccio, *The Decameron*, Albert and Charles Boni, 1926.

THE LATE MEDIEVAL VISION OF DEATH
J. Huizinga

No other epoch has laid so much stress as the expiring Middle Ages on the thought of death. An everlasting call of *memento mori* resounds through life. Denis the Carthusian, in his *Directory of the Life of Nobles,* exhorts them: "And when going to bed at night, he should consider how, just as he now lies down himself, soon strange hands will lay his body in the grave." In earlier times, too, religion had insisted on the constant thought of death, but the pious treatises of these ages only reached those who had already turned away from the world. Since the thirteenth century, the popular preaching of the mendicant orders had made the eternal admonition to remember death swell into a sombre chorus ringing throughout the world. Towards the fifteenth century, a new means of inculcating the awful thought into all minds was added to the words of the preacher, namely, the popular woodcut. Now these two means of expression, sermons and woodcuts, both addressing themselves to the multitude and limited to crude effects, could only represent death in a simple and striking form. All that the meditations on death of the monks of yore had produced, was now condensed into a very primitive image. This vivid image, continually impressed upon all minds, had hardly assimilated more than a single element of the great complex of ideas relating to death, namely, the sense of the perishable nature of all things. It would seem, at times, as if the soul of the declining Middle Ages only succeeded in seeing death under this aspect.

The endless complaint of the frailty of all earthly glory was sung to various melodies. Three motifs may be distinguished. The first is expressed by the question: where are now all those who once filled the world with their splendour? The second motif swells on the frightful spectacle of human beauty gone to decay. The third is the death-dance: death dragging along men of all conditions and ages.

At the close of the Middle Ages the whole vision of death may be summed up in the word *macabre,* in its modern meaning. Of course, this meaning is the outcome of a long process. But the sentiment it embodies, of something gruesome and dismal, is precisely the conception of death which arose during the last centuries of the Middle Ages. This bizarre word appeared in French in the fourteenth century, under the form *macabré,* and, whatever may be its etymology, as a proper name. A line of the poet Jean Le Fèvre, "Je fis de Macabré la dance," which may be dated 1376, remains the birth-certificate of the word for us.

Towards 1400 the conception of death in art and literature took a spectral and fantastic shape. A new and vivid shudder was added to the great primitive horror of death. The macabre vision arose from deep psychological strata of fear; religious thought at once reduced it to a means of moral exhortation. As such it was a great cultural idea, till in its turn it went out of fashion, lingering on in epitaphs and symbols in village cemeteries.

The idea of the death-dance is the central point of a whole group of connected conceptions. The priority belongs to the motif of the three dead and three living men, which is found in French literature from the thirteenth century onward. Three young noblemen suddenly meet three hideous dead men, who tell them of their past grandeur and warn them of their own near end. Art soon took hold of this suggestive theme. We can see it still in the striking frescoes of the *Campo santo* of Pisa. The sculpture of the portal of the church of the Innocents at Paris, which the duke of Berry had carved in 1408, but which has not been preserved, represented the same subject. Miniature painting and woodcuts spread it broadcast.

The theme of the three dead and three living men connects the horrible motif of putrefaction with that of the death-dance. This theme, too, seems to have originated in France, but it is unknown whether the pictorial representation preceded the scenic or the reverse. The thesis of Monsieur Emile Mâle, according to which the sculptural and pictorial motifs of the fifteenth century were supposed as a rule to be derived from dramatic representations, has not been able to keep its ground, on critical examination. It may be, however, that we should make an exception in favour of the death-dance. Anyhow, the Dance of the Dead has been acted as well as painted and engraved. The duke of Burgundy had it performed in his mansion at Bruges in 1449. If we could form an idea of the effect produced by such a dance, with vague lights and shadows gliding over the moving figures, we should no doubt be better able to understand the horror inspired by the subject, than we are by the aid of the pictures of Guyot Marchant or Holbein.

The woodcuts with which the Parisian printer, Guyot Marchant, ornamented the first edition of the *Danse Macabré* in 1485 were, very probably, imitated from the most celebrated of these painted death-dances, namely, that which, since 1424, covered the walls of the cloister of the churchyard of the Innocents at Paris. The stanzas printed by Marchant were those written under these mural paintings; perhaps they even hail back to the lost poetry of Jean Le Fèvre, who in his turn seems to have followed a Latin model. The wood-cuts of 1485 can give but a feeble impression of the paintings of the Innocents, of which they are not exact copies, as the costumes prove. To have a notion of the effect of these frescoes, one should rather look at the mural paintings of the church of La Chaise-Dieu, where the unfinished condition of the work heightens the spectral effect.

The dancing person whom we see coming back forty times to lead away the living, originally does not repre-sent Death itself, but a corpse: the living man such as he will presently be. In the stanzas the dancer is called "the dead man" or "the dead woman." It is a dance of the dead and not of Death; the researches of Monsieur Gédéon Huet have made it probable that the primitive subject was a roundabout dance of dead people, come forth from their graves, a theme which Goethe revived in his *Totentanz*. The indefatigable dancer is the living man himself in his future shape, a frightful double of his person. "It is yourself," said the horrible vision to each of the spectators. It is only towards the end of the century that the figure of the great dancer, of a corpse with hollow and fleshless body, becomes a skeleton, as Holbein depicts it. Death in person has then replaced the individual dead man.

While it reminded the spectators of the frailty and the vanity of earthly things, the death-dance at the same time preached social equality as the Middle Ages understood it, Death levelling the various ranks and professions. At first only men appeared in the picture. The success of his publication, however, suggested to Guyot the idea of a dance macabre of women. Martial d'Auvergne wrote the poetry; an unknown artist, with-out equalling his model, completed the pictures by a series of feminine figures dragged along by a corpse. Now it was impossible to enumerate forty dignities and professions of women. After the queen, the abbess, the nun, the saleswoman, the nurse, and a few others, it was necessary to fall back on the different states of feminine life: the virgin, the beloved, the bride, the woman newly married, the woman with child. And here the sensual note reappears, to which we referred above. In lamenting the frailty of the lives of women, it is still the briefness of joy that is deplored, and with the grave tone of the *memento mori* is mixed the regret for lost beauty.

From J. Huizinga, *The Waning of the Middle Ages*, New York: St. Martin's Press, 1949.

THE IMITATION OF CHRIST
Thomas à Kempis

OF THE IMITATION OF CHRIST, AND OF CONTEMPT OF THE WORLD AND ALL ITS VANITIES

He that followeth me shall not walk in darkness,[1] saith the Lord. These are the words of Christ; and they teach us how far we must imitate His life and character, if we seek true illumination, and deliverance from all blindness of heart. Let it be our most earnest study, therefore, to dwell upon the life of Jesus Christ.

2. His teaching surpasseth all teaching of holy men, and such as have His Spirit find therein *the hidden manna*.[2] But there are many who, though they fre-quently hear the Gospel, yet feel but little longing after it, because they have not the mind of Christ. He, therefore, that will fully and with true wisdom understand the words of Christ, let him strive to conform his whole life to that mind of Christ.

3. What doth it profit thee to enter into deep dis-cussion concerning the Holy Trinity, if thou lack hu-mility, and be thus displeasing to the Trinity? For verily it is not deep words that make a man holy and upright; it is a good life which maketh a man dear to God. I had rather feel contrition than be skilful in the definition thereof. If thou knewest the whole Bi-ble, and the sayings of all the philosophers, what should all this profit thee without the love and grace of God? *Vanity of vanities, all is vanity*, save to love God, and Him only to serve. That is the highest wisdom, to cast the world behind us, and to reach forward to the heavenly kingdom.

4. It is vanity then to seek after, and to trust in, the riches that shall perish. It is vanity, too, to covet honours, and to lift up ourselves on high. It is vanity to follow the desires of the flesh and be led by them, for this shall bring misery at the last. It is vanity to desire a long life, and to have little care for a good life. It is vanity to take thought only for the life which now is, and not to look forward to the things which shall be hereafter. It is vanity to love that which quickly passeth away, and not to hasten where eternal joy abideth.

5. Be ofttimes mindful of the saying,[3] *The eye is not satisfied with seeing, nor the ear with hearing.* Strive, therefore, to turn away thy heart from the love of the things that are seen, and to set it upon the things that are not seen. For they who follow after their own fleshly lusts, defile the conscience, and destroy the grace of God. . . .

THERE is naturally in every man a desire to know, but what profiteth knowledge without the fear of God? Better of a surety is a lowly peasant who serveth God, than a proud philosopher who watcheth the

93

stars and neglecteth the knowledge of himself. He who knoweth himself well is vile in his own sight; neither regardeth he the praises of men. If I knew all the things that are in the world, and were not in charity, what should it help me before God, who is to judge me according to my deeds?

2. Rest from inordinate desire of knowledge, for therein is found much distraction and deceit. Those who have knowledge desire to appear learned, and to be called wise. Many things there are to know which profiteth little or nothing to the soul. And foolish out of measure is he who attendeth upon other things rather than those which serve to his soul's health.

1. John viii. 12.
2. Revelations ii. 17.
3. Ecclesiastes i. 8.

From *The Harvard Classics*, ed. Charles W. Eliot, New York: Collier & Son, 1909, Vol. VII.

ANALYSIS AND INTERPRETATION OF THE READINGS

1. How does the attitude toward death expressed in Boccaccio's *The Decameron* differ from that typified by the death-dance as described by Huizinga? Considering the year to which *The Decameron* was attributed, how do you account for this difference?

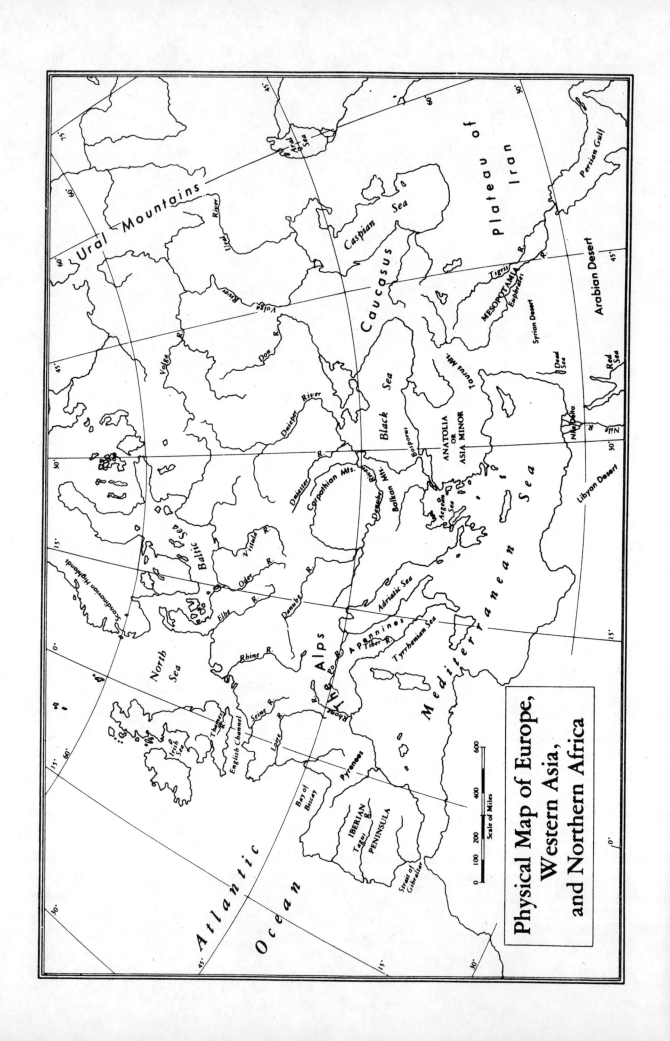

Ural Mountains

Atlantic Ocean

North Sea

Baltic Sea

Scandinavian Highlands

Irish Sea

English Channel

Bay of Biscay

Thames R.

Seine R.

Loire R.

Rhine R.

Elbe R.

Oder R.

Vistula R.

Danube R.

Pyrenees

IBERIAN PENINSULA

Tagus R.

Strait of Gibraltar

The Alps

Po R.

Rhone R.

Apennines

Tiber R.

Tyrrhenian Sea

Adriatic Sea

Mediterranean Sea

Dniester River

Dniester R.

Carpathian Mts.

Danube R.

Dnieper R.

Balkan Mts.

Bosporus

Aegean Sea

Black Sea

Caspian Sea

Caucasus

Volga R.

Don R.

Ural River

Aral Sea

ANATOLIA OR ASIA MINOR

Taurus Mts.

MESOPOTAMIA

Tigris

Euphrates

Syrian Desert

Dead Sea

Red Sea

Nile Delta

Nile R.

Libyan Desert

Arabian Desert

Plateau of Iran

Persian Gulf

Scale of Miles
0   100   200   400   600

Physical Map of Europe,
Western Asia,
and Northern Africa

REVIEW of PART 3

(Chapters 9–12)
The Middle Ages

MAP WORK

Locate each of the following by writing the appropriate letter on the map opposite.

a. Region where Albigensian heresy flourished
b. University where St. Thomas Aquinas taught
c. University where John Wyclif taught
d. City recaptured by the French to end the Hundred Years' War
e. Site of Council that ended the Great Schism
f. Papal headquarters during the "Babylonian Captivity"
g. Capital of the Abbasid Caliphate
h. Site of Charles Martel's defeat of the Muslims in 732
i. Dante's native city
j. Great Christian capital sacked during the Fourth Crusade
k. Grand Duchy of Moscow

CHRONOLOGICAL REVIEW

In the blanks below, write the correct date of each event, selected from the following list:

622	751	800	1453
1071	1135	1417	1054
1250	910	1066	1321
1215	1358		1505

_____Death of Dante

_____Founding of monastery of Cluny

_____The *Jacquerie*

_____Crowning of Charlemagne as Emperor

_____Separation of Greek and Roman churches

_____Turkish conquest of Constantinople

_____Battle of Manzikert

_____Norman invasion of England

_____The Hegira (*Hijrah*)

_____End of Merovingian rule

_____Signing of Magna Carta

_____Beginning of Capetian dynasty

_____Death of emperor Frederick II

_____End of the Great Schism

_____Death of Ivan the Great

CHAPTER

13 The Civilization of the Renaissance (c. 1350–c. 1550)

CHRONOLOGY

Rather than memorizing arbitrary dates, you should be able to distinguish between the early and the High Renaissance in terms of leading figures. Before each of the following names indicate the half-century in which the individual was active (e.g., 1450–1500 Pico della Mirandola).

_____Ariosto   _____Raphael

_____Petrarch   _____Botticelli

_____Masaccio   _____Pico della Mirandola

_____Michelangelo _____Albrecht Dürer

_____da Vinci   _____Erasmus

_____Palestrina   _____Servetus

IDENTIFICATIONS

In the blanks, write the correct names selected from the list below:

Lorenzo de Medici   Botticelli
Marsilio Ficino   da Vinci
Petrarch   Raphael
Ariosto   Michelangelo
Niccolo Machiavelli   Donatello
Cesare Borgia   Copernicus
Castiglione   Galileo
Vesalius   Johann Kepler
Giordano Bruno   Lorenzo Valla
Masaccio   Palestrina

1. This Neoplatonic philosopher was condemned by the Inquisition and burned at the stake in 1600 for his belief in the plurality of worlds.

_____

2. A superb and sensitive Florentine painter, he is famed for his *The Allegory of Spring* and *Birth of Venus*, which reflect Neoplatonic concepts.

_____

3. Noted for his statue of David triumphant over Goliath, this sculptor executed the first monumental bronze equestrian statue since the Romans.

_____

4. A short-lived, early master of the High Renaissance, perhaps the most popular of all Renaissance painters, he portrayed human beings as temperate, wise, and dignified.

_____

5. Although he was the first Italian humanist, he upheld the medieval Christian ideal, and his famous sonnets to Laura were written in the style of the troubadours.

_____

6. Styled the Magnificent, this Florentine ruler and patron of art was for a time the patron of Leonardo da Vinci.

_____

7. His astronomical observations helped prove the heliocentric theory, and his experiments in physics established the law of falling bodies.

_____

8. His *Orlando Furioso* incorporated medieval legends but in its point of view differed sharply from the typical medieval epic.

_____

9. This giant of the High Renaissance was both a great painter and a great sculptor as his paintings in the Sistine Chapel and his tomb figures show.

_____

10. Author of *Discourses on Livy* and *The Prince*, he is best known for his realistic views of the nature of politics and the duties of heads of state.

_____

11. Architect, musician, inventor, and painter, he created in the *Last Supper* and the *Mona Lisa* two of the most famous paintings in the Western World.

_____

12. Inspired by Neoplatonic teachings, this Polish astronomer attempted to prove the validity of the heliocentric theory.

_____

13. One of the earliest prominent Florentine painters, a remarkable naturalist, he died at the age of twenty-seven.

_____

14. A leading member of the Platonic Academy in Florence, he translated Plato's works into Latin.

_____

15. The son of a pope, his shrewd and ruthless statecraft provided a fascinating study for Machiavelli.

_____

16. This diplomat wrote a book depicting the ideal Renaissance man.

_____

17. This mystical but indefatigable thinker discovered the elliptical orbits of the planets.

_____

18. A native of Brussels, he is considered the father of the science of anatomy.

_____

19. A skilled grammarian who exposed the fraudulent "Donation of Constantine," he applied vigorous critical scholarship to his *Notes on the New Testament*.

_____

20. An Italian composer of the high Renaissance, he is noted for his religious choral works.

_____

Below are listed a number of famous Renaissance works, including both paintings and writings. In the blank after each, put the name of the painter or author selected from the following list:

On the Structure of the Human Body_____

On the Family_____

Gargantua and Pantagruel _____

Oration on the Dignity of Man_____

Utopia _____

The Faërie Queene _____

Praise of Folly _____

School of Athens_____

Moses_____

Portraits of Erasmus and More_____

Knight, Death, and Devil_____

On the Revolutions of the Heavenly Spheres _____

Ulrich von Hutten
Albrecht Dürer
Hans Holbein
Johann Kepler
Erasmus
Copernicus
Vesalius

Raphael
François Rabelais
Sir Thomas More
Edmund Spenser
Pico della Mirandola
Leon Battista Alberti
Michelango

STUDY QUESTIONS

1. Why does the long popular concept of a "Renaissance Period" need to be modified? To what aspects of the two centuries under consideration can the term "Renaissance" be most usefully applied?

2. How did Renaissance knowledge and interpretation of ancient classical literature differ from that exhibited by medieval scholars?
3. Explain the meanings of humanism—in its specific and its more general sense—as applied to the Renaissance.
4. Why did the Renaissance begin in Italy?
5. How do you account for the growing aversion to medieval Scholasticism? Was it based purely upon intellectual considerations?
6. What were the objectives of the civic humanists?
7. What did the Neoplatonists have in common with the "civic humanists" in spite of the differences between the two groups?
8. What was Machiavelli's contribution to political philosophy?
9. What technical improvements between 1300 and 1500 made possible the full flowering of Italian painting?
10. What was Leonardo da Vinci's conception of painting? What relationship did he see between art and science?
11. Compare Florentine and Venetian painting.
12. "If Leonardo was a naturalist, Michelangelo was an idealist." Show how this is exemplified in the works of these two supreme artists.
13. How do you account for the contrast in style between Michelangelo's ceiling frescoes and his *Last Judgment* in the Sistine Chapel?
14. What developments account for the decline of the Italian Renaissance?
15. Point out the chief differences between the Renaissance in Italy and that in northern and western Europe. How do you account for these differences?
16. Erasmus is generally regarded as "the prince of the Christian humanists." Show how his writings entitled him to such a distinction.
17. What did Erasmus mean by the "philosophy of Christ"?
18. How does More's *Utopia* illustrate the ideals of humanism?
19. How are the manifestations of the Renaissance in Germany illustrated by the *Letters of Obscure Men*?
20. Compare the effects of the Counter-Reformation and the rise of Protestantism upon Renaissance culture.

21. How do the writings of Rabelais contrast with those of Erasmus as examples of Renaissance humanism?
22. In view of their criticisms of the contemporary Church, why did most humanists choose to remain within the Catholic fold?
23. How were the developments in music related to other aspects of the Renaissance?
24. Why was Renaissance humanism less of a stimulus to scientific progress than was the mystical philosophy of Neoplatonism?
25. What other factors aided in the development of science?
26. Trace the steps in the achievement of the "Copernican Revolution."

PROBLEMS

1. If the instability of political life in Italy contributed to the ending of the Renaissance thereafter 1550, why did not the political instability of the preceding 250 years prevent a Renaissance in the first place?
2. Investigate the causes of the waning of the Italian Renaissance.
3. Investigate further any of the following: (a) the Florence of the Medicis; (b) Petrarch's sonnets; (c) Machiavelli's *The Prince*; (d) Leonardo da Vinci's inventions; (e) Galileo's discoveries; (f) the Renaissance papacy.
4. Was the Renaissance more medieval than modern? Support your answer with evidence.
5. Study the illustrations of paintings in the text. If possible, study in detail the works of one or more of the great painters mentioned in Chapter 14.
6. Explain the relationship between Machiavelli's personal career, the fate of the Florentine republic, and his political philosophy. Was he primarily a cynic or a disillusioned idealist?
7. Why was the Renaissance in northern and western Europe so different from the Italian Renaissance?
8. Read Castiglione's *The Book of the Courtier* and make a critique of his view of the respective roles of men and women.
9. Read More's *Utopia* to discover what aspects of humanism it illustrates.

AIDS TO AN UNDERSTANDING OF THE CIVILIZATION OF THE RENAISSANCE

THE CONFLICT BETWEEN HUMANISM AND MEDIEVAL ASCETICISM: Letter of Petrarch to His Brother, a Carthusian Monk

In the three following respects I have complied with your injunctions. In the first place, I have by means of solitary confession, laid open the secret uncleanness of my transgressions, which would otherwise have fatally putrified, through neglect and long silence. I have learned to do this frequently, and have accustomed myself to submit the secret wounds of my soul to the healing balm of Heaven. Next, I have learned to send up songs of praise to Christ, not only by day but in the night. And following your admonitions I have put away habits of sloth, so that even in these short summer nights the dawn never finds me asleep or silent, however wearied I am by the vigils of the evening before. I have taken the words of the Psalmist to heart, "Seven time a day do I praise thee"; and never since I began this custom have I allowed anything to distract me from my daily devotions. I observe, likewise, the admonition, "At midnight I will rise to give thanks unto thee." When the hour arrives I feel a mysterious stimulus which will not allow me to sleep, however oppressed I may be with weariness.

In the third place, I have learned to fear more than death itself that association with women which I once thought I could not live without. And, although I am still subject to severe and frequent temptations, I have but to recollect what woman really is, in order to dispel all temptation and return to my normal peace and liberty. In such straits I believe myself aided by your loving prayers, and I trust and beg that you will continue your good offices, in the name of him who had mercy on you, and led you from the darkness of your errors into the brightness of his day. In all this you are most happy, and show a most consistent contempt for false and fleeting joys. May God uphold you. Do not forget me in your prayers.

From J. H. Robinson, *Petrarch, the First Modern Scholar and Man of Letters.*

THE REALISM OF LEONARDO DA VINCI: As Described in His *Notebooks*

THE PAINTER'S NEED FOR ALERTNESS

The mind of the painter should be like a mirror which always takes the color of the thing that it reflects, and which is filled by as many images as there are things placed before it. Knowing therefore that you cannot be a good master unless you have a universal power of representing by your art all the varieties of the forms which nature produces — which indeed you will not know how to do unless you see them and retain them in your mind — look to it, O Painter, that when you go into the fields you give your attention to the various objects, and look carefully in turn first at one thing and then at another, making a bundle of different things selected and chosen from among those of less value. And do not after the manner of some painters who when tired by imaginative work, lay aside their task and take exercise by walking, in order to find relaxation, keeping, however, such weariness of mind as prevents them either seeing or being conscious of different objects.

OF THE WAY TO FIX IN YOUR MIND THE FORM OF A FACE

If you desire to acquire facility in keeping in your mind the expression of a face, first learn by heart the various different kinds of heads, eyes, noses, mouths, chins, throats, and also necks and shoulders. Take as an instance noses: they are of ten types: straight, bulbous, hollow, prominent either above or below the centre, aquiline, regular, simian, round, and pointed. These divisions hold good as regards profile. Seen from in front, noses are of twelve types: thick in the middle, thin in the middle, with the tip broad, and narrow at the base, and narrow at the tip, and broad at the base, with nostrils broad or narrow, or high or low, and with the openings either visible or hidden by the tip. And similarly you will find variety in the other features; of which things you ought to make studies from nature and so fix them in your mind. Or when you have to draw a face from memory, carry with you a small notebook in which you have noted down such features, and then when you have cast a glance at the face of the person whom you wish to draw you can look privately and see which nose or mouth has a resemblance to it, and make a tiny mark against it in order to recognise it again at home. Of abnormal faces I here say nothing, for they are kept in mind without difficulty.

HOW IT IS NECESSARY FOR THE PAINTER TO KNOW THE INNER STRUCTURE OF MAN

The painter who has acquired a knowledge of the nature of the sinews, muscles, and tendons will know exactly in the movement of any limb how many and which of the sinews are the cause of it, and which muscle by its swelling is the cause of the sinew's contracting, and which sinews having been changed into most delicate cartilage surround and contain the said muscle. So he will be able in divers ways and universally to indicate the various muscles by means of the different attitudes of his figures; and he will not do like many who in different actions always make the same things appear in the arm, the back, the breast, and the legs; for such things as these ought not to rank in the category of minor faults.

Of The Conformity Of The Limbs

Further I remind you to pay great attention in giving limbs to your figures, so that they may not merely appear to harmonize with the size of the body but also with its age. So the limbs of youths should have few muscles and veins, and have a soft surface and be rounded and pleasing in color; in men they should be sinewy and full of muscles; in old men the surface should be wrinkled, and rough, and covered with veins, and with the sinews greatly protruding.

From Edward MacCurdy, *The Notebooks of Leonardo da Vinci,* Vol. II, Reynal & Hitchcock, Inc., 1938.

PHILOSOPHY AND SCIENCE: The Cynicism and Realism of Machiavelli

From hence arises a dispute, whether it is better to be belov'd or feard: I answer, a man would wish he might be the one and the other: but because hardly can they subsist both together, it is much safer to be feard, than be loved; being that one of the two must needs fail; for touching men, we may say this in general, they are unthankful, unconstant, dissemblers, they avoyd dangers, and are covetous of gain; and whilest thou doest them good, they are wholly thine; their blood, their fortunes, lives and children are at thy service, as is said before, when the danger is remote; but when it approaches, they revolt. And that Prince who wholly relies upon their words, unfurnished of all other preparations, goes to wrack: for the friendships that are gotten with rewards, and not by the magnificence and worth of the mind, are dearly bought indeed; but they will neither keep long, nor serve well in time of need: and men do less regard to offend one that is supported by love, than fear. For love is held by a certainty of obligation, which because men are mischievous, is broken upon any occasion of their own profit. But fear restrains with a dread of punishment which never forsakes a man. Yet ought a Prince cause himself to be belov'd in such a manner, that if he gains not love, he may avoid hatred: for it may well stand together, that a man may be feard and not hated; which shall never fail, if he abstain from his subjects goods, and their wives; and whensoever he should be forc'd to proceed against any of their lives, do it when it is to be done upon a just cause, and apparent conviction; but above all things forbeare to lay his hands on other mens goods; for men forget sooner the death of their father, than the loss of their patrimony. Moreover the occasions of taking from men their goods, do never fail: and alwaies he that begins to live by rapine, finds occasion to lay hold upon other mens goods: but against mens lives, they are seldome found, and sooner fail.

• • •

For a people in command, if it be duly restrained, will have the same prudence and the same gratitude as a prince has, or even more, however wise he may be reckoned; and a prince on the other hand, if freed from the control of the laws, will be more ungrateful, fickle, and short-sighted than a people. And further, I say that any difference in their methods of acting results not from any difference in their nature, that being the same in both, or, if there be advantage on either side, the advantage resting with the people, but from their having more or less respect for the laws under which each lives. And whosoever attentively considers the history of the Roman people, may see that for four hundred years they never relaxed in their hatred of the regal name, and were constantly devoted to the glory and welfare of their country, and will find numberless proofs given by them of their consistency in both particulars. And should any allege against me the ingratitude they showed to Scipio, I reply by what has already been said at length on that head, where I proved that peoples are less ungrateful than princes. But as for prudence and stability of purpose, I affirm that a people is more prudent, more stable, and of better judgment than a prince. Nor is it without reason that the voice of the people has been likened to the voice of God; for we see that wide-spread beliefs fulfil themselves, and bring about marvellous results, so as to have the appearance of presaging by some occult quality either weal or woe. Again, as to the justice of their opinions on public affairs, we seldom find that after hearing two speakers of equal ability urging them in opposite directions, they do not adopt the sounder view, or are unable to decide on the truth of what they hear. And if, as I have said, a people errs in adopting courses which appear to it bold and advantageous, princes will likewise err when their passions are touched, as is far oftener the case with them than with a people.

We see, too, that in the choice of magistrates a people will choose far more honestly than a prince; so that while you shall never persuade a people that it is advantageous to confer dignities on the infamous and profligate, a prince may readily, and in a thousand ways, be drawn to do so. Again, it may be seen that a people, when once they have come to hold a thing in abhorrence, remain for many ages of the same mind; which we do not find happen with princes.

• • •

Nor would I have it thought that anything our historian may have affirmed in the passage cited, or elsewhere, controverts these my opinions. For if all the glories and all the defects both of peoples and of princes be carefully weighed, it will appear that both for goodness and for glory a people is to be preferred. And if princes surpass peoples in the work of legislation, in shaping civil institutions, in moulding statutes, and framing new ordinances, so far do the latter surpass the former in maintaining what has once been established, as to merit no less praise than they.

And to state the sum of the whole matter shortly, I say that popular governments have endured for long periods in the same way as the governments of princes, and that both have need to be regulated by the laws; because the prince who can do what he pleases is a madman, and the people which can do as it pleases is never wise. If, then, we assume the case of a prince bound, and of a people chained down by the laws, greater virtue will appear in the people than in the prince; while if we assume the case of each of them freed from all control, it will be seen that the people commits fewer errors than the prince, and less serious errors, and such as admit of readier cure. For a turbulent and unruly people may be spoken to by a good man, and readily brought back to good ways; but none can speak to a wicked prince, nor any remedy be found against him but by the sword.

• • •

. . . when the entire safety of our country is at stake, no consideration of what is just or unjust, merciful or cruel, praiseworthy or shameful, must intervene. On the contrary, every other consideration being set aside, that course alone must be taken which preserves the existence of the country and maintains its liberty.

From Niccolò Machiavelli, *The Prince* and *Discourses on the First Ten Books of Titus Livius*, E. Dacres trans.

PHILOSOPHY AND SCIENCE: The Founding of the Science of Anatomy
H. O. Taylor

A few years after Leonardo's death the method of direct examination of the pertinent physical facts was established in the most direct and simple form in that very science of anatomy to which he had set himself so zealously. Andreas Vesalius was the author of this achievement. Judging by results and their continuity, it was he, rather than Leonardo, who founded the modern method and science of anatomy, and prepared the way for physiology. He was born at Brussels in 1514, just as the bells were ringing out the old year. For generations his forbears had been doctors. He went to school at Louvain, and entered the university. But his constant and passionate occupation was the dissection of animals. In his eighteenth year he made his way to Paris to hear Jacobus Sylvius (Jacques Du Bois) the most famous master of anatomy at that time. Sylvius was a hard conservative, who taught after Galen, and used dissections to illustrate that great authority rather than as independent means of gaining knowledge. Vesalius could not endure that Sylvius should lecture from a book while barbers clumsily cut up a human body or far more frequently a dog's. What knowledge could be gained from having the roughly extracted viscera shown to him? This masterful auditor

insisted upon conducting the dissection himself. "I had to put my own hand to the business." Outside of the lecture-room, Vesalius dissected dogs, and haunted the cemeteries, where there were piles of human bones. He became so familiar with them that he could recognize any part of the human skeleton by touch, and name it with his eyes blindfolded.

After some three years of medical study in Paris, Vesalius returned to Louvain, and then went to Venice and soon to Padua, where at the end of the year 1537 he was made professor in the university. He was scarcely twenty-three.

Quickly casting aside "the ridiculous method of the schools," he demonstrated and dissected before his students, practicing also the vivisection of animals. But he used Galen in lecturing, at least until he became convinced that Galen had made his dissections and descriptions from apes, rather than from human bodies. After that, braving all opposition, he gradually freed himself and his demonstrations from the older author; and even used the bodies under dissection to show the many errors in Galen's descriptions when applied to the parts and organs of the human body. He was now demonstrating and lecturing from the facts alone, and from books no longer. He had five hundred students, and was already known beyond the university through his reputation and his *Anatomical Tables* which circulated widely.

From H. O. Taylor, *Thought and Expression in the Sixteenth Century*, Vol. II.

THE SATIRICAL HUMANISM OF ERASMUS: *The Praise of Folly*

The merchants, however, are the biggest fools of all. They carry on the most sordid business and by the most corrupt methods. Whenever it is necessary, they will lie, perjure themselves, steal, cheat, and mislead the public. Nevertheless, they are highly respected because of their money. There is no lack of flattering friars to kowtow to them . . . [because] they are after some of the loot.

• • •

After the lawyers come the philosophers, who are reverenced for their beards and the fur on their gowns. They announce that they alone are wise, and that the rest of men are only passing shadows. Their folly is a pleasant one. They frame countless worlds and measure the sun, moon, stars, and spheres as with thumb and line. They unhesitatingly explain the causes of lightning, winds, eclipses, and other inexplicable things. One would think that they had access to the secrets of nature, who is the maker of all things, or that they had just come from a council of the gods. Actually, nature laughs uproariously at them all the time. The fact that they can never explain why they constantly disagree with each other is sufficient proof that they do not know the truth about anything. They know nothing at all, yet profess to know everything. They are ignorant even of themselves, and are often too absent-minded or near-sighted to see the ditch or stone in front of them. At the same time, they assert that they can see ideas, universals, pure forms, original matter, and essences — things so shadowy that I doubt if Lynceus could perceive them. They show their scorn of the layman whenever they produce their triangles, quadrangles, circles, and other mathematical forms, lay one on another or entangle them into a labyrinth, then maneuver letters as if in battle formation, and presently reverse the arrangement. It is all designed to fool the uninitiated. Among these philosophers are some who predict future events by consulting the stars, and others who promise even greater wonders. And these fortunate fellows find people to believe them.

Perhaps it would be wise to pass over the theologians in silence. That short-tempered and supercilious crew is as unpleasant to deal with as Lake Camarina or *Anagyris foetida*. They may attack me with an army of six hundred syllogisms; and if I do not recant, they will proclaim me a heretic. With this thunderbolt they terrify the people they don't like. They are extremely reluctant to acknowledge my benefits to them, which are nevertheless considerable. Their opinion of themselves is so great that they behave as if they were already in heaven; they look down pityingly on other men as so many worms. A wall of imposing definitions, conclusions, corollaries, and explicit and implicit propositions protects them. They have so many hideouts that even Vulcan could not catch them with his net. They escape through distinctions, and cut knots as easily as with a double-bitted axe from Tenedos. They are full of big words and newly-invented terms.

They explain (to suit themselves) the most difficult mysteries: how the world was created and set in order; through what channels original sin has passed to successive generations; by what means, in what form, and for how long the perfect Christ was in the womb of the Virgin; and how accidents subsist in the Eucharist without their subject. But these are nothing. Here are questions worthy of these great and reputedly illuminated theologians. If they encounter these questions they will have to extend themselves. Was divine generation at a particular instant? Are there several son-ships in Christ? Is this a possible proposition: God the Father hates the Son? Could God have assumed the form of a woman, a devil, an ass, a gourd, a stone? If so, how could the gourd have preached, performed miracles, and been crucified? What would Peter have consecrated if he had administered the sacrament when Christ's body hung on the Cross? And was Christ at that moment a man? After the resurrection will it be forbidden to eat and drink? (They are providing now against hunger and thirst!) These subtleties are countless, and include even more refined propositions dealing with instants of time, opinions, relations, accidents, quiddities, entities, which

no one can discern unless, like Lynceus, he can see in blackest darkness things that are not there.

There are in addition those moral maxims, or rather, contradictions, that make the so-called Stoic paradoxes seem like child's play. For example: it is less of a sin to cut the throats of a thousand men than to stitch a poor man's shoe on Sunday; it is better to commit the whole world to destruction than to tell a single lie, even a white one. These subtlest of subtleties are made more subtle by the methods of the scholastic philosophers. It is easier to escape from a maze than from the tangles of Realists, Nominalists, Thomists, Albertists, Occamists, and Scotists, to name the chief ones only. There is so much erudition and obscurity in the various schools that I imagine the apostles themselves would need some other spiritual assistance if they were to argue these topics with modern theologians. . . .

THE GOOD PRINCE: As Described by Erasmus

The good prince ought to have the same attitude toward his subjects, as a good *paterfamilias* toward his household — for what else is a kingdom but a great family? What is the king if not the father to a great multitude? As a *paterfamilias* thinks whatever increase of wealth has fallen to any of his house is [the same as if it had been] added to his own private goods, so he who has the true attitude of a prince considers the possessions of his subjects to represent his own wealth. Them he holds bound over to him through love, so that they have nothing to fear at all from the prince for either their lives or their possessions.

A prince who is about to assume control of the state must be advised at once that the man hope of a state lies in the proper education of its youth. This Xenophon wisely taught in his *Cyropaedia*. Pliable youth is amenable to any system of training. Therefore the greatest care should be exercised over public and private schools and over the education of the girls so that the children may be placed under the best and most trustworthy instructors and may learn the teachings of Christ and that good literature which is beneficial to the state. As a result of this scheme of things, there will be no need for many laws or punishments, for the people will of their own free will follow the course of right. . . .

Education exerts such a powerful influence, as Plato says, that a man who has been trained in the right develops into a sort of divine creature, while . . . a person who has received a perverted training degenerates into a monstrous sort of savage beast. Nothing is of more importance to a prince than to have the best possible subjects.

The prince should try to prevent too great an inequality of wealth. I should not want to see anyone deprived of his goods, but the prince should employ certain measures to prevent the wealth of the multitude being hoarded by a few. Plato did not want his citizens to be too rich, neither did he want them extremely poor, for the pauper is of no use and the rich man will not use his ability for public service.

A good prince will tax as lightly as possible those commodities which are used even by the poorest members of society; e.g., grain, bread, beer, wine, clothing, and all the other staples without which human life could not exist. But it so happens that these very things bear the heaviest tax in several ways; in the first place, by the oppressive extortion of the tax farmers, commonly called *assisiae*, then by import duties which call for their own set of extortionists, and finally by the monopolies by which the poor are sadly drained of their funds in order that the prince may gain a mere trifling interest.

As I have brought out, the best way of increasing the prince's treasury is to follow the old proverb, "Parsimony is a great revenue," and carefully check expenditures. However, if some taxation is absolutely necessary and the affairs of the people render it essential, barbarous foreign goods should be heavily taxed because they are not the essentials of livelihood but the extravagant luxuries and delicacies which only the wealthy enjoy; for example, linen, silks, dyes, pepper, spices, unguents, precious stones, and all the rest of that same category. But by this system only those who can well afford it feel the pinch. They will not be reduced to straightened circumstances as a result of this outlay but perchance may be made more moderate in their desires so that the loss of money may be replaced by a change for the better in their habits.

From Desiderius Erasmus, *The Education of a Christian Prince*, L. K. Born trans., Columbia University Press. Reprinted by permission of the publisher.

THE HUMANISM OF SIR THOMAS MORE: *Utopia*

OF WARFARE

War or battle as a thing very beastly, and yet to no kind of beasts in so much use as to man, they [the Utopians] do detest and abhor. And contrary to the custom almost of all other nations, they count nothing so much against glory, as glory gotten in war. And therefore though they do daily practise and exercise themselves in the discipline of war, and not only the men, but also the women upon certain appointed days, lest they should be to seek in the feat of arms, if need should require, yet they never go to battle, but either in the defence of their own country, or to drive out of their friend's land the enemies that have invaded it, or by their power to deliver from the yoke of bondage of tyranny some people, that be therewith oppressed. Which thing they do of mere pity and compassion. Howbeit they send help to their friends; not ever in their defence, but sometimes also to requite and revenge injuries before to them done. But this they do not unless their counsel and advice in the matter be asked, whiles it is yet new and fresh.

From Sir Thomas More, *Utopia*, Maurice Adams ed.

ANALYSIS AND INTERPRETATION OF THE READINGS

1. Why do you think Petrarch had such a strong aversion toward women?
2. Are there evidences of democracy in political theory of Machiavelli?
3. Compare the "Good Prince" of Erasmus with the type of Prince admired by Machiavelli.
4. Do you think Sir Thomas More could be classified as a pacifist?

CHAPTER 14

Europe Expands and Divides: Overseas Discoveries and Protestant Reformation

CHRONOLOGY

In the blanks write the correct dates selected from the list below:

1415	1517	1540
1460	1519–1521	1545–1563
1502	1525	1546–1547
1513	1534	1564

Death of Calvin_____

Council of Trent_____

Death of Henry the Navigator_____

Index of Prohibited Books_____

Founding of the Jesuit order_____

Peasants' Revolt in Germany_____

Balboa's discovery of the Pacific Ocean_____

Cortés's conquest of the Aztec empire_____

Posting of the Ninety-Five Theses_____

Founding of the University of Wittenberg_____

_____2. Early leadership in overseas discovery and trade was taken by (a) France; (b) England; (c) Spain; (d) Portugal.

_____3. A factor which delayed discovery of the New World until the end of the fifteenth century was (a) belief that the earth was flat; (b) the profitability of African trade; (c) the lack of ships capable of crossing the Atlantic; (d) papal prohibition of intercourse with heathen lands.

_____4. Vasco da Gama's exploits extended Portuguese trade to (a) India; (b) Africa; (c) the West Indies; (d) the East Indies.

_____5. Christopher Columbus (a) advanced the novel theory of the earth's sphericity; (b) was the first European to land on the American continent; (c) greatly underestimated the earth's circumference; (d) was bitterly disappointed by his failure to reach Asia.

_____6. The *conquistadores* obtained for Spain (a) a direct water route to India; (b) raw materials which stimulated industrial development; (c) the eastern seaboard of North America; (d) control of Central and South America except for Brazil.

IDENTIFICATIONS

In the blank before each statement write the letter identifying the correct completion:

_____1. The voyages of overseas discovery can best be accounted for by (a) the Renaissance interest in science; (b) the pursuit of late medieval economic goals; (c) the need for emigration from overpopulated European countries; (d) knowledge of the New World acquired by the Vikings.

You should know what the following are and what their significance was in relation to the Reformation:

indulgences	Anabaptists
dispensation	Lollards
transubstantiation	*Spiritual Exercises*
Eucharist	predestination
"good works"	Calvin's *Institutes*
Treasury of Merits	Elizabethan compromise
justification by faith	Council of Trent
Augustinianism	millenarianism

In the blanks, write the appropriate names from the following list:

Charles V
Elector Frederick the Wise
Julius II
Leo X
Martin Luther
John of Leyden
Ulrich Zwingli
John Calvin

Henry VIII
Thomas Cranmer
Mary I
John Knox
Cardinal Ximenes
Paul III
Elizabeth I
Ignatius Loyola

1. A German prince who protected Luther from arrest by Catholic authorities.

_____

2. An Anabaptist leader who declared himself successor of David and king of the New Jerusalem of Münster.

_____

3. An archibishop of Canterbury who with the dukes of Somerset and Northumberland made the Church of England more decidedly Protestant during the reign of Edward VI.

_____

4. A Protestant Reformer who is said to have reduced church service to "four bare walls and a sermon."

_____

5. A Spanish nobleman and ex-soldier who founded a militant religious order in the sixteenth century.

_____

6. A pope whose authorization of the sale of indulgences in Germany incensed Luther.

_____

7. The Holy Roman emperor who summoned a Diet that condemned Luther.

_____

8. A pope of the Counter-Reformation who convoked the Council of Trent.

_____

9. An English queen whose determined efforts to restore Catholicism to her country ended in failure.

_____

10. A Swiss reformer who converted much of northern Switzerland to Protestantism.

_____

STUDY QUESTIONS

1. "As quickly as Europeans took hold of the world, they lost their spiritual unity." Why did the rupture of European unity not prevent the extension of European power and influence?
2. What were the threefold results of European overseas expansion and colonization?
3. Whatever may have helped bring on the Protestant Reformation, abuses within the Roman Catholic Church were an important factor. What were some characteristic abuses on the eve of the Lutheran upheaval?
4. Why was Germany in the early sixteenth century especially likely to be the scene of any considerable revolt against the Church?
5. "Luther preferred a rigorously Augustinian system of theology to a medieval Thomistic one." Explain these terms.
6. What did Luther mean by "the priesthood of all believers"? How did he reconcile this concept with the retention of ecclesiastical authority?
7. Explain why German political authorities supported Luther's cause and why their support was essential to its success.
8. What were the important changes that Luther wrought in the Church in Germany?
9. Why did Luther harshly condemn the revolt of the German peasants?
10. If their political objectives were similar to those of the German princes, why did the kings of Spain and France not likewise break with the Catholic Church?
11. How did King Henry VIII's marital difficulties lead to a break with Rome? What elements of Catholicism did Henry retain in the Church of England?

12. What is meant by the Elizabethan compromise?
13. What were the chief emphases in the creed of the Anabaptists? Why were they almost entirely suppressed?
14. How did Calvin's religious ideas differ from those of Luther? Which was the more medieval in his outlook (in answering this, explain in what sense you are interpreting the word "medieval")?
15. Describe the work of the Council of Trent.
16. How did the Jesuits differ from previous monastic orders? Why was their organization so peculiarly fit to serve the Catholic Reformation?
17. What was the relationship of the Protestant Reformation to the Renaissance and what were the differences between the two movements?
18. Point out the effects of the Protestant Reformation upon (a) the theory and practice of state sovereignty; (b) the growth of nationalism; (c) the position of women in society.
19. Compare or contrast the effects of the Catholic Reformation (Counter-Reformation) in these same respects.

d. The career of Ignatius Loyola
e. The Anabaptists
f. The career of Zwingli
4. Explain the conflict between the Augustinian and Scholastic systems of theology. What was the significance of this conflict?
5. How did capitalism relate to the Protestant Reformation? Consult R. H. Tawney, *Religion and the Rise of Capitalism.*
6. What relationship can you show between the Lutheran movement and the later history of Germany?
7. Read Luther's *Address to the Christian Nobility of the German Nation.* What sorts of arguments does he use in urging resistance to the papacy?
8. To what extent was the Catholic Reformation a Counter-Reformation?
9. Prove or disprove that the Reformation was a great milestone on the road to progress.
10. What is the justification for considering European overseas expansion and the Protestant Reformation as related movements in spite of the fundamental differences between them?

PROBLEMS

1. How did Lutheranism penetrate Scandinavia?
2. How did the Jesuits go about reconverting much of central Europe to Roman Catholicism?
3. Investigate further any of the following:
   a. Martin Luther and the German Bible
   b. John Calvin's rule in Geneva
   c. Henry VIII and the confiscation of monastic lands

GEOGRAPHICAL IDENTIFICATIONS

Trent	Calais
Wittenberg	Geneva
Saxony	Ceuta
Worms	Azores
Münster	Cape of Good Hope
Basel	Gold Coast
Zürich	Malacca

AIDS TO AN UNDERSTANDING OF OVERSEAS DISCOVERIES AND PROTESTANT REFORMATION

CHRISTOPHER COLUMBUS' Report of His First Voyage

LETTER FROM COLUMBUS TO LOUIS DE SANTANGEL, 1493

Sir, – Believing that you will take pleasure in hearing of the great success which our Lord has granted me in my voyage. I write you this letter, whereby you will learn how in thirty-three day's time I reached the Indies with the fleet which the most illustrious King and Queen, our Sovereigns, gave to me, where I found very many islands thickly peopled, of all which I took possession without resistance for their Highnesses by proclamation made and with the royal standard unfurled. To the first island that I found I gave the name of *San Salvador*, in remembrance of His High Majesty, who hath marvelously brought all these things to pass; the Indians call it *Guanaham*. To the second Island I gave the name of *Santa-Maria de Concepción*; the third I called *Fernandina*, the fourth, *Isabella*; the fifth, *Juana*; and so to each one I gave a new name. When I reached *Juana*, I followed its coast to the westward, and found it so large that I thought it must be the mainland – the province of Cathay; and, as I found neither towns nor villages on the sea-coast, but only a few hamlets, with the inhabitants of which I could not hold conversation, because they all immediately fled, I kept on the same route, thinking that I could not fail to light upon some large cities and towns. At length . . . [having] learned from some . . . Indians whom I had seized, that this land was certainly an island . . . I followed the coast eastward for a distance of one hundred and seven leagues, where it ended in a cape. From this cape, I saw another island to the eastward at a distance of eighteen leagues from the former, to which I gave the name of *La Española* [Hispaniola]. Thither I went, and followed its northern coast to the eastward . . . one hundred and seventy-eight full leagues due east. This island, like all the others, is extraordinarily large. . . . The lands are high, and there are many very lofty mountains . . . covered with trees of a thousand kinds of such great height that they seemed to reach the skies. Some were in bloom, others bearing fruit. . . . The nightingale was singing . . . and that, in November. . . . In the interior there are many mines of metals and a population innumerable. *Española* is a wonder. Its mountains and plains, and meadows, and fields, are so beautiful and rich for planting and sowing, and rearing cattle of all kinds, and for building towns and villages. The harbours on the coast, and the number and size and wholesomeness of the rivers, most of them bearing gold, surpass anything that would be believed by one who has not seen them. There is a great difference between the trees, fruits, and plants of this island and those of

Juana. In this island there are many spices and extensive mines of gold and other metals. The inhabitants of this and of all the other islands I have found or gained intelligence of, both men and women, go as naked as they were born, with the exception that some of the women cover one part only with a single leaf of grass or with a piece of cotton, made for that purpose. They have neither iron, nor steel, nor arms, nor are they competent to use them, not that they are not well-formed and of handsome stature, but because they are timid to a surprising degree. . . . It is true that when they are reassured and have thrown off this fear, they are guileless. . . . They never refuse anything that they possess when it is asked of them; on the contrary, they offer it themselves . . . and, whether it be something of value or of little worth that is offered to them, they are satisfied. . . . They are not acquainted with any kind of worship, and are not idolators; but believe that all power and, indeed, all good things are in heaven, and they are firmly convinced that I, with my vessels and crews, came from heaven, and with this belief received me at every place at which I touched, after they had overcome their apprehension. . . . On my reaching the Indies, I took by force . . . some of these natives, that they might learn our language and give me information in regard to what existed in these parts; . . . [they] are still with me, and, from repeated conversations . . . I find that they still believe that I come from heaven. . . . Although I have taken possession of all these islands in the name of their Highnesses, and they are all more abundant in wealth than I am able to express; and although I hold them all for their Highnesses, so that they can dispose of them quite as absolutely as they can of the kingdoms of Castile, yet there was one large town in *Española* of which especially I took possession, situated in a locality well adapted for the working of the gold mines, and for all kinds of commerce, either with the mainland on this side, or with that beyond which is the land of the great Khan, with which there will be vast commerce and great profit. To that city I gave the name of *Villa de Navidad*, and fortified it with a fortress, which by this time will be quite completed, and I have left in it a sufficient number of men with arms, artillery, and provisions for more than a year, a barge, and a sailing master skilful in the arts necessary for building others. I have also established the greatest friendship with the king of that country, so much so that he took pride in calling me his brother, and treating me as such. Even should these people change their intentions towards us and become hostile, they do not know what arms are, but, as I have said, go naked, and are the most timid people in the world; so that the men I have left could, alone, destroy the whole country, and this island has no danger for them, if they only know how to conduct themselves.... Finally, and speaking only of what has taken place in this voyage, which has been so hasty, their Highnesses may see that I shall give them all the gold they require, if they will give me but a very little assistance; spices also, and cotton, as much as their Highnesses shall command to be shipped; and mastic, hitherto found only in Greece, in the island of Chios ... slaves, as many of these idolators as their Highnesses shall command to be shipped. I think also I have found rhubarb and cinnamon, and I shall find a thousand other valuable things by means of the men that I have left behind me, for I tarried at no point so long as the wind allowed me to proceed.... Much more I would have done if my vessels had been in as good a condition as by rights they ought to have been. This is much, and praised be the eternal God, our Lord, who gives to all those who walk in his ways victory over things which seem impossible; ... although others may have spoken or written concerning these countries, no one could say that he had seen them.... But our Redeemer hath granted this victory to our illustrious King and Queen and their kingdoms, which have acquired great fame by an event of such high importance, in which all Christendom ought to rejoice, and which it ought to celebrate with great festivals and the offering of solemn thanks to the Holy Trinity with many solemn prayers, both for the great exaltation which may accrue to them in turning so many nations to our holy faith, and also for the temporal benefits which will bring great refreshment and gain, not only to Spain, but to all Christians. This, thus briefly, in accordance with the events.

Done on board the caravel, off the Canary Islands, on the fifteenth of February, fourteen hundred and ninety-three.

At your orders.

The Admiral

From R. H. Major ed., *Select Letters of Christopher Columbus*.

THE CONQUISTADORES: CORTES AND THE INVASION OF MEXICO
Boies Penrose

After Columbus' Fourth Voyage, there was a pause of several years in the progress of discovery, during which the Greater Antilles were exploited and settled, but during which no effort was made to penetrate the mainland of Central and South America. By the end of the first decade of the new century, however, the logical sequel of the development of the Islands reveals itself, and Spanish enterprise embarked on a second phase even grander, and more heroic than the first — the conquest of the barbaric empires of the New World. This period lasted almost until midcentury and may be divided into four stages: the conquest of the Central American Isthmus, 1509–1519; the conquest of Mexico, 1517–1525; the conquest of Peru, 1530–1548;

and the conquest of New Granada, 1535–1539. It might be argued that the conquests belong more to history than to geography; actually the men who undertook them were primarily conquerors and only incidentally explorers, yet many thousands of square miles of territory were for the first time traversed by Europeans, and man's knowledge of the globe was immeasurably increased by the wanderings of these unprincipled adventurers.

The men who performed these mighty feats have become known to us as the Conquistadores, and they indeed embodied much of the best and much of the worst of which the human soul is capable. Their courage was peerless, their cruelty revolting; their endurance was heroic, their lust for riches despicable; their devotion to their leaders was often the personification of fidelity, but the treachery of the leaders to one another was often beneath contempt. As John Fiske well put it: "The Spanish adventurers in America need all the allowances that charity can make for them." Another historian of the conquests, Sir Arthur Helps, asks the reader to picture to himself "what his own nature might have become, if he formed one of such a band toiling in a fierce new clime, enduring miseries unimagined by him before, gradually giving up all civilised ways, growing more and more indifferent to the destruction of life — the life of animals, of his adversaries, of his companions, even his own — retaining the adroitness and sagacity of man and becoming fell, reckless, and rapacious as the fiercest brute of the forest." Yet for all this, one cannot withhold admiration from these little bands of Renaissance Spaniards, whose dauntless courage enabled them to overthrow mighty kingdoms defended by huge armies. Truly the conquistadores were men of superlative extremes....

All the Spanish conquests began with preliminary reconnaissances, and the conquest of Mexico was no exception. Determination to solve the riddle of the rumors of a wealthy empire was largely due to the vitality and drive of the governor of Cuba, Diego Velasquez, who in 1517 dispatched Francisco Fernandez de Cordoba on a westward journey of discovery. This voyage no sooner scratched the surface than it met with disaster. Cordoba reached Yucatan at its northeastern corner and probably coasted as far as Campeche; he and his men found people in dyed cotton clothing cultivating cornfields, and they saw monstrous idols and a towering city of masonry so wonderful that they christened it Grand Cairo. But the natives were everywhere bitterly hostile, and after several battles Cordoba returned to Cuba to die of his wounds. A few battered survivors of his crews returned with him.

This reverse only whetted Velasquez's appetite. The next year he sent out another expedition, three times as large, commanded by his cousin, Juan de Grijalva. This venture was indeed memorable; Grijalva reached Yucatan near Cape Catoche and sailed southward into the Gulf of Honduras. Then, retracing his course, he rounded the Yucatan peninsula, and made the discovery of Mexico itself. Grijalva was cautious and prudent; he had read the lesson of Cordoba's failure too well to try any excursions inland, and he took great care to avoid hostilities. Even then he had a bloody skirmish at Campeche, in which thirteen Spaniards were killed, but elsewhere on his long coasting voyage his caution and diplomatic mein won him a friendly reception. His course extended as far as Tampico, and he returned to Cuba with tales of the Aztec Empire, whose ruler Montezuma lived in a great city in a mountain lake — with tales also of Mexican picture writing, and of the runners, who brought word of the white men to Montezuma even while Grijalva's vessels were still off the coast — and best of all with tales of gold.

Grijalva was too cautious and too obedient to his instructions to satisfy the aggressive Velasquez. who expected much more than a mere coasting voyage; so a third expedition was prepared. Its command fell to Hernando Cortes, who had come to Cuba as Velasquez's secretary; a man distinguished among the Conquistadores for being a university man (he had attended Salamanca), and no less distinguished for his numerous affairs of gallantry, which brought him on one occasion to prison and on another to unintended matrimony. Yet he was to show himself neither a scholar nor a Casanova, but as a fearless, ruthless, determined, and insubordinate man of action. Velasquez, perhaps too late, realized this strain in Cortes' character and revoked the appointment, but Cortes had the intuition to anticipate him, and sailed from Santiago to western Cuba before the governor could act. Cortes was temporarily at least beyond the governor's reach, and along the coast he proceeded to gather recruits and collect stores, for which he could not pay. Whatever his other failings, Cortes must have been an inspiring leader, for he quickly gathered around him as devoted a gang of desperadoes as ever engaged in a desperate venture: Alvarado, Olid, Sandoval, Bernal Diaz, and even the governor's own nephew, Diego de Velasquez, later to be slain during the retreat from Tenochtitlan on the *Noche Triste.*

With this picturesque following, Cortes sailed in early 1519, before the irate Velasquez could lay hands on him. His course took him along the coast from Yucatan to Tobasco, where he landed and had a desperate battle with the natives — his first, but by no means his last. He then moved farther up the coast to a point which native information revealed as the harbor nearest to the Aztec capital. Landing there on Good Friday 1519, Cortes set up a municipality with all the high-sounding officials and elaborate organization of a Spanish town, and he christened the newborn metropolis Vera Cruz. Four months were spent there, during which Cortes consolidated his position, won the allegiance of the coastal regions, and planned his daring campaign upcountry. Then, with a profound touch of the dramatic, he had his ships burned and set off in mid-August with four hundred Spanish infantry to pit his strength against unknown odds. The march to Mexico took nearly three months, although the air-line distance is but two hundred miles. But savage tribes had to be vanquished and mountain passes negotiated. As the Spaniards ascended the barrier between the tropical shores of the Caribbean and the lofty Valley of Mexico, they entered the territory of the Tlaxcalans, a warlike race, the traditional enemies of the Aztecs. Three times the great hordes of Tlaxcalans attacked the Spaniards, as often to be repulsed with great slaughter; then, and not until then, did the Tlaxcalans yield. In winning the peace Cortes gained a mighty ally, for the Tlaxcalan state became from then on a loyal friend of the Spanish vanquisher. Without their help Cortes could never have overthrown the empire of Montezuma.

After the Tlaxcalan campaign, Cortes pursued his way to Mexico City (Tenochtitlan), which he reached early in November. One of his soldiers, Bernal Diaz del Castillo, wrote of the Conquistadores' approach through the Valley of Mexico: "When we saw so many cities and villages built in the water and other great towns on dry land and that straight and level causeway going towards Mexico, we were amazed and said it was like the enchantments they tell of in the legend of Amadis, on account of the great towers and *cues* and buildings rising from the water, and all built of masonry. And some of our soldiers even asked whether the things we saw were not all a dream . . . I do not know how to describe it, seeing things as we did that had never been heard of or seen before, not even dreamed about. . . . Gazing on such wonderful sights, we did not know what to say, or whether what appeared before us was real, for on one side, on the land, there were great cities, and in the lake ever so many more, and the lake itself was crowded with canoes . . . and in front of us stood the great City of Mexico, and we — we did not even number four hundred soldiers!"

Cortes and his men entered the city peaceably and amid much ceremony. But within a few days Cortes, by an arrant bit of treachery, had seized the person of Montezuma and held him in honorable, but none the less close, captivity among the Spanish soldiery. With the ruler in his possession, Cortes was able to amass a huge amount of gold and silver, and most of the winter was spent in collecting treasure from throughout the Aztec lands. With the spring (1520) came bad news from the coast; Velasquez had sent an expedition from Cuba under Panfilo de Narvaez to arrest Cortes as a traitor. Leaving a garrison under Pedro de Alvarado in Tenochtitlan, where the unfortunate Montezuma was still in custody, Cortes returned to the coast and decisively defeated Narvaez. Most of Narvaez's men thereupon joined Cortes' force, which immediately returned to the capital. Cortes found that things had taken a very serious turn in his absence; the whole populace was in rebellion against the Spaniards, provoked by the needless slaughter of some Aztec nobles during a ceremonial dance — a deed as tactless as it was cruel. In the hope of quieting the populace, Cortes made Montezuma show himself to his subjects, but when the ruler declared himself a friend of the Spaniards, one of the stones hurled by the angry mob struck his head, and the poor Montezuma, refusing any treatment, died of his wound as well as of a broken heart soon after.

This tragedy was a bitter blow to Cortes' plans, for as

long as Montezuma lived, he was a powerful instrument in the Spaniards' hands. With his removal, there was but one course left for the isolated group of invaders in the hostile city: to get out as soon as possible. This was accomplished with tremendous losses in one of the most difficult operations in military annals: a night march over the western causeway to the mainland, during which the Spaniards and their Tlaxcalan allies were beset every foot by fanatical foes; a night so terrible that it has been known ever afterwards as the *Noche Triste* (June 30, 1520). Hopeful of annihilating the hated invader, the Aztecs pursued closely, but in the desperate Battle of Otumba the Spaniards defeated the natives and were able to get through to Tlaxcala. There, among a population of loyal friends, they spent many months regaining their strength.

From Boies Penrose, *Travel and Discovery in the Renaissance*, Harvard University Press, 1952. Reprinted by permission of the publisher. For permission to photocopy this selection, please contact Harvard University Press.

THE THEOLOGY OF THE PROTESTANT REVOLUTION: Luther's Idea of Good Works and Justification by Faith

The first and highest, the most precious of all good works is faith in Christ, as He says, John vi. When the Jews asked Him: "What shall we do that we may work the works of God?" He answered: "This is the work of God, that ye believe on Him Whom He hath sent." When we hear or preach this word, we hasten over it and deem it a very little thing and easy to do, whereas we ought here to pause a long time and to ponder it well. For in this work all good works must be done and receive from it the inflow of their goodness, like a loan. This we must put bluntly, that men may understand it.

We find many who pray, fast, establish endowments, do this or that, lead a good life before men, and yet if you should ask them whether they are sure that what they do pleases God, they say, "No"; they do not know, or they doubt. And there are some very learned men, who mislead them, and say that it is not necessary to be sure of this; and yet, on the other hand, these same men do nothing else but teach good works. Now all these works are done outside of faith, therefore they are nothing and altogether dead. For as their conscience stands toward God and as it believes, so also are the works which grow out of it. Now they have no faith, no good conscience toward God, therefore the works lack their head, and all their life and goodness is nothing. Hence it comes that when I exalt faith and reject such works done without faith, they accuse me of forbidding good works, when in truth I am trying hard to teach real good works of faith.

From Martin Luther, "Treatise on Good Works," in *Collected Works of Martin Luther*, A. J. Holman Co., 1915—, Vol. I, pp 187-188. Reprinted by permission of United Lutheran Publication House.

ON REBELLION AGAINST RULERS
Martin Luther

Here stands the law, and says, "No one shall fight or make war against his overlord; for a man owes his overlord obedience, honor and fear" (Romans xiii). If one chops over one's head, the chips fall in one's eyes, and as Solomon says, "He who throws stones in the air, upon his head they fall." That is the law in a nutshell. God Himself has instituted it and men have accepted it, for it does not fit together that men shall both obey and resist, be subject and not put up with their lords.

But we have already said that justice ought to be mistress of law, and where circumstances demand, guide the law, or even command and permit men to act against it. Therefore the question here is whether it can be just, i.e., whether a case can arise in which one can act against this law, be disobedient to rulers and fight against them, depose them or put them in bonds. . . .

The peasants in their rebellion alleged that the lords would not allow the Gospel to be preached and robbed the poor people, and, therefore that they must be overthrown; but I have answered this by saying that although the lords did wrong in this, it would not therefore be just or right to do wrong in return, that is, to be disobedient and destroy God's ordinance, which is not ours. On the contrary, we ought to suffer wrong and if prince or lord will not tolerate the Gospel, then we ought to go into another princedom where the Gospel is preached, as Christ says in Matthew x, "If they persecute you in one city flee into another."

It is just, to be sure, that if a prince, king, or lord goes crazy, he should be deposed and put under restraint, for he is not to be considered a man since his reason is gone. Yes, you say a raving tyrant is crazy, too, or is to be considered even worse than a madman, for he does much more harm. That answer puts me in a tight place, for such a statement makes a great appearance and seems to be in accord with justice. Nevertheless, it is my opinion that the cases of madmen and tyrants are not the same; for a madman can neither do nor tolerate anything reasonable, nor is there any hope for him because the light of reason has gone out. But a tyrant, however much of this kind of thing he does, knows that he does wrong. He has his conscience and his knowledge, and there is hope that he may do better, allow himself to be instructed, and learn, and follow advice, none of which things can be hoped for in a crazy man, who is like a clod or a stone. . . .

Here you will say, perhaps, "Yes, if everything is to be endured from the tyrants, you give them too much and their wickedness only becomes stronger and greater by such teaching. Is it to be endured then that every man's wife and child, body and goods, are to be in danger? Who can start any good thing if that is the way we are to live?" I reply: My teaching is not for you, if you will to do whatever you think good and whatever pleases you. Follow your own notion and slay all your lords, and see what good it does you. My teaching is only for those who would like to do right. To these I say that rulers are not to be opposed with violence and rebellion, as the Romans, the Greeks, the Swiss and the Danes have done; but there are other ways of dealing with them.

In the first place, if they see that the rulers think so little of their soul's salvation that they rage and do wrong, of what importance is it that they ruin your property, body, wife and child? They cannot hurt your soul, and they do themselves more harm than they do you, because they damn their own souls and the ruin of body and property must then follow. Do you think that you are not already sufficiently revenged upon them?

In the second place, what would you do if these rulers of yours were at war and not only your goods and wives and children, but you yourself must be broken, imprisoned, burned and slain for your lord's sake? Would you for that reason slay your lord? . . .

In the third place, if the rulers are bad, what of it? God is there, and He has fire, water, iron, stone and numberless ways of killing. How quickly He has slain a tyrant! He would do it, too, but our sins do not permit it; for He says in Job, "He letteth a knave rule because of the people's sins." It is easy enough to see that a knave rules, but no one is willing to see that he is ruling not because of his knavery, but because of the people's sin. The people do not look at their own sin, and think that the tyrant rules because of his knavery; so blinded, perverse and mad is the world! That is why things go as they went with the peasants in the revolt. They wanted to punish the sins of the rulers, just as though they were themselves pure and guiltless; therefore, God had to show them the beam in their eye in order to make them forget another's splinter.

In the fourth place, the tyrants run the risk that, by God's decree, their subjects may rise up, as has been said, and slay them or drive them out. For we are here giving instruction to those who want to do what is right, and they are very few; the great multitude remain heathen, godless, and unchristian, and these, if God so decrees, set themselves wrongfully against the rules and create disaster, as the Jews and Greeks and Romans often did. Therefore you have no right to complain that by our doctrine the tyrants and rulers gain security to do evil; nay, they are certainly not secure. . . .

In the fifth place, God has still another way to punish rulers, so that you have no need to revenge yourself. He can raise up foreign rulers, like the Goths against the Romans, the Assyrians against the Jews, etc., so that there is vengeance, punishment, and danger enough hanging over tyrants and rulers, and God does not allow them to be wicked and have peace and joy; He is right behind them, and has them between spurs and under bridle. This agrees, also, with the natural law that Christ teaches, in Matthew vii, "What ye would that people do to you, that do you to them." No father would be driven out by his own family, slain, or ruined because of his

misdeeds (especially if the family did it out of disregard of authority and love of violence, in order to revenge themselves and be judges in their own case) without previous complaint to a higher authority. It ought to be just as wrong for any subject to act against his tyrant.

From Martin Luther, *A Compendium of Luther's Theology*, Hugh Thomson Kerr, Jr., ed.

THE THEOLOGY OF THE PROTESTANT REVOLUTION: Calvin's Doctrine of Predestination
John Calvin

In conformity, therefore, to the clear doctrine of the Scripture, we assert, that by an eternal and immutable counsel, God has once for all determined, both whom he would admit to salvation, and whom he would condemn to destruction. We affirm that this counsel, as far as concerns the elect, is founded on his gratuitous mercy, totally irrespective of human merit; but that to those whom he devotes to condemnation, the gate of life is closed by a just and irreprehensible, but incomprehensible, judgment. In the elect, we consider calling as an evidence of election, and justification as another token of its manifestation, till they arrive in glory, which constitutes its completion. As God seals his elect by vocation and justification, so by excluding the reprobate from the knowledge of his name and the sanctification of his Spirit, he affords an indication of the judgment that awaits them.

From John Calvin, *Institutes of the Christian Religion*, John Allen trans.

ON CIVIL GOVERNMENT
John Calvin

And for private men, who have no authority to deliberate on the regulation of any public affairs, it would surely be a vain occupation to dispute which would be the best form of government in the place where they live. Besides, this could not be simply determined, as an abstract question, without great impropriety, since the principle to guide the decision must depend on circumstances. And even if we compare the different forms together, without their circumstances, their advantages are so nearly equal, that it will not be easy to discover of which the utility preponderates. The forms of civil government are considered to be of three kinds: Monarchy, which is the dominion of one person, whether called a king, or a duke, or any other title; Aristocracy, or the dominion of the principal persons of a nation; and Democracy, or popular government, in which the power resides in the people at large. It is true that the transition is easy from monarchy to despotism; it is not much more difficult from aristocracy to oligarchy, or the faction of a few; but it is most easy of all from democracy to sedition. Indeed, if these three forms of government, which are stated by philosophers, be considered in themselves, I shall by no means deny, that either aristocracy, or a mixture of aristocracy and democracy, far excels all others; and that indeed not of itself, but because it very rarely happens that kings regulate themselves so that their will is never at variance with justice and rectitude; or, in the next place, that are they endued with such penetration and prudence, as in all cases to discover what is best. The vice or imperfection of men therefore renders it safer and more tolerable for the government to be in the hands of many, that they may afford each other mutual assistance and admonition, and that if any one arrogate to himself more than is right, the many may act as censors and masters to restrain his ambition. This has always been proved by experience, and the Lord confirmed it by his authority, when he established a government of this kind among the people of Israel, with a view to preserve them in the most desirable condition, till he exhibited in David a type of Christ. And as I readily acknowledge that no kind of government is more happy than this, where liberty is regulated with becoming moderation, and properly established on a durable basis, so also I consider those as the most happy people, who are permitted to enjoy such a condition; and if they exert their strenuous and constant efforts for its preservation and retention, I admit that they act in perfect consistence with their duty. And to this object the magistrates likewise ought to apply their greatest diligence, that they suffer not the liberty, of which they are constituted guardians, to be in any respect diminished, much less to be violated: if they are inactive and unconcerned about this, they are perfidious to their office, and traitors to their country. But if those, to whom the will of God has assigned another form of government, transfer this to themselves so as to be tempted to desire a revolution, the very thought will be not only foolish and useless, but altogether criminal. If we limit not our views to one city, but look round and take a comprehensive survey of the whole world, or at least extend our observations to distant lands, we shall certainly find it to be a wise arrangement of Divine Providence that various countries are governed by different forms of civil polity; or they are admirably held together with a certain inequality, as the elements are combined in very unequal proportions. All these remarks, however, will be unnecessary to those who are satisfied with the will of the Lord. For if it be his pleasure to appoint kings over kingdoms, and senators or other magistrates over free cities, it is our duty to be obedient to any governors whom God has established over the places in which we reside.

———

From John Calvin, *Institutes of the Christian Religion,* John Allen trans.

THE CATHOLIC REFORMATION: SIGNIFICANT DECREES OF THE COUNCIL OF TRENT

The universal Church has always understood, that the entire confession of sins was also intuted by the Lord, and is of divine right necessary for all who have fallen after baptism; because that our Lord Jesus Christ, when about to ascend from earth to heaven, left priests His own vicars, as presidents and judges, unto whom all the mortal crimes, into which the faithful of Christ may have fallen, should be carried, in order that, in accordance with the power of the keys, they may pronounce the sentence of forgiveness or retention of sins. For it is manifest, that priests could not have exercised this judgment without knowledge of the cause; neither indeed could they have observed equity in enjoining punishments, if the said faithful should have declared their sins in general only, and not rather specifically, and one by one. Whence it is gathered that all the mortal sins, of which, after a diligent examination of themselves, they are conscious, must needs be by penitents enumerated in confession.... Venial sins, whereby we are not excluded from the grace of God, and into which we fall more frequently, although they be rightly and profitably, and without any presumption, declared in confession, as the custom of pious persons demonstrates, yet they may be omitted without guilt, and be expiated by many other remedies. But, whereas all mortal sins, even those of thought, render men *children of wrath,* and enemies of God, it is necessary to seek also for the pardon of them all from God, with an open and modest confession.... It is ... impious to assert, that confession, enjoined to be made in this manner, is impossible, or to call it *a slaughter-house of consciences:* for it is certain, that in the Church nothing else is required of penitents, but that, after each has examined himself diligently, and searched all the folds and recesses of his conscience, he confess those sins by which he shall remember that he has mortally offended his Lord and God: whilst the other sins, which do not occur to him after diligent thought, are understood to be included as a whole in that same confession; for which sins we confidently say with the prophet: *From my secret sins cleanse me, O Lord.*

The holy Synod enjoins on all bishops, and others who sustain the office and charge of teaching, that ... they especially instruct the faithful diligently concerning the intercession and invocation of saints; the honour (paid) to relics; and the legitimate use of images: teaching them, that the saints, who reign together with Christ, offer up their own prayers to God for men; that it is good and useful suppliantly to invoke them, and to have recourse to their prayers, aid, (and) help for obtaining benefits from God, through His Son, Jesus Christ our Lord, who is our alone Redeemer and Saviour; but that they think impiously, who deny that the saints, who enjoy eternal happiness in heaven, are to be invocated; or who assert either that they do not pray for men, or that the invocation of them to pray for each of us even in particular, is idolatry; or, that it is repugnant to the word of God; and is opposed to the honour of the *one mediator of God and men, Christ Jesus;* or, that it is foolish to supplicate, vocally or mentally, those who reign in heaven. Also, that the holy bodies of holy martyrs, and of others now living with Christ, — which bodies were the living members of Christ, and *the temple of the Holy Ghost,* and which are by Him to be raised unto eternal life, and to be glorified, — are to be venerated by the faithful, through which (bodies) many benefits are bestowed by God on men; so that they who affirm that veneration and honour are not due to the relics of saints; or, that these, and other sacred monuments, are uselessly honoured by the faithful; and that the places dedicated to the memories of the saints are in vain visited with the view of obtaining their aid; are wholly to be condemned, and now also condemns them.

Moreover, that the images of Christ, of the Virgin Mother of God, and of the other saints are to be had and retained patricularly in temples; and that due honour and veneration are to be given them; not that any divinity, or virtue, is believed to be in them, on account of which they are to be worshipped; or that anything is to be asked of them; or, that trust is to be reposed in images, as was of old done by the Gentiles who placed their hope in idols; but because the honour which is shown them is referred to the prototypes which those images represent; in such wise that by the images which we kiss, and before which we uncover the head, and prostrate ourselves, we adore Christ; and we venerate the saints, whose similitude they bear. . . .

From J. Waterworth trans., *The Canons and Decrees of the . . . Council of Trent.*

ANALYSIS AND INTERPRETATION OF THE READINGS

1. To what extent was Columbus guilty of exaggeration in describing the new lands he had discovered?
2. What does the account of Cortés's invasion of Mexico tell us about the character of the *conquistadores*?
3. Explain Luther's interpretation of "good works."
4. In relation to the theory of predestination, what does Calvin mean by the statement, "We consider calling as an evidence of election"?
5. What differences do you detect between Luther and Calvin in their views of government and the role of the people under government?

CHAPTER
15

A Century of Crisis for Early-Modern Europe (c. 1560–c. 1660)

CHRONOLOGY

1555	1588	1648
1562	1598	1649
1572	1609	1659

From the above list, select the correct date for each of the following:

Massacre of St. Bartholomew's Day_____

Peace of the Pyrenees_____

Edict of Nantes_____

Defeat of the Spanish Armada_____

Recognition of independent Dutch Republic_____

Execution of Charles I_____

Religious Peace of Augsburg_____

Peace of Westphalia_____

Outbreak of civil war in France_____

IDENTIFICATIONS

In the blanks write the correct names selected from the list below:

Gustavus Adolphus   Oliver Cromwell
Pope Innocent VIII   William the Silent
Cardinal Richelieu   Emperor Charles V
Henry of Navarre   James I

1. Although he was a deadly foe of the Stuarts and their abuses, he ended by exercising more arbitrary power than any Stuart ever knew.

_____

2. This king of Scotland and England was, in the opinion of a French contemporary, "the wisest fool in Christendom."

_____

3. This seventeenth-century prince of the church was instrumental in making his country the most powerful in Europe and in leading it far along the road to royal despotism.

_____

4. A convert from Catholicism, this wealthy nobleman led the Dutch struggle against the rule of Philip II of Spain.

_____

5. Although a Lutheran, this Scandinavian ruler fought in Germany as an ally of Catholic France.

_____

6. This king who converted to Catholicism for political reasons gave France one of the most benevolent and progressive reigns in the country's history.

_____

Select the appropriate letter for completion of each of the following:

_____1. Montaigne's *Essays* are characterized by: (a) mystical pietism; (b) rationalism and materialism; (c) carefully disguised atheism; (d) skepticism and tolerance.

_____2. The author of *Six Books on the Commonwealth* was (a) Jean Bodin; (b) Oliver Cromwell; (c) Thomas Hobbes; (d) the duke of Sully.

_____3. The most radical political and economic theories in seventeenth-century England were those advanced by (a) the Puritans; (b) the Presbyterians; (c) the Diggers; (d) the Levellers.

_____4. The political philosopher Thomas Hobbes (a) upheld the right of revolution; (b) viewed the ideal state as a theocracy; (c) regarded the state of nature as a condition of war; (d) stressed the inherent goodness of human nature.

_____5. Blaise Pascal, the author of *Pensées*, (a) was a French Lutheran; (b) persecuted the Huguenots; (c) upheld the supremacy of reason; (d) believed that faith alone could save man from his wretched state.

_____6. A common characteristic of the works of the great Elizabethan dramatists was (a) an exuberant national pride; (b) unmitigated optimism; (c) glorification of royal absolutism; (d) weariness and disillusionment.

_____7. John Milton (a) was the author of a major poem, classical in form, Christian in content; (b) was a classical scholar who wrote a great Latin epic; (c) protested against the execution of King Charles I; (d) was a Puritan zealot who advocated censorship of the press.

_____8. The colonnade in front of St. Peter's basilica was the work of (a) Michelangelo; (b) El Greco; (c) Bernini; (d) Byzantine sculptors.

Explain the meaning of each of the following (if a literary or artistic work, name the author or artist):

Massacre of the Innocents	"No bishop, no king"
Volpone	Huguenots
Cavaliers and Roundheads	intendants
Petition of Right	The *Fronde*
ship money	prerogative courts
Commonwealth	*The Tempest*
Leviathan	*Paradise Lost*

STUDY QUESTIONS

1. What other period or periods of history that you have already studied offer parallels to Europe's "iron century"? What difference do you detect between the problems of the fourteenth century and those of the period 1560–1660?

2. What were the causes of the "price revolution"? Why was inflation harder on the poor than on the rich?

3. What was the impact of the price revolution upon governments?

4. Why were the religious wars of the latter half of the sixteenth century more brutal than any previously fought by Europeans, including the medieval crusades?

5. Summarize the provisions of Henry IV's Edict of Nantes. Did it grant complete religious freedom?

6. Explain why antagonisms between Catholics and Protestants in the Netherlands led to a revolt against Spanish rule.

7. Why was the defeat of the Spanish Armada "one of the most decisive battles of Western history"?

8. How did religious disputes contribute to the outbreak of the Thirty Years' War? Why did religion become subordinated to other issues in the course of the conflict?

9. Explain why access to huge quantities of American silver failed to prevent Spain's economic decline.

10. What did each of the following contribute to the development of strong central government in France: Henry IV, the duke of Sully, Cardinal Richelieu?

11. Why did the revolt known as the *Fronde* fail to check the growth of centralized absolutism in France?

12. What were the reasons for the unpopularity of King James I among his English subjects? Did he fully deserve this unpopularity?

13. What part did each of the following play in causing the English Civil War: the Puritan religious movement, the Crown's struggle for increased revenue, the Stuart rulers' political doctrines, the Scottish war of 1640?

14. The period of the Commonwealth and Protectorate constitutes England's only experiment with a republican form of government. Why was the experiment abandoned? Was it a complete failure?

15. To what extent was the witchcraft hysteria of the period 1550–1660 a religious phenomenon? What other factors help account for it?

16. Compare the political theories of Jean Bodin and Thomas Hobbes. Which of them was the more absolutist in his point of view? Why was Hobbes generally unpopular with royalists in spite of his championing of absolutism?

17. What is the social and the psychological significance of Cervantes' greatest work?

18. Describe briefly the characteristics of Shakespeare's plays from each of the three periods that mark his career as a dramatist.

19. Both the Mannerist and the Baroque styles of painting reflected the influence of religion. What were the differences between these two styles?

20. What Baroque characteristics are found in the works of Rubens? In what ways were his paintings more typically Baroque than those of Velázquez?

21. What is the justification for claiming Rembrandt as the greatest of all Netherlandish painters?

PROBLEMS

1. Why did absolutism decline in England at a time when it was rising on the Continent?
2. Compare the political role of the Huguenots in France with that of the Puritans in England.
3. Investigate further any of the following:
   a. The Huguenot communities in southern France
   b. The witchcraft hysteria
   c. The impact of the price revolution of the late sixteenth century
   d. The French court under the Cardinals Richelieu and Mazarin
   e. The Dutch struggle for independence
   f. The reign of Henry IV of France
   g. The influence of the Puritans upon English thought and English politics in the seventeenth century
   h. The career of Oliver Cromwell
4. Read several of Montaigne's *Essays* to discover what light they throw on the character of the age in which he wrote.
5. How does the Baroque style in painting, sculpture, or architecture reflect the dominant interests, ideals, or passions of the period? Illustrate your judgments by citing specific works.

GEOGRAPHICAL INDENTIFICATIONS

Flanders	Ghent	Aragon
Seville	Bohemia	Provence
Geneva	Alsace	Brittany
Navarre	Castile	Burgundy
Antwerp	Catalonia	Stratford

THE GOOD-HUMORED SATIRE OF MONTAIGNE:
The Essays

But, to speak seriously, is not man a miserable creature? Scarcely is it in his power, constituted as he is by nature, to enjoy a single pure and entire pleasure, yet he is at pains, by reasoning about it, to curtail it: he is not wretched enough, except by art and study he augment his misery:

By art we multiply the woes of Fortune. (PROPERTIUS.)

Man in his wisdom very foolishly exercises his ingenuity in lessening the number and sweetness of the pleasures that we have a right to; as he industriously and successfully employs his artifices in tricking out and disguising the ills and alleviating the sense of them.

Had I ruled the roast, I should have taken another more natural course, which is to say, a true, meet, and holy one, and I should perhaps have made myself strong enough to set bounds to it. What of our spiritual and bodily physicians, who, as if conspiring together, find no cure or remedy for the maladies of body and soul, except by way of misery, pain, and torment? Vigils, fasts, hair-shirts, remote and solitary exiles, perpetual imprisonments, scourges, and other afflictions, have been introduced to that end; the understanding being that they shall be really afflictions, with bitterness and sting; and that it shall not fall out as in the case of one Gallio, who had been banished to the isle of Lesbos. News having been brought to Rome that he was giving himself a good time, and that what had been imposed on him as a penance was turned to his advantage, they changed their minds and recalled him home to his wife and family, and commanded him to stay in his house, in order to make him fittingly sensible to their punishment. For, to a man whose health and cheerfulness are sharpened by fasting, or to whom fish is more appetizing than flesh, these would cease to be salutary remedies; just as in the other kind of medicine drugs have no effect on him who takes them with appetite and pleasure. . . .

From E. J. Trechmann trans., *The Essays of Montaigne*, Oxford University Press, 1927. Reprinted by permission of the publisher.

KING JAMES I's Conception of the Divine Right of Kings

The state of monarchy is the supremest thing upon earth; for kings are not only God's lieutenants upon earth, and sit upon God's throne, but even by God himself are called gods. There be three principal similitudes that illustrate the state of monarchy: one taken out of the word of God; and the two other out of the grounds of policy and philosophy. In the Scriptures kings are called gods, and so their power after a certain relation compared to the divine power. Kings are also compared to fathers of families: for a king is truly *Parens patriae*, the politique father of his people. And lastly, kings are compared to the head of this microcosm of the body of man.

Kings are justly called gods, for that they exercise a manner or resemblance of divine power upon earth: for if you will consider the attributes to God, you shall see how they agree in the person of a king. God hath power to create or destroy, make or unmake at his pleasure, to give life or send death, to judge all and to be judged nor accountable to none; to raise low things and to make high things low at his pleasure, and to God are both souls and body due. And the like power have kings: they make and unmake their subjects, they have power of raising and casting down, of life and of death, judges over all their subjects and in all causes and yet accountable to none but God only. . . .

I conclude then this point touching the power of kings with this axiom of divinity, That as to dispute what God may do is blasphemy. . . . so is it sedition in subjects to dispute what a king may do in the height of his power. But just kings will ever be willing to declare what they will do, if they will not incur the curse of God. I will not be content that my power be disputed upon; but I shall ever be willing to make the reason appear of all my doings, and rule my actions according to my laws. . . . I would wish you to be careful to avoid three things in the matter of grievances:

First, that you do not meddle with the main points of government; that is my craft . . . to meddle with that were to lesson me. . . . I must not be taught my office.

Secondly, I would not have you meddle with such ancient rights of mine as I have received from my predecessors. . . . All novelties are dangerous as well in a politic as in a natural body, and therefore I would be loath to be quarreled in my ancient rights and possessions; for that were to judge me unworthy of that which my predecessors had and left me.

And lastly, I pray you beware to exhibit for grievance anything that is established by a settled law, and whereunto . . . you know I will never give a plausible answer; for it is an undutiful part in subjects to press their king, wherein they know beforehand he will refuse them.

From King James I, *Works* (1609).

REPLY OF THE HOUSE OF COMMONS TO KING JAMES I, 1604

Most Gracious Sovereign:

... With all humble and due respect to your Majesty, our sovereign lord and head, against these misinformations we most truly avouch, first, that our privileges and liberties are our right and due inheritance, no less than our very lands and goods. Secondly, that they cannot be withheld from us, denied, or impaired, but with apparent wrong to the whole state of the realm. Thirdly, that our making of request in the entrance of parliament to enjoy our privilege is an act only of manners, and doth weaken our right no more than our suing to the king for our lands by petition, which form, though new and more decent than the old by *praecipe*, yet the subject's right is no less than of old. Fourthly, we avouch also that our House is a court of record, and so ever esteemed. Fifthly, that there is not the highest standing court in this land that ought to enter into competency either for dignity or authority with this high court of parliament, which with your Majesty's royal assent gives laws to other courts, but from other courts receives neither laws or orders.

Sixthly, and lastly, we avouch that the House of Commons is the sole proper judge of return of all such writs, and of the election of all such members as belong unto it, without which the freedom of election were not entire; and that the chancery, though a standing court under your majesty, be to send out those writs and receive the returns and to preserve them, yet the same is done only for the use of the parliament; over which neither the chancery nor any other court ever had or ought to have any manner of jurisdiction.

The rights and liberties of the Commons of England consisteth chiefly of these three things: first, that the shires, cities, and boroughs of England, by representation to be present, have free choice of such persons as they shall put in trust to represent them; secondly, that the persons chosen, during the time of the parliament, as also of their access and recess, be free from restraint, arrest and imprisonment; thirdly, that in parliament they may speak freely their consciences without check and controlment, doing the same with due reverence to the sovereign court of parliament, that is, to your Majesty and both the Houses, who all in this case make but one politic body, whereof your Highness is the head. ...

From *Journals of the House of Commons*, Vol. I, 1547-1629.

AN ENGLISH JUSTIFICATION OF ABSOLUTISM
Thomas Hobbes

The only way to erect such a common power as may be able to defend them from the invasion of foreigners and the injuries of one another, and thereby to secure them in such sort as that by their own industry and by the fruits of the earth they may nourish themselves and live contentedly, is to confer all their power and strength upon one man, or upon one assembly of men, that may reduce all their wills by plurality of voices unto one will; which is as much to say, to appoint one man or assembly of men to bear their person; and every one to own and acknowledge himself to be author of whatsoever he that so beareth their person shall act, or cause to be acted, in those things which concern the common peace and safety; and therein to submit their wills, every one to his will, and their judgments to his judgment. This is more than consent or concord: it is a real unity of them all, in one and the same person, made by covenant of every man with every man, in such manner as if every man should say to every man, 'I authorize and give up my right of governing myself to this man, or to this assembly of men, on this condition, that thou give up thy right to him and authorize all his actions in like manner.' This done, the multitude so united in one person is called a 'commonwealth,' in Latin *civitas*. This is the generation of that great 'leviathan,' or, rather, to speak more reverently, of that 'mortal god,' to which we owe under the 'immortal God,' our peace and defence. For by this authority, given him by every particular man in the commonwealth, he hath the use of so much power and strength conferred on him that by terror thereof he is enabled to perform the wills of them all, to peace at home and mutual aid against their enemies abroad. And in him consisteth the essence of the commonwealth; which, to define it, is 'one person, of whose acts a great multitude by mutual covenants one with another have made themselves every one the author, to the end he may use the strength and means of them all as he shall think expedient for their peace and common defence.'

And he that carrieth this person is called 'sovereign,' and said to have 'sovereign power'; and every one besides his 'subject.'

The attaining to this sovereign power is by two ways. One by natural force, as when a man maketh his children to submit themselves and their children to his government, as being able to destroy them if they refuse; or by war subdueth his enemies to his will, giving them their lives on that condition. The other is when men agree amongst themselves to submit to some man, or assembly of men, voluntarily, on confidence to be protected by him against all others. This latter may be called a political commonwealth, or commonwealth by 'institution'; and the former, a commonwealth by 'acquisition.'

From Thomas Hobbes, *Leviathan*.

REASON SHOULD GUIDE THE GOVERNING OF A STATE
Cardinal Richelieu

Common sense leads each one of us to understand that man, having been endowed with reason, should do nothing except that which is reasonable, since otherwise he would be acting contrary to his nature, and by consequence contrary to Him Who is its Creator. It further teaches us that the more a man is great and conspicuous, the more he ought to be conscious of this principle and the less he ought to abuse the rational process which constitutes his being, because the ascendency he has over other men requires him to preserve that part of his nature and his purpose which was specifically given to him by Him Who chose him for elevation.

From these two principles it clearly follows that if man is sovereignly reasonable he ought to make reason sovereign, which requires not only that he do nothing not in conformity with it, but also that he make all those who are under his authority reverence it and follow it religiously. This precept is the source of another, which teaches us that since we should never want the accomplishment of anything not reasonable and just, neither should we ever want the accomplishment of anything without having it carried out and our commands followed by complete obedience, because otherwise reason would not really reign sovereign. The practice of this rule is quite easy because love is a most powerful motive in winning obedience, and it is impossible for subjects not to love a prince if they know that reason is the guide of all his actions. Authority constrains obedience, but reason captivates it. It is much more expedient to lead men by means which imperceptibly win their wills than, as is more the practice, by those which coerce them.

If it is true that reason ought to be the torch which lights the conduct of both princes and their states, it is also true that there is nothing in nature less compatible with reason than emotion. It can so blind a person that it makes the shadow seem like the substance, and a prince must above all avoid acting upon such a basis. It would make him doubly odious, since it is directly contrary to what distinguishes man from the animals. One often has to repent at leisure what emotion has hastily engendered, but such results never occur when action springs from reasonable consideration. It is for such reasons necessary to back one's decision with a firm will, because this is the only way to make oneself obeyed, and just as humility is the first foundation of Christian perfection, so obedience is the most important part of the subjection so necessary to the wellbeing of states, which, if it is defective, cannot flourish.

There are many things which by their very nature are difficult neither to order nor to carry out, but it is necessary to will them efficaciously, that is to say, with complete firmness and lasting attention, and so that after the execution has been ordered, severe punishment falls on any who disobey. Those tasks which appear the most difficult, even almost impossible, seem so only because of the lack of determination with which we view them and command their execution. And it is true that subjects will always religiously obey when princes are firm and relentless in their commands, from which it follows that if states are poorly governed princes are all the more responsible for it, since it is certain that their weakness and indifference are the cause of it. In a word,

just as to will firmly and to do what one wills are the same thing in a true prince, so too to will weakly or not to will at all are alike in the opposite sense in that nothing is ever accomplished.

The government of kingdoms requires a manly bearing and an inflexible will, contrary to indecision which exposes those who are its victims to the schemes of their enemies. It is necessary, in all cases, to act with vigor, principally because even if the outcome of an undertaking is not good, at least we can know that having omitted nothing which could have made it succeed we can spare ourselves the shame of responsibility although we cannot avoid the evil of a real misfortune. Even when one fails in honestly trying to do his duty the disgrace should make him happy, while contrariwise, if success comes to him accidentally when not abiding by what he is obligated to by honor and conscience, he should be considered most unfortunate since he can draw no satisfaction from it equal to the real losses arising from the knowledge of the means he has employed. In the past the larger part of the great plans drafted for France have come to naught because the first serious obstacle confronting them has been sufficient to cause an end of effort on the part of those who in all justice should have carried them through, and if things have resulted differently during the reign of Your Majesty it is because of the perseverance with which matters have constantly been pursued.

If, at a given time, it seems inexpedient to attempt to carry out a particular plan, one should postpone action and turn to something else, and if this is also interrupted good sense indicates we should again take up the first project as soon as the time and circumstances are favorable. In a word, nothing ought to be allowed to turn us permanently away from a good objective unless some untoward accident makes it entirely unachievable, and we must never fail to do whatever is necessary to bring about the execution of that which we have rightly resolved to accomplish.

It is this which obliges me to speak here of secrecy and diligence, both of which are so necessary to the success of affairs as to dwarf all other attributes. Both experience and reason make it evident that what is suddenly presented ordinarily astonishes in such a fashion as to deprive one of the means of opposing it, while if the execution of a plan is undertaken slowly the gradual revelation of it can create the impression that it is only being projected and will not necessarily be executed. From this it follows that women, by nature indolent and unable to keep secrets, are little suited to government, particularly if one also considers that they are subject to their emotions and consequently little susceptible to reason and justice, attributes which should exclude them from all public office. This is not to say that a few might be found so free of these faults as to make them admissible to public service. There are few general rules for which no exceptions can be found. This era itself bears witness to several women whose deeds cannot be praised enough. But it is true that their weakness denies them the masculine vigor necessary to public administration, and it is almost impossible for them to govern without a base exploitation of their sex, or without acts of injustice and cruelty arising from the disorderly ascendency of their emotions.

From *The Political Testament of Cardinal Richelieu*, tr. by Henry Betram Hill, University of Wisconsin Press, 1961. Reprinted by permission of publisher.

THE NEGATIVE EFFECTS OF OVERSEAS CONQUESTS ON EUROPEAN SOCIETY
A. Kent MacDougall

Newspaper, magazine, and television celebrations of the 1492 "discovery" have paid scant attention to its effects on Europeans themselves. The unspoken assumption is that the Americans' and Africans' loss must have been Europeans' gain, that all that misery, destruction, and death in the New World must have benefited people in the Old. Progress, however uneven, must have been served.

The opposite is true. Ordinary Europeans suffered terribly, and for centuries, from the conquest and the military arms race, inflation, and falling living standards that Europeanization of the Americas touched off. How this happened and the parallels with the present provide an instructive warning of what's to come in the contemporary world if current trends continue.

The gold and silver mined with forced labor in Mexico and what is now Bolivia constituted a windfall that could have been used to develop Spanish agriculture, industry, and commerce and help the country catch up with northwestern Europe's more developed economies. Such development would sooner or later have benefited the impoverished peasantry that comprised 95 per cent of Spain's population.

But Spain was in the grip of a tiny ruling class of royalty, Catholic Church hierarchy, and landed aristocracy. Two to three per cent of the population owned 97 per cent of the land in Castile, Spain's heartland. The great landowners had no incentive to modernize Spain. They just wanted to raise more sheep and sell more wool. The environmental degradation that overgrazing vast numbers of sheep entailed seems to have bothered the ruling class no more than did the cutting of forests for timber to build ships and provide charcoal to smelt domestic Spanish silver ore. And so what if the wool went to Holland to be manufactured into cloth rather than being processed in Spain itself.

Meanwhile, successes in the New World swelled the Spanish monarchy's ambitions in the Old. The bonanza of bullion from the Americas encouraged Spain's rulers to build up their army into Europe's largest military force, setting off an arms race that forced rivals to multiply their armed forces as well. Spain hired German, Italian, and Irish mercenaries and built and bought a vast fleet of heavily armed ships. Hegemonic wars against the French, Dutch, and English followed.

These wars were as costly as they were ill-advised, as economically ruinous as they were militarily unsuccessful. To pay for them, the Spanish crown raised taxes, bleeding the peasantry even more mercilessly, and borrowed heavily from foreign bankers, incurring mounting interest obligations that eventually proved unsupportable. The gold and silver flowing from the Americas flowed swiftly out again to foreign bankers and military suppliers. Little trickled down to benefit Spaniards themselves.

The most lasting and far-reaching effect of the increase of money in circulation was to set off a long wave of inflation that spread throughout Western Europe. To be sure, debasement of coinage by monarchs in search of additional royal revenue contributed to the run-up in prices, as did deficit spending on unproductive armies, navies, and wars. So did the pressure of growing populations on scarce resources and lagging production of goods. But the trigger was the 20 per cent increase in Europe's stock of gold by 1660 and the tripling of its silver supply.

By 1600, prices had risen five-fold in Andalusia, two-and-a-half-fold in France, and four-fold in England, without anything like a comparable increase in wages. Before long, English carpenters and masons had to work four times as long to buy a loaf of bread, and their real wages did not return to the pre-1540 level until 1880. As British historian John Burnett recounts in *A History of the Cost of Living*, inflation created "a new category of the poor—those who had employment but whose wages were inadequate to support life at a reasonable level." The deterioration continued for centuries; in 1850 one of every seven persons in England and Wales was still a pauper.

An excerpt from "The Empire Strikes Back at Itself," *The Progressive*, March 1992. Reprinted by permission of the author.

ANALYSIS AND INTERPRETATION OF THE READINGS

1. Why does Montaigne think man has become a "miserable creature"? Could he have become otherwise?

2. What part did the rights of the people play in the struggle between James I and the English Parliament?
3. What was the real point at issue between king and parliament?
4. Upon what grounds does Thomas Hobbes justify absolute government?
5. According to Cardinal Richelieu, what qualities must a ruler possess to govern well? Why does he consider women ill-suited to govern?

The Economy and Society of Early-Modern Europe

CHRONOLOGY

1602	1694
1607	1720
1651	1769
1657	1793
1666	1807

From the list above, select the correct date for each of the following items:

First English Navigation Act_____

Dissolution of French East India Company_____

Abolition of slavery in French colonies_____

Founding of the Bank of Sweden_____

Founding of the Bank of England_____

Ending of the British slave trade_____

South Sea and Mississippi Bubbles_____

Establishment of first English colony in
North America_____

Founding of the Dutch East India Company_____

Great Fire of London_____

IDENTIFICATIONS

In the blanks, write the appropriate names from the list following:

Frederick II and Maria Theresa	Viscount Charles Townsend
Fuggers	John Kay
John Law	Duke of Bridgewater
Jean Baptiste Colbert	Molière

Inventor of the fly-shuttle_____

Developer of French sugar-producing colonies_____

_____

Promoter of the Mississippi Company_____

_____

English canal builder_____

Author of *The Bourgeois Gentleman*_____

Instituted systems of compulsory education_____

Austrian banking house_____

Advocate of turnip husbandry_____

You should be able to define or explain each of the following terms:

regulated company	"middle passage"
joint-stock company	open-field system
chartered company	putting-out system
corvée	"deserving" poor
seigneur	"world turned upside down"

STUDY QUESTIONS

1. What factors explain Europe's unprecedented population increase after 1750?
2. What was the relationship between shifts in population during the seventeenth and eighteenth centuries and changes in agriculture and industry?
3. What were the most prized agricultural products from America? From the Far East?
4. What advances toward scientific farming by the introduction of new methods and of new crops were made during these centuries, and where were they most prominent? How did these advances affect small peasant proprietors?
5. What was the purpose of the enclosure movement in agriculture, and what were its social effects? How did the movement in England differ from that in France? During what period was it most rapid in England?
6. Explain the putting-out system that developed in the textile industry. What were its advantages both for entrepreneurs and for workers? What were its disadvantages?
7. What industries other than textiles were developing in rural areas?
8. Why were technical innovations in industry sometimes resisted by workers or banned by governments?

9. What were the obstacles to efficient and economical transportation, and what attempts were made in the eighteenth century to overcome them?

10. What two related but diverging economic systems guided the development of commerce and industry during the early modern world? Define each of the two systems.

11. What assumptions did mercantilism and capitalism have in common? In what respects did they differ?

12. What medieval social or institutional patterns were evident in mercantilism?

13. How did Spain's colonial policy illustrate the objectives of mercantilism, and in what respects was its policy deficient?

14. What variations on the mercantilist theme did the Dutch employ, and how successful were they in competition with their rivals?

15. How do you account for the outstanding success of France and England in the age of mercantilism?

16. Why were the growth of banks and improvement in the monetary system essential to the success of the commercial revolution?

17. Chartered companies "were an example of the way capitalist and mercantilist interests might coincide." How is this demonstrated by the British and French East India companies?

18. Why were the early English colonial settlements less strictly regulated than the Spanish colonies? Why did English colonial policy change in the late seventeenth century?

19. Explain the notorious "triangular" trade pattern that proved so profitable to British merchants.

20. About how many black slaves were transported from Africa during the history of the slave trade? What percentage of this total came during the eighteenth century?

21. How was the concept of "freedom" interpreted in a "society of orders"?

22. What similarities and what differences did the aristocracies of the leading European countries show?

23. What legal and economic disabilities rested upon the peasantry? Why were the peasants of western Europe generally more free than those in eastern Europe?

24. Name three European cities that had attained populations of 200,000 or more by 1800. Which of these had the largest?

25. What change in the structure of society, especially in France, is represented by the rise of the *bourgeoisie*?

26. How did the decay of the guild system affect the status of workers?

27. What was the rationale behind the English Poor Law of 1601?

28. Describe briefly the character of education during this period.

PROBLEMS

1. Investigate further any of the following topics:
   a. The social and economic effects of the enclosure movement
   b. The role of the potato and maize in improving the European diet
   c. The African slave trade
   d. Canal building in England and France
   e. Living conditions in populous cities
   f. The changing status of labor accompanying the decay of the guilds
   g. Village festivals, folklore, and pasttimes

2. Explore the relationship between the Commercial Revolution and the Protestant and Catholic Reformations.

3. In what respects is mercantilism still an influential force?

4. Trace the changes in the structure of society and changes in beliefs concerning the "social orders" and the relationships between them.

5. Support or refute the proposition: "The Commercial Revolution was of substantial benefit to the inhabitants of western Europe."

GEOGRAPHICAL IDENTIFICATIONS

Bombay	Madras
Bristol	Madrid
Amsterdam	Augsburg
Venice	Seville
Cadiz	St. Lawrence River
Orléans	Berlin
Barbados	Jamaica
Spice Islands	Surinam
Dominique	Lyons
Sumatra	St. Petersburg
Veracruz	Manila

AIDS TO AN UNDERSTANDING OF THE ECONOMY AND SOCIETY OF EARLY-MODERN EUROPE

THE PIRATICAL EXPLOITS OF FRANCIS DRAKE

Our Generall seeing this stayed her no longer, but wayed anchor, and set sayle towards the coast of Chili, and drawing towards it, we mette neere to the shore an Indian in a Canoa, who thinking us to have bene Spaniards, came to us and tolde us, that at a place called S. Iago, there was a great Spanish ship laden from the kingdome of Peru: for which good newes our Generall gave him divers trifles, wherof he was glad, and went along with us and brought us to the place, which is called the port of Valparizo.

When we came thither, we found indeede the ship riding at anker, having in her eight Spaniards and three Negros, who thinking us to have bene Spaniards and their friends, welcommed us with a drumme, and made ready a Bottija of wine of Chili to drinke to us: but as soone as we were entred, one of our company called Thomas Moone began to lay about him, and strooke one of the Spanyards, and sayd unto him, "Abaxo Perro," that is in English, "Goe downe dogge." One of these Spaniards seeing persons of that quality in those seas, all to crossed, and blessed himselfe: but to be short, wee stowed them under hatches all save one Spaniard, who suddenly and desperately leapt over boord into the sea, and swamme ashore to the towne of S. Iago, to give them warning of our arrivall.

They of the towne being not above 9. households, presently fled away and abandoned the towne. Our generall manned his boate, and the Spanish ships boate, and went to the Towne, and being come to it, we rifled it, and came to a small chappell which wee entred, and found therin a silver chalice, two cruets, and one altar-cloth, the spoyle whereof our Generall gave to M. Fletcher, his minister. . . .

Not farre from hence going on land for fresh water, we met with a Spaniard and an Indian boy driving 8. Llamas or sheepe of Peru which are as big as asses; every of which sheepe had on his backe 2. bags of leather, each bagge conteining 50. li. weight of fine silver: so that bringing both the sheepe and their burden to the ships we found in all the bags 800. weight of silver.

Here hence we sailed to a place called Arica, and being entred the port, we found there three small barkes which we rifled, and found in one of them 57 wedges of silver, each of them weighing about 20 pound weight, and every of these wedges were of the fashion and bignesse of a brickbat. In all these 3 barkes we found not one person: for they mistrusting no strangers, were all gone aland to the Towne which consisteth of about twentie houses, which we would have ransacked if our company had bene better and more in number. But our Generall contented with the spoyle of the ships, left the Towne and put off againe to sea and set sayle for Lima, and by the way met with a small barke, which he boorded, and found in her good store of linen cloth, whereof taking some quantitie, he let her goe. . . .

From E. P. Cheyney, *Readings in English History*, New York: Ginn and Company, 1908, pp. 399-401. Reprinted by permission of the publisher.

SOME RESULTS OF THE ENCLOSURE MOVEMENT IN ENGLAND
Sir Thomas More

But yet this is not only the necessary cause of stealing. There is another, which, as I suppose, is proper and peculiar to you Englishmen alone. What is that, quoth the Cardinal? forsooth my lord (quoth I) your sheep that were wont to be so meek and tame, and so small eaters, now, as I hear say, be become so great devourers and so wild, that they eat up, and swallow down the very men themselves. They consume, destroy, and devour whole fields, houses, and cities. For look in what parts of the realm doth grow the finest and therefore dearest wool, there noblemen and gentlemen, yea and certain abbots, holy men no doubt, not contenting themselves with the yearly revenues and profits, that were wont to grow to their forefathers and predecessors of their lands, nor being content that they live in rest and pleasure nothing profiting, yea much annoying the weal public, leave no ground for tillage, they inclose all into pastures; they throw down houses; they pluck down towns, and leave nothing standing, but only the church to be made a sheep-house. And as though you lost no small quantity of grounds by forests, chases, lawns, and parks, those good holy men turn all dwelling-places and all glebeland into desolation and wilderness. Therefore that one covetous and insatiable cormorant and very plague of his native country may compass about and inclose many thousand acres of ground together within one pale or hedge, the husbandmen be thrust out of their own, or else either by cunning and fraud, or by violent oppression they be put besides it, or by wrongs and injuries they be so wearied, that they be compelled to sell all: by one means therefore or by other, either by hook or crook they must needs depart away, poor, silly, wretched souls, men, women, husbands, wives, fatherless children, widows, woeful mothers, with their young babes, and their whole household small in substance and much in number, as husbandry requireth many hands. Away they trudge, I say, out of their known and accustomed houses, finding no place to rest in. All their household stuff, which is very little worth, though it might well abide the sale: yet being suddenly thrust out, they be constrained to sell it for a thing of nought. And when they have wandered abroad till that be spent, what can they then else do but steal, and then justly pardy be hanged, or else go about a begging.

From Sir Thomas More, *Utopia*, Maurice Adams ed.

POLITICAL CONSEQUENCES OF THE GROWTH OF BANKING
R. H. Tawney

Nourished by the growth of peaceful commerce, the financial capitalism of the age fared not less sumptuously, if more dangerously, at the courts of princes. Mankind, it seems, hates nothing so much as its own prosperity. Menaced with an accession of riches which would lighten its toil, it makes haste to redouble its labors, and to pour away the perilous stuff, which might deprive of plausibility the complaint that it is poor. Applied to the arts of peace, the new resources commanded by Europe during the first half of the sixteenth century might have done something to exorcise the specters of pestilence and famine, and to raise the material fabric of civilization to undreamed-of heights. Its rulers, secular and ecclesiastical alike, thought otherwise. When pestilence and famine were ceasing to be necessities imposed by nature, they reëstablished them by political art.

The sluice which they opened to drain away each new accession of superfluous wealth was war. "Of all birds," wrote the sharpest pen of the age, "the eagle alone has seemed to wise men the type of royalty — not beautiful, not musical, not fit for food, but carnivorous, greedy, hateful to all, the curse of all, and, with its great powers of doing harm, surpassing them in its desire of doing it." The words of Erasmus, uttered in 1517, were only too prophetic. For approximately three-quarters both of the sixteenth and of the seventeenth centuries, Europe tore itself to pieces. In the course of the conflict the spiritual fires of Renaissance and Reformation alike were trampled out beneath the feet of bravos as malicious and mischievous as the vain, bloody-minded and futile generals who strut and posture, to the hateful laughter of Thersites, in the most despairing of Shakespeare's tragedies. By the middle of the sixteenth century the English Government, after an orgy of debasement and confiscation, was in a state of financial collapse, and by the end of it Spain, the southern Netherlands including Antwerp, and a great part of France, including the financial capital of southern Europe, Lyons, were ruined. By the middle of the seventeenth century wide tracts of Germany were a desert, and by the end of it the French finances had relapsed into worse confusion than that from which they had been temporarily rescued by the genius of Colbert. The victors compared their position with that of the vanquished, and congratulated themselves on their spoils. It rarely occurred to them to ask what it would have been, had there been neither victors nor vanquished, but only peace.

It is possible that the bankruptcies of Governments have, on the whole, done less harm to mankind than their ability to raise loans, and the mobilization of economic power on a scale unknown before armed the fierce nationalism of the age with a weapon more deadly than gunpowder and cannon. The centralized States which were rising in the age of Renaissance were everywhere faced with a desperate financial situation. It sprang from the combination of modern administrative and military methods with medieval systems of finance. They entrusted to bureaucracies work which, if done at all, had formerly been done as an incident of tenure, or by boroughs and gilds; officials had to be paid. They were constantly at war; and the new technique of war, involving the use of masses of professional infantry and artillery — which Rabelais said was invented by the inspiration of the devil, as a counterpoise to the invention of printing inspired by God — was making it, as after 1870, a highly capitalized industry. Government after Government, undeterred, with rare exceptions, by the disasters of its neighbors, trod a familiar round of expedients, each of which was more disastrous than the last. They hoarded treasure, only to see the accumulations of a thrifty Henry VII or Frederick III dissipated by a Henry VIII or a Maximilian. They debased the currency and ruined trade. They sold offices, or established monopolies, and crushed the taxpayer beneath a load of indirect taxation. They plundered the Church, and spent gorgeously as income property which should have been treated as capital. They parted with Crown estates, and left an insoluble problem to their successors.

These agreeable devices had, however, obvious limits. What remained, when they were exhausted, was the money-market, and to the rulers of the money-market sooner or later all States came. Their dependence on the financier was that of an Ismail or an Abdul, and its results were not less disastrous. Naturally, the City interest was one of the great Powers of Europe. Publicists might write that the new Messiah was the Prince, and reformers that the Prince was Pope. But behind Prince and Pope alike, financing impartially Henry VII, Edward VI and Elizabeth, Francis, Charles and Philip, stood in the last resort a little German banker, with branches in every capital in Europe, who played in the world of finance the part of the *condottieri* in war, and represented in the economic sphere the morality typified in that of politics by Machiavelli's Prince. Compared with these financial dynasties, Hapsburgs, Valois and Tudors were puppets dancing on wires held by a money-power to which political struggles were irrelevant except as an opportunity for gain.

From R. H. Tawney, *Religion and the Rise of Capitalism*. Copyright 1926 by Harcourt, Brace & World, Inc.; renewed 1954 by R. H. Tawney. Reprinted by permission of Harcourt, Brace & World, Inc., and John Murray.

ADAM SMITH ON THE PRINCIPLE OF MERCANTILISM

That wealth consists in money, or in gold and silver, is a popular notion which naturally arises from the double function of money as the instrument of commerce, and as the measure of value. In consequence of its being the instrument of commerce, when we have money we can more readily obtain whatever else we have occasion for, than by means of any other commodity. The great affair, we always find, is to get money. When that is obtained, there is no difficulty in making any subsequent purchase. In consequence of its being the measure of value, we estimate that of all other commodities by the quantity of money which they will exchange for. We say of a rich man that he is worth a great deal, and of a poor man that he is worth very little money. A frugal man, or a man eager to be rich, is said to love money; and a careless, a generous, or a profuse man, is said to be indifferent about it. To grow rich is to get money; and wealth and money, in short, are, in common language, considered as in every respect synonymous.

It is not because wealth consists more essentially in money than in goods, that the merchant finds it generally more easy to buy goods with money, than to buy money with goods; but because money is the known and established instrument of commerce, for which every thing is readily given in exchange, but which is not always with equal readiness to be got in exchange for every thing. The greater part of goods besides are more perishable than money, and he may frequently sustain a much greater loss by keeping them. When his goods are upon hand too, he is more liable to such demands for money as he may not be able to answer, than when he has got their price in his coffers. Over and above all this, his profit arises more directly from selling than from buying, and he is upon all these accounts generally much more anxious to exchange his goods for money, than his money for goods. But though a particular merchant, with abundance of goods in his warehouse, may sometimes be ruined by not being able to sell them in time, a nation or country is not liable to the same accident. The whole capital of a merchant frequently consists in perishable goods destined for purchasing money. But it is but a very small part of the annual produce of the land and labour of a country which can ever be destined for purchasing gold and silver from their neighbours. The far greater part is circulated and consumed among themselves; and even of the surplus which is sent abroad, the greater part is generally destined for the purchase of other foreign goods. Though gold and silver, therefore, could not be had in exchange for the goods destined to purchase them, the nation would not be ruined. It might, indeed, suffer some loss and inconveniency, and be forced upon some of those expedients which are necessary for supplying the place of money. The annual produce of its land and labour, however, would be the same, or very nearly the same, as usual, because the same, or very nearly the same consumable capital would be employed in maintaining it. And though goods do not always draw money so readily as money draws goods, in the long-run they draw it more necessarily than even it draws them. Goods can serve many other purposes besides purchasing money, but money can serve no other purpose besides purchasing goods. Money, therefore, necessarily runs after goods, but goods do not always or necessarily run after money. The man who buys, does not always mean to sell again, but frequently to use or to consume; whereas he who sells, always means to buy again. The one may frequently have done the whole, but the other can never have done more than the one-half of his business. It is not for its own sake that men desire money, but for the sake of what they can purchase with it.

From Adam Smith, *An Inquiry into the Nature and Causes of the Wealth of Nations,* Edwin Cannan ed.

LIFE IN SIXTEENTH-CENTURY ENGLAND: As Described by Erasmus

. . . I am frequently astonished and grieved to think how it is that England has been now for so many years troubled by a continual pestilence, especially by a deadly sweat, which appears in a great measure to be peculiar to your country. I have read how a city was once delivered from a plague by a change in the houses, made at the suggestion of a philosopher. I am inclined to think that this, also, must be the deliverance for England.

First of all, Englishmen never consider the aspect of their doors or windows; next, their chambers are built in such a way as to admit of no ventilation. Then a great part of the walls of the house is occupied with glass casements, which admit light but exclude the air, and yet they let in the draught through holes and corners, which is often pestilential and stagnates there. The floors are, in general, laid with white clay, and are covered with rushes, occasionally renewed, but so imperfectly that the bottom layer is left undisturbed, sometimes for twenty years, harboring expectorations, vomitings, the leakage of dogs and men, ale droppings, scraps of fish, and other abominations not fit to be mentioned. Whenever the weather changes a vapor is exhaled, which I consider very detrimental to health. I may add that England is not only everywhere surrounded by sea, but is, in many places, swampy and marshy, intersected by salt rivers, to say nothing of salt provisions, in which the common people take so much delight. I am confident the island would be much more salubrious if the use of rushes were abandoned, and if the rooms were built in such a way as to be exposed to the sky on two or three sides, and all the windows so built as to be opened or closed at once, and so completely closed as not to admit the foul air through chinks; for as it is beneficial to health to admit the air, so it is equally beneficial at times to exclude it. The common people laugh at you if you complain of a cloudy or foggy day. Thirty years ago, if ever I entered a room which had not been occupied for some months, I was sure to take a fever. More moderation in diet, and especially in the use of salt meats, might be of service; more particularly were public officers appointed to see the streets cleaned from mud and filth, and the suburbs kept in better order. . . .

From E. P. Cheyney, *Readings in English History*, New York: Ginn and Company, 1908, pp. 316–17.

ANALYSIS AND INTERPRETATION OF THE READINGS

1. Did Sir Thomas More conceive of the enclosure movement as an economic problem or a moral problem?
2. What did R. H. Tawney mean by saying "Mankind, it seems, hates nothing so much as its own prosperity"?
3. Do you think Tawney exaggerated when he accused the bankers of the sixteenth and seventeenth centuries of so great a responsibility for the growth of militarism?

The Age of Absolutism (1660–1789)

IDENTIFICATIONS

In the blanks write the correct names selected from the list below:

James I
Charles I
Charles II
James II
Louis XIV
Louis XV
William of Orange
Jean Bodin
Elector Frederick William
Hugo Grotius

Frederick William I
Frederick II
Maria Theresa
Joseph II
Peter the Great
Catherine the Great
Robert Walpole
Emelyan Pugachev
George III
Thaddeus
    Kosciuszko

1. This Habsburg ruler's 1780 "Edict on Idle Institutions" closed thousands of monastic houses.

_____

2. He cut off the beards of his subjects, annihilated their self-government, published a book of manners, and carried his country to the shores of the Baltic, all in the name of its westernization.

_____

3. His violation of Parliamentary Acts dealing with Catholics and his unexpected son by his second wife helped bring on the Glorious Revolution and make him the last Stuart king.

_____

4. Whether he said it or not, the phrase *l'état c'est moi* perfectly expressed this monarch's conception of his proper authority.

_____

5. This Dutch prince, in accepting the offer of the English throne, acknowledged the supremacy of Parliament.

_____

6. An "enlightened absolutist" who corresponded with French philosophers, this German-born empress helped westernize her country but did little to relieve the woes of its peasants.

_____

7. A cynical contemporary remarked of this ruler's reluctance to share in the dismemberment of Poland: "She weeps, but she takes her share."

_____

8. The second Prussian ruler with the title of king, he greatly increased the size of Prussia's army.

_____

9. This political leader, called Britain's "first prime minister," was important in developing the cabinet system of parliamentary government.

_____

10. Self-declared "first servant of the state," this industrious despot built the most efficient bureaucracy in Europe and involved his country in a series of wars.

_____

11. Witty, sensuous, and dissembling, this monarch by his policies sowed the whirlwind his more stubborn brother reaped in 1688.

_____

12. Claiming to be Tsar Peter III, he led an unsuccessful peasant-serf revolt which stiffened the absolutist tendencies of the empress Catherine.

_____

13. His determination to "be king" brought his political downfall after England's loss of her most valuable overseas colonies.

_____

14. A veteran of the American War of Independence, his efforts to free Poland from foreign domination were crushed in 1794-1795.

_____

Select the letter most appropriate for completion of each of the following statements:

_____Bishop Bossuet's *Politics Drawn from the Very Words of Scripture* (a) proclaimed the doctrine of papal supremacy; (b) traced the origin of governments to a social contract; (c) asserted that kings ruled by divine right; (d) claimed that the king was answerable to no one, not even to God.

_____The French Estates General (a) had powers similar to those of the British Parliament; (b) were large estates owned by the royal family; (c) were abolished by Louis XIV; (d) did not meet between 1614 and 1789.

_____By revoking the Edict of Nantes in 1685 Louis XIV (a) established religious toleration in France; (b) removed the disabilities imposed on Catholics; (c) demonstrated a statesmanship that ensured the loyalty of all his subjects; (d) contributed to industrial progress in rival Protestant countries by driving large numbers of Huguenots out of France.

_____To finance his projects, Tsar Peter the Great laid heaviest exactions upon (a) peasants; (b) the Church; (c) the nobles; (d) bankers and industrialists.

_____The Eurocentric world view of Peter the Great is most evident in his (a) democratic reforms; (b) abolition of serfdom; (c) pacific relations with his western neighbors; (d) military conquests.

_____The Clarendon Code (a) was broken by French cryptographers during the War of the Spanish Succession; (b) penalized English Catholics and Protestant dissenters; (c) prescribed the public behavior of the English aristocracy; (d) was abolished by King Charles I.

_____A factor facilitating the dismemberment of Poland was (a) retention of "liberties" by the Polish nobility; (b) outbreak of the Seven Years' War; (c) aggressive policies of Polish kings; (d) Catholic-Protestant conflict.

_____John Locke, in his *Two Treatises of Civil Government*, declared that the right to life, liberty, and property was derived from (a) the law of nature; (b) the Bible; (c) custom; (d) acts of the legislature.

_____The "diplomatic revolution" of 1756 (a) brought a rapprochement between France and Austria; (b) overthrew the Habsburg monarchy; (c) created an international peace-keeping organization; (d) pitted Prussia against Great Britain.

You should be able to place in context or define each of the following:

streltsy	"Sun King"
boyar	intendants
Tories	*taille*
Whigs	*parlements*
Bill of Rights (English)	*Junkers*
Cossacks	*asiento*

STUDY QUESTIONS

1. How did the economic system of mercantilism support political absolutism?
2. What factors, if any, limited the exercise of complete absolutism?
3. What elements within European states were most likely to oppose absolutism and what tactics did the rulers use in dealing with these elements?
4. Describe Louis XIV's use of theater to centralize state power in the royal person.
5. How did Colbert's policies as finance minister illustrate the objectives of mercantilism?
6. What aspect of Colbert's reform program was most successful? Did his sovereign master help or hinder its success?
7. What were the difficulties in the way of establishing absolutism in Germany? Did these difficulties discourage the various princes from trying?
8. By what instruments did Frederick William the "Great Elector" make Brandenburg-Prussia a strongly centralized state?

9. Which elements of society under absolutist regimes were best able to retain their privileges in succeeding eras?

10. How did the absolutism of Peter the Great (Tsar Peter I) differ from that of his western European contemporaries?

11. Both Charles II and his brother James II favored absolute rule. Why did revolution come under James rather than under Charles?

12. How did the "Glorious Revolution" of 1688 and its aftermath ensure that the English monarchy would henceforth be limited?

13. What aspects or consequences of the Revolution of 1688 could be considered as less than "glorious"?

14. On what grounds did John Locke establish the right of revolution? Why were his theories particularly useful to the leaders of the English Revolution of 1688?

15. The growth of foreign ministries and embassies in European capitals reflected a desire to achieve international stability. What other objectives emerged? Why was diplomacy also "a weapon in the army of the absolutist state"?

16. How was the character of warfare changing during this period?

17. What wars resulted from Louis XIV's threat to the European balance of power? What were the stakes at issue in the War of the Spanish Succession?

18. Summarize the provisions of the Treaty of Utrecht of 1713. What particular advantages accrued to the British?

19. Explain the term "enlightened absolutism." To what extent did the absolutism of eighteenth-century rulers become enlightened?

20. Explain why the religious movements Quietism and Jansenism were hostile to French absolutism.

21. Explain the authors' statement that European cities of the age of absolutism, in contrast to medieval cities, celebrated inequality.

22. Why did the Catholic rulers Maria Theresa and Joseph II enact measures restricting the liberties of the Church?

23. Why was Catherine the Great able to establish a more nearly total absolutism in Russia than were contemporary Habsburg rulers in Austria?

24. How did the role of the English gentry in local government differ from that of the Continental aristocracy? By what means did they maintain their preponderant influence in the central government of England during the eighteenth century?

25. What significant shift in the European balance of power occurred in the second half of the eighteenth century?

26. Summarize the provisions of the Treaty of Paris of 1763.

27. What is the significance of the Treaty of Paris signed by the British in 1783?

28. Although seemingly essential to the maintenance of a European balance of power, Poland was unable to retain its independent existence. Explain why.

PROBLEMS

1. A longing for stability after exhausting crises and conflicts helps explain popular support of, or tolerance for, absolutist rulers. Does the rise of totalitarian regimes in our own day offer a parallel? Develop this theme as concretely as you can.

2. The year is 1689. You are twenty years old and live in London. How does the prospect before you differ from the one that would confront you if you were living in Moscow?

3. To what extent was the English Glorious Revolution a conservative revolution?

4. Make a critique of "enlightened absolutism" as exemplified by the personality, character, and rule of Frederick the Great.

5. Study the career of Catherine the Great and assess the effects of her rule.

GEOGRAPHICAL IDENTIFICATIONS

Brandenburg
Prussia
Bohemia
Moravia
Silesia
Cologne
Blenheim
Hanover

Ukraine
St. Petersburg
Volga River
Strassburg
Luxembourg
Alsace
Utrecht
Vienna

THE THEORY OF DIVINE RIGHT: From *Politics Drawn From the Holy Scriptures* *Bishop Bossuet*

There are four qualities essential to royal authority. First, the royal authority is sacred; second, it is paternal; third, it is absolute; fourth, it is submitted to reason. . . .

Thus, as we have seen, the royal throne is not the throne of a man, but the throne of God himself. "Jehovah hath chosen Solomon my son to sit upon the throne of the kingdom of Jehovah over Israel" (I Chronicles 28:5). . . .

It appears from all this that the person of kings is sacred, and that to make an attempt on their lives is a sacrilege.

God causes them to be anointed by his prophets with a sacred unction, in the same way that he causes pontiffs and his ministry to be anointed.

But even without the exterior application of this unction, they are sacred by their charge, being representatives of the divine majesty, deputed by his providence to the execution of his designs. . . .

St. Paul, after having said that the prince is the minister of God, concludes thus: "Wherefore ye must needs be in subjection, not only because of the wrath, but also for conscience' sake" (Romans 13:5). . . .

And again: "Servants, obey in all things your masters according to the flesh. . . . And whatsoever ye do, do it heartily, as to the Lord, and not unto men" (Colossians 3:22-3). . . .

If the apostle speaks thus of servitude, an unnatural state, what ought we to think of legitimate subjection to princes and magistrates who are the protectors of public liberty. . . .

Even when princes do not do their duty, we must respect their office and ministry. "Servants, be subject to your masters with all fear; not only to the good and gentle, but also to the froward" (I Peter 2:18).

There is then something religious in the respect we pay to the prince. The service of God and the respect for kings are one and the same thing; and St. Peter puts these two duties together: "Fear God. Honour the king" (I Peter 2:17). . . .

However, because their power comes from above, princes must not think that they are free to use it at their pleasure; rather must they use it with fear and discretion, as a thing which comes to them from God, and of which God will demand a strict account. . . .

Kings should therefore tremble while using their God-given power, and think what a horrible sacrilege it is to misuse it. . . .

The royal authority is absolute.

In order to render this term odious and insupportable, some people try to confuse absolute and arbitrary government. But there is nothing more different, as we shall see when we speak of justice.

The prince is accountable to no one for what he orders. . . .

We must obey princes as justice itself, without which there would be no order nor purpose in human affairs.

They are gods, and participate in the divine independence. . . .

Whoever becomes a sovereign prince, holds in his hands everything together, both the sovereign authority to judge, and all the forces of the state. . . .

The end of government is the good and conservation of the state. . . .

The good constitution of the body of the state consists in two things: in religion and justice: these are the interior and constitutive principles of states. By the one, we render to God what is due to him; and by the other, we render to men what belongs to them. . . .

The prince must employ his authority to destroy false religions in his state. . . .

He is the protector of the public peace which depends upon religion; and he must sustain his throne, of which it is the foundation, as we have seen. Those who would not suffer the prince to act strictly in matters of religion because religion ought to be free, are in impious error. Otherwise it would be necessary to suffer, among his subjects and in the whole state, idolatry, Mohammedanism, Judaism, every false religion, blasphemy, even atheism, and the greatest crimes, would go unpunished. . . .

From Franklin L. Baumer, *Main Currents of Western Thought*, 2nd ed., New York: Alfred A. Knopf Inc., 1964.

THE POLITICAL PHILOSOPHY OF A RUSSIAN ABSOLUTIST: The "Instructions" of Catherine the Great

6. Russia is a European State.

7. This is clearly demonstrated by the following Observations: The Alterations which *Peter the Great* undertook in Russia succeeded with the greater Ease, because the Manners, which prevailed at that Time, and had been introduced amongst us by a Mixture of different Nations, and the Conquest of foreign Territories, were quite unsuitable to the Climate. *Peter the First*, by introducing the Manners and Customs of Europe among the European People in his Dominions, found at that Time such Means as even he himself was not sanguine enough to expect. . . .

9. The Sovereign is absolute; for there is no other Authority but that which centers in his single Person,

that can act with a Vigour proportionate to the Extent of such a vast Dominion.

10. The Extent of the Dominion requires an absolute Power to be vested in that Person who rules over it. It is expedient so to be, that the quick Dispatch of Affairs, sent from distant Parts, might make ample Amends for the Delay occasioned by the great Distance of the Places. . . .

13. What is the true End of Monarchy? Not to deprive People of their natural Liberty; but to correct their Actions, in order to attain the *supreme Good*.

14. The Form of Government, therefore, which best attains this End, and at the same Time sets less Bounds than others to natural Liberty, is that which coincides with the Views and Purposes of rational Creatures, and answers the End, upon which we ought to fix a steadfast Eye in the Regulations of civil Polity.

15. The Intention and the End of Monarchy, is the Glory of the Citizens, of the State, and of the Sovereign.

16. But, from this Glory, a Sense of Liberty arises in a people governed by a Monarch; which may produce in these States as much Energy in transacting the most important Affairs, and may contribute as much to the Happiness of the Subjects, as even Liberty itself. . . .

33. The Laws ought to be so framed, as to secure the Safety of every Citizen as much as possible.

34. The Equality of the Citizens consists in this; that they should all be subject to the same Laws.

35. This Equality requires Institutions so well adapted, as to prevent the Rich from oppressing those who are not so wealthy as themselves, and converting all the Charges and Employments intrusted to them as Magistrates only, to their own private Emolument.

36. General or political Liberty does not consist in that licentious Notion, *That a Man may do whatever he pleases*.

37. In a State or Assemblage of People that live together in a Community, where there are Laws, Liberty can only consist *in doing that which every One ought to do, and not to be constrained to do that which One ought not to do*.

38. A Man ought to form in his own Mind an exact and clear Idea of what Liberty is. *Liberty is the Right of doing whatsoever the Laws allow:* And if any one Citizen could do what the Laws forbid, there would be no more Liberty; because others would have an equal Power of doing the same. . . .

96. Good Laws keep strictly a just Medium: They do not always inflict pecuniary, nor always subject Malefactors to corporal, Punishment.

All Punishments, by which the human Body might be maimed, ought to be abolished. . . .

240. It is better to *prevent* Crimes, than to *punish* them.

241. To *prevent* Crimes is the *Intention*, and the *End* of every *good* Legislation; which is nothing more than the Art of conducting People to the *greatest* Good, or to leave the *least* Evil possible amongst them, if it should prove impracticable to *exterminate* the whole. . . .

243. Would you *prevent* Crimes? order it *so*, That

the laws might rather favour every *Individual*, than any particular Rank of Citizens, in the Community. . . .

245. Would you prevent Crimes? order it so, that the *Light of Knowledge may be diffused* among the people. . . .

248. Finally, the *most sure*, but, at the same Time, the *most difficult* Expedient to mend the Morals of the People, is a perfect System of Education.

———

From W. F. Reddaway, *Documents of Catherine the Great*, Cambridge University Press, 1931. Reprinted by permission of the publisher.

THE LIBERAL POLITICAL THEORY OF JOHN LOCKE: From *Of Civil Government*

But though this be a state of liberty, yet it is not a state of licence; though man in that state have an uncontrollable liberty to dispose of his person or possessions, yet he has not liberty to destroy himself, or so much as any creature in his possession, but where some nobler use than its bare preservation calls for it. The state of Nature has a law of Nature to govern it, which obliges every one, and reason, which is that law, teaches all mankind who will but consult it, that being all equal and independent, no one ought to harm another in his life, health, liberty or possessions; for men being all the workmanship of one omnipotent and infinitely wise Maker; all the servants of one sovereign Master, sent into the world by His order and about his business; they are His property, whose workmanship they are made to last during His, not one another's pleasure. And, being furnished with like faculties, sharing all in one community of Nature, there cannot be supposed any such subordination among us that may authorise us to destroy one another, as if we were made for one another's uses, as the inferior ranks of creatures are for ours. Every one as he is bound to preserve himself, and not to quit his station wilfully, so by the like reason, when his own preservation comes not in competition, ought he as much as he can to preserve the rest of mankind, and not unless it be to do justice on an offender, take away or impair the life, or what tends to the preservation of the life, the liberty, health, limb, or goods of another.

And that all men may be restrained from invading others' rights, and from doing hurt to one another, and the law of Nature be observed, which willeth the peace and preservation of all mankind, the execution of the law of Nature is in that state put into every man's hands, whereby every one has a right to punish the transgressors of that law to such a degree as may hinder its violation. For the law of Nature would, as all other laws that concern men in this world, be in vain if there were nobody that in the state of Nature had a power to execute that law, and thereby preserve the innocent and restrain offenders; and if any one in the state of Nature may punish another for any evil he has done, every one may do so. For in that state of perfect equality, where naturally there is no superiority or jurisdiction of one over another, what any may do in prosecution of that law, every one must needs have a right to do.

• • •

Though the legislative, whether placed in one or more, whether it be always in being or only by intervals, though it be the supreme power in every commonwealth, yet, first, it is not, nor can possibly be, absolutely arbitrary over the lives and fortunes of the people. For it being but the joint power of every member of the society given up to that person or assembly which is legislator, it can be no more than those persons had in a state of Nature before they entered into society, and gave it up to the community. For nobody can transfer to another more power than he has in himself, and nobody has an absolute arbitrary power over himself, or over any other, to destroy his own life, or take away the life or property of another. A man, as has been proved, cannot subject himself to the arbitrary power of another; and having, in the state of Nature, no arbitrary power over the life, liberty, or possession of another, but only so much as the law of Nature gave him for the preservation of himself and the rest of mankind, this is all he doth, or can give up to the commonwealth, and by it to the legislative power, so that the legislative can have no more than this. Their power in the utmost bounds of it is limited to the public good of the society. It is a power that hath no other end but preservation, and therefore can never have a right to destroy, enslave, or designedly to impoverish the subjects; the obligations of the law of Nature cease not in society, but only in many cases are drawn closer, and have, by human laws, known penalties annexed to them to enforce their observation. Thus the law of Nature stands as an eternal rule of all men, legislators as well as others. The rules that they make for other men's actions must, as well as their own and other men's actions, be conformable to the law of Nature — i.e., to the will of God, of which that is a declaration, and the fundamental law of Nature being the preservation of mankind, no human sanction can be good or valid against it.

From John Locke, *Two Treatises on Civil Government.*

Extracts from the English Bill of Rights

1. That the pretended power of suspending of laws, or for the execution of laws, by regal authority, without consent of Parliament is illegal.

2. That the pretended power of dispensing with laws, or the execution of laws, by regal authority, as it hath been assumed and exercised of late, is illegal.

3. That the commission for erecting the late Court of Commissioners for Ecclesiastical Causes, and all other commissions and courts of like nature, are illegal and pernicious.

4. That levying money for or to the use of the Crown, by pretence of prerogative, without grant of Parliament, for longer time, or in other manner than the same is or shall be granted, is illegal.

5. That it is the right of the subjects to petition the King, and all commitments and prosecutions for such petitioning are illegal.

6. That the raising or keeping a standing army within the kingdom in time of peace, unless it be with consent of Parliament, is against law.

7. That the subjects which are Protestants may have arms for their defence, suitable to their conditions, and as allowed by law.

8. That election of Members of Parliament ought to be free.

9. That the freedom of speech, and debates or proceedings in Parliament, ought not to be impeached or questioned in any court or place out of Parliament.

10. That excessive bail ought not to be required, nor excessive fines imposed; nor cruel and unusual punishments inflicted.

11. That jurors ought to be duly impanelled and returned, and jurors which pass upon men in trials for high treason ought to be freeholders.

12. That all grants and promises of fines and forfeitures of particular persons before conviction, are illegal and void.

13. And that for redress of all grievances, and for the amending, strengthening, and preserving of the laws, Parliaments ought to be held frequently. . . .

From John Fairburn, ed., *Magna Charta, the Bill of Rights; with the Petition of Right . . .*

ANALYSIS AND INTERPRETATION OF THE READINGS

1. What restraints on royal power does Bossuet postulate? Would these restraints be very effective?
2. According to Bossuet, what are the proper relations between church and state?
3. According to Locke, in what ways is the law-making power limited in political society?
4. What are the implications of the Empress Catherine's definition of liberty?
5. Why has the English Bill of Rights come to be regarded as an essential part of the British Constitution?
6. Compare the English Bill of Rights with the American Bill of Rights.

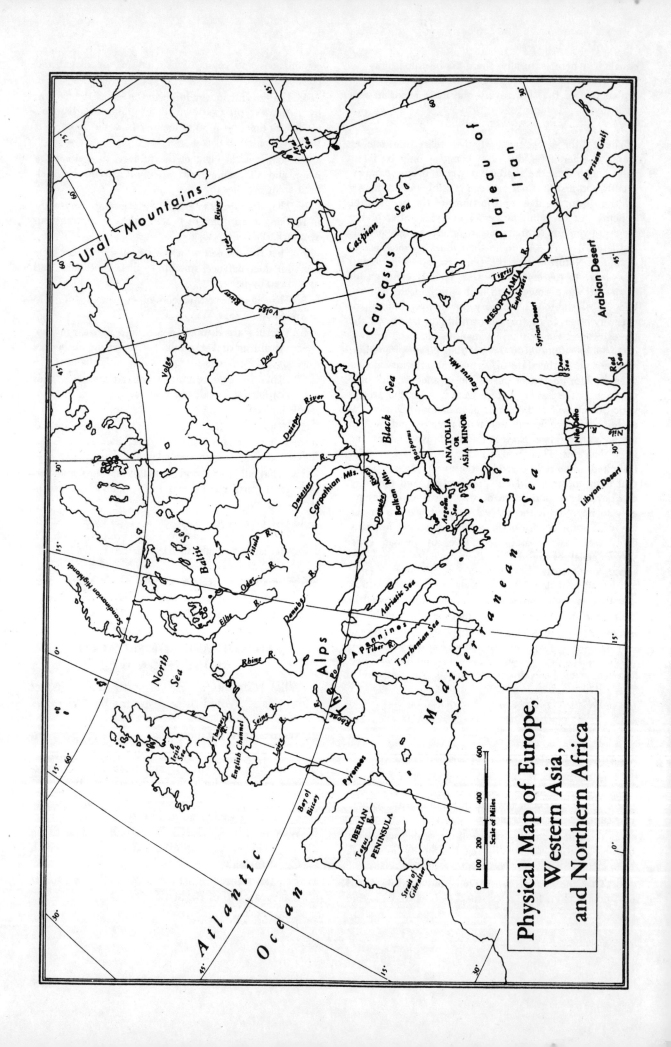

Physical Map of Europe,
Western Asia,
and Northern Africa

(Chapters 13–17)
The Early-Modern World

MAP WORK

On the map opposite indicate the political divisions of Europe in 1648, that is, at the end of the Thirty Years' War.

CHRONOLOGICAL REVIEW

In the lists below, circle the individuals, events, or items that do not belong in the period under which they have been listed.

FIFTEENTH CENTURY

Masaccio
Botticelli
Pico della Mirandola
Blaise Pascal
Sir Thomas More
Lorenzo Valla

SIXTEENTH CENTURY

Beginning of Tudor Dynasty
William the Silent
Peace of Westphalia
Edict of Nantes
Vasco da Gama's Voyage to India
John Locke
Spanish Armada
Castiglione
Peter the Great
Montaigne
Michelangelo

SEVENTEENTH CENTURY

Cromwell's Protectorate
Revocation of the Edict of Nantes
Petition of Right
Louis XV
Rembrandt van Rijn
Ascendancy of Cardinal Richelieu
South Sea Bubble
Voltaire
Leonardo da Vinci
Dürer
Colbert

EIGHTEENTH CENTURY

Galileo
Frederick the Great
Catherine the Great
Glorious Revolution
Seven Years' War
Peter Paul Rubens
Building of Versailles
Thomas Hobbes
St. Bartholomew's Day Massacre
Machiavelli

Now, in the space provided below, assign all the individual events or items you have circled above to their correct centuries.

FIFTEENTH CENTURY

SIXTEENTH CENTURY

SEVENTEENTH CENTURY

EIGHTEENTH CENTURY